Read My Lips

Read My Lips

Stories of a Hollywood Life

SALLY KELLERMAN

WEINSTEIN
BOOKS

Printed in the United States of America.

Editorial production by *Marra*thon Production Services. www.marrathon.net
Book Design by Lisa Diercks.
Cataloging-in-Publication data for this book is available from the Library of Congress.
ISBN: 978–1–60286–167–1 (print)
ISBN: 978–1–60286–201–2 (e-book)

Published by Weinstein Books
A member of the Perseus Books Group
www.weinsteinbooks.com

Weinstein Books are available at special discounts for bulk purchases in the U.S. by
corporations, institutions and other organizations. For more information, please
contact the Special Markets Department at the Perseus Books Group, 2300 Chestnut
Street, Suite 200, Philadelphia, PA 19103, call (800) 810–4145, ext. 5000, or e-mail
special.markets@perseusbooks.com.

First edition

10 9 8 7 6 5 4 3 2 1

To my fascinating, uber-mensch of a husband and my precious children, who lovingly dragged me kicking and screaming into adulthood. I love you all madly.

Contents

Preface   ix

Prologue: Just a Small Town Girl   xi

CHAPTER 1: The Day I Ruined My Life   1

CHAPTER 2: Make Believe   15

CHAPTER 3: Check, Please   30

CHAPTER 4: Loss and Longing   45

CHAPTER 5: Pushing the Limits   53

CHAPTER 6: Hit the Deck   78

CHAPTER 7: Never the Same Again   92

CHAPTER 8: The Wheel of Fortune   105

CHAPTER 9: Flirting with Politics   123

CHAPTER 10: Advice Given and Ignored   135

CHAPTER 11: Reaching Down, Reaching Out   154

CHAPTER 12: Chasing Garbo   167

CHAPTER 13: Love and Therapy   178

CHAPTER 14: God Laughs While We Make Plans   190

CHAPTER 15: Two, No Three, Little Surprises   208

CHAPTER 16: Lost and Found   225

CHAPTER 17: The Next Chapter   239

Acknowledgments   245

Index   248

Preface

To my readers . . .

This is my memoir. In my case, that means anything I can remember.

It is a collection of experiences that made me laugh or cry—stories of people I've loved, of lessons I've learned and have yet to learn. There is some X-rated language and the odd X-rated visual description.

My mom—a darling, five-foot-two Arkansan, New Orleans, piano-playing, warm, a-tad-judgmental, spiritual, generous, thoughtful, kind mom—wanted a lady. My dad—a funny, handsome, sentimental, good man who said what was on his mind, was a tad controlling, and worried about how I'd turn out—wanted a lady too.

Instead they got an actress, a singer, an entertainer.

"Please don't be like Carole Lombard," my mom said to me when I was little. She once overheard Lombard say "shit" in Bullock's Department Store. "And please don't be like Aunt Moatsie. She wore slippers to the market . . ."

I wasn't enough like Carole Lombard when I tested for her life story, but I did wear slippers to the market.

Just a Small Town Girl

IT WAS HALLOWEEN. I CAME ONSTAGE WITH MY BACK TO THE audience, dressed in black from head to toe. I had some of my favorite guys backing me that night: Lyman Medeiros on bass, my wonderful musical director Ed Martel on keyboards, and Dick Weller on drums. The band was playing spooky music from *Phantom of the Opera*, and the lighting was eerie green. The room, I'm so happy to say, was packed.

These days Vitello's is my club of choice when I'm in town, somewhere to develop my show, try out new material, and keep on singing. Over the years I've worked many different clubs in LA, my hometown, where I've had all my successes and made all my mistakes.

Vitello's is a little Italian spot on Tujunga Avenue in Studio City, an upscale Mediterranean restaurant serving the kind of food that I could eat every night—and do. Spaghetti marinara, thin-crust pizza, delicious salads—you get the idea—served on white tablecloths, with lit candles, by waiters so good you don't know they're there. The club has about a hundred seats, and guests can eat a little dinner, sip a little wine, and enjoy music from all kinds of top-notch performers, like the great arranger-songwriter Johnny Mandel who wrote "The Shadow of Your Smile."

Since it was Halloween, I opened with an eerie version of "I Put a Spell on You," then moved on to songs like "Spooky" and "Love Potion Number Nine." At one point in the show, I went into the audience, as I always do (I love to see all the faces and sing to them up close), greeting every table. That night I passed out candy wrapped as eyeballs. "I've got a crush on you . . ." I'd croon. "Would you care for an eyeball?" I talked a little, joked with the band, and sang a lot. It was an especially silly night, but for me, singing is freedom. I was in heaven. Before I knew it, it was time to take a bow, hug some friends, and pack up to go home.

Don Heckman, a well-known music journalist who now heads up the *International Review of Music*, came to see me perform. He loved the show and reviewed it the next day. "Even when she's not doing a mini-Halloween celebration," he wrote, "Sally's performances are all utterly mesmerizing, overflowing with humor, atmosphere, and musicality. . . . At her best, and in a crowded female vocal field, she is one of the rare true originals."

It feels good to get such encouragement from a critic I respect, especially for doing something I love as much as performing live.

Yes, I was one of those kids who wanted to perform from the very first moment I could stand on two legs, find my lungs, and hold a makeshift prop. Sure, I'm better known to audiences as an actress than as a singer. However, for me, there's never been a separation between singing and acting. Singing is acting; it's telling a story through music. Acting may have been my chief role for a long while, but singing has always been its understudy; now it's taking the lead. Over my more than fifty years as a performer, I've done a lot, seen a lot, screwed up a lot up and gotten some things right. And I've done it all here, where I call home: Los Angeles.

I love Los Angeles. It may be a huge metropolis but it is still my little town, the one I've known all my life, for better or worse, through richer and poorer, through blue skies and smog. I have always lived within a twenty-file-mile radius of where I was born and raised, so I feel like a real small town girl in many ways.

Today, LA is sprawling and still growing. There's so much traffic that I can take a nap between signals.

Down the hill to the south from my home in the Hollywood Hills is the entertainment capital of the world. I've watched West Hollywood grow from a little burg to an incorporated city. I've seen wide open spaces get gobbled up, from the Hollywood Hills and the Valley to Studio City and Santa Monica, with builders scrambling to make their creations safer from inevitable earthquakes.

But to me Hollywood is still the place where Santa Monica Boulevard had one shoe repair joint, Coombs Hardware store, and a five and dime. It's where I stood in front of Schwab's Pharmacy on Sunset Boulevard—the main drag of much of my life—talking to my friends about acting or boys. It's where I got malts on Hollywood Boulevard; and at night, left the door to my apartment unlocked. Open. Free.

We have grown and changed a lot over the years, my town and me. If Hollywood is about anything, it's about reinvention and survival. Hollywood has taught me plenty about both, whether I wanted to learn those lessons or not.

I have always known I would never live anywhere else, no matter what my life held in store. After all: Every great Hollywood story needs a strong third act. I'm working on mine.

CHAPTER 1

The Day I Ruined My Life

TO ME HOLLYWOOD WAS NEVER ABOUT GLAMOUR OR FAME. IT was about the work, going to class, doing plays. But that didn't mean I was immune to its charms. I've always loved movie stars—Ingrid Bergman, Humphrey Bogart, Cary Grant, Gregory Peck, Greta Garbo, Vivian Leigh, and my darling Jennifer Jones—as well as musical stars like Bing Crosby, Danny Kaye, and, of course, Doris Day.

Then one day, when I was around fifteen years old, I saw Marlon Brando in *Viva Zapata!* Marlon was changing the face of acting then—and with it, my life. There he was on the screen, gazing casually out the window, wearing white Mexican drawstring pajamas, with Jean Peters spread out behind him in bed. The minute I saw him in those pants—no shirt—standing at the window with that steamy sexuality oozing from his every pore, everything changed. I changed. There was a new reality, and it was his raw vulnerable emotion and sex. From then on out I saw every one of Brando's pictures five, six, even seven times. *The Wild One, On the Waterfront, The Men, Guys and Dolls, Sayonara*—I never missed a one.

And then one night lightning struck: I actually met Marlon in the flesh at Cosmo Alley. Just south of Hollywood Boulevard, it was a club behind the Ivar Theater that was a quick stroll from some great fixtures of 1950s Hollywood that are still going strong today: the Pantages and Musso and Frank's. You could hear folk and blues at the Cosmo, and it was one of my favorite places to hear jazz. It was dark, nothing fancy to it. Just throw on some jeans and go hear some music and forget your troubles. I even subbed there as a waitress a few times.

That night I had gone to the Cosmo with a friend to hear Stan Getz play. Working the door was Al Lettieri, a good friend and great character actor who would go on to play Virgil "The Turk" Sollozzo in *The Godfather*.

"Come on," Al said. "I'll sit you right over here."

Al sat us down right beside—guess who? Marlon Brando.

Taking my seat next to my idol, I stared straight ahead, afraid to breathe.

Suddenly a star-struck tourist spotted Marlon. "Hey!" he called out in an exuberant Southern accent. "Marlon Brando! *Sayonara! On the Waterfront!* How Do You DO?!"

Marlon loved it. He threw his head back and laughed.

I still didn't look. I didn't budge. Eyes front, wishing all the time that I had the confidence, the freedom to express my great excitement.

But that's how I stayed. For two entire sets of one of my favorite musicians, I was frozen, not so much as tapping a toe. Before I knew it, the music had stopped and the lights came up.

"I'm gonna go," my friend said.

As he got up to leave, I remained rooted, and without looking, I uttered weakly, "Bye."

Then Marlon turned to me and started to speak.

"Okay, so, what are you, an actress?" he asked.

Breaking free of my spell, I whirled around to face him. "Yes, I am, and I don't think that's funny!"

"Well, would you like to go for a ride with me?" he said.

"Yes, I would."

I followed Marlon out to his rather nondescript white car.

Once I'd spotted him driving it down Hollywood Boulevard and was so excited that I almost wrecked my own dilapidated Chevy. I couldn't believe he wasn't being chauffeured around in a limo. Another time, when it was raining, I spied him going into the movies on Sunset, wearing white pants. White pants in the rain?! My mother would have gasped in horror. Of course, I ran out and bought my own pair as soon as I could scrape together enough tip money.

But now here I was with Marlon, Marlon Brando, slipping his frame behind the wheel, and I was sitting in the front seat right next to him. He pulled out of the parking lot and began driving down the alley. I looked around, quiet, trying to be nonchalant about it all.

Then, after about half a block, he leaned over and touched my arm. That was enough to send me reeling, feeling so many conflicting impulses at once. I was so hopelessly in love with him that I was both scared and thrilled. I immediately pulled away. I didn't know what to do, and I had no idea how to act.

"Riiiight," Marlon said, a little pissed off. "I wouldn't want to spoil this 'beautiful friendship' we have."

He turned the car around and dropped me off back at the club.

I stood there, watching my hero drive off into the night. I was bursting out of my skin with excitement. I ran to the nearest pay phone to call my best friend, Luana, to tell her I had just been in Marlon Brando's car. I was twenty years old and I had actually been in Marlon Brando's car.

• • •

I MUST HAVE COME OUT OF THE WOMB SINGING AND ACTING. I knew I wanted to be a performer ever since I was a skinny little kid growing up in Granada Hills in the San Fernando Valley. In the middle of my sophomore year we moved to Park La Brea in Los Angeles, and I went to Hollywood High School. By then I was a five-foot-ten, 170-pound, thick-wristed, moon-faced, duck-billed blonde in saddle shoes and a very unflattering blue wool skirt that hid layers of crinoline and chub held in place by a Playtex girdle. The term "leading lady" didn't exactly jump to mind.

I remember sitting down with my bag lunch on a bench under a tree in the tiny quad on my first day at school when, like a vision emerging from the midday sun, came these four beautiful girls. They were so stylish, they wore makeup—just enough—and they floated up to me in their high-heeled shoes. I'd never seen anything like them. *Wow*, I thought, *fashion*.

I looked up at them, my tomato and mayonnaise sandwich sticking halfway out of my mouth.

"Evidently someone doesn't know whose bench they're sitting on," one of the fashionable foursome said.

I stood up, grabbed my sack lunch, and went straight to the girls' bathroom. There I pulled myself together and stood in front of the bathroom mirror. I had a mantra for times like these: "Someday . . ." I said to my reflection, "Someday . . ." I did this in times of stress. It was a quiet reminder that things would always get better. I was on a path to somewhere better, somewhere different. Someday . . .

I had started the mirror pep talks as a young child. I was constantly putting on shows for anyone who would watch, singing for anyone who would listen, and even for those who wouldn't. But the self-chats were my secret. And as long as I was banishing myself to the bathroom for lunch—I ate there for the next three weeks—I was going to make good use of my time. Every time somebody came into the bathroom, I hid in the stall, sandwich and all.

I soon learned that each bench outside in the quad was for a different club. There were bad-girl clubs (they smoked) and wholesome-girl clubs (they studied and dressed cute). Some clubs had mild hazing; some had auditions. As time passed and my personality beamed out, I got more comfortable and made friends. I had to brave a little rejection at first, and I was sure that no club would want me because of my size. But I eventually got into one of the more goody-goody clubs. My friend Mary Finwall was in the bad-girl smoking club, but I loved hanging out with her.

Despite that rocky beginning, I ended up having a ball in high school. No boyfriends, mind you, but lots and lots of friends. Boys still teased me—calling me names like "Barge!" "Boat!" "Klondike Sal!" I hit five-foot-nine in fifth grade, so being self-conscious about my size was nothing new. I coped the way a lot of people do—I began to embrace my role as class clown and being one of the guys. A friend of mine once told me that he heard I was the most popular girl at Hollywood High. Excited, I told my mom. She simply said, "Dear, you don't want to be popular. You want to be beloved."

My grades were poor, but I did get As in choir and gym. I was always putting together trios with my best pals, especially my friend Barbara Black. Our accompanist was often our classmate Lincoln Majorga, a fabulous keyboardist who went on to play with Quincy Jones. We sang after school; we performed at school events. Anywhere and everywhere. In high school it was all about Nat King Cole, the Four Freshmen, and Shake, Rattle and Roll. My friend Dawn Adams's family knew Norman Granz, the founder and head of Verve Records, and Dawn promised to help me get a demo to him. Lincoln and I would record it before graduation.

My friend Norma Jean Nielsen was the only person—besides the mirror—to whom I admitted my *big secret*, my performing secret: my desire to be up onstage. I was afraid to admit it out loud. Singing was one thing—it was about your voice. But saying out loud that I wanted to act felt different. I was afraid that people would think that I, the clown, suddenly believed that I was pretty enough to act. But by twelfth grade I was ready to dive in. With a little encouragement—and thanks to my imposing size—I got to play the mother in Hollywood High's production of *Meet Me in St. Louis*. I even got to sing in the show.

Lavender blue . . . dilly dilly. . . . .

My friend Hooper C. Dunbar III brought his mom to the play. Hooper really did look like a "Hooper C. Dunbar the Third." He had big owl glasses, and though I can't remember whether he wore a neat little sweater vest, I feel like maybe he should have. But he was spiritual and had an innate kindness that made me feel safe. Unbeknownst to me, his mother enjoyed my performance so much that she got hold of a copy of my high school picture and submitted me for a real movie audition.

"You'd be perfect for it!" she later enthused.

That's how I found myself in the running to play Joan of Arc in Otto Preminger's film adaptation of the George Bernard Shaw play *Saint Joan*. Soon I was standing in line with about three hundred other girls from all over the world at a big theater in Los Angeles. The way the auditions were set up, you could see the person in line ahead of you audition and hear a bit of the judges' response. The girl who went right before me was very talented, or so I thought. I watched her closely and saw her raise her arms skyward to God. Such enthusiasm! The judges appeared to be very impressed, and she looked quite pleased with herself as she exited. *Wow. That was something,* I thought. I had to give it a go.

I walked in, introduced myself, flung my arms to the heavens, and exclaimed, "Oh God . . ."

"Next!!!"

Oh God, indeed.

Jean Seberg got the part, but I couldn't be stopped. Once my desire to perform had transformed from lonely pep talks in front of the mirror into full-blown, on-stage singing in front of an audience, I knew my life was about to change, even if I couldn't say how. That feeling of being up on a stage with other people, people like me who had something to say, something to share, was exhilarating. I loved being able to connect with them and with an audience, to belong. As high school drew to an end I began to explore Los Angeles, to soak up as much theater as I could.

· · ·

ONE NIGHT I WENT WITH FRIENDS TO THE PICO PLAYHOUSE IN the Cheviot Hills neighborhood. When we exited I saw a vision of 1950s cool: Eddie Byrnes, who would soon go on to play the comb-wielding valet sidekick on TV's 77 *Sunset Strip*. He was just standing there in a slick monogrammed shirt, leaning back against a powder-blue T-bird convertible. Dreamy.

Somebody introduced the two of us, and that was that: I had my first proper boyfriend.

It was right after high school, and I was living with my older sister Diana on Havenhurst, near the legendary Garden of Allah Hotel and bungalows and across from the Chateau Marmont, even then a place to be seen and a playground for movie stars. The Garden of Allah was party central for Hollywood's Golden Age royalty—John Barrymore, Ernest Hemingway, Orson Welles, Marlene Dietrich, Dorothy Parker, Greta Garbo, and many more actors, writers, and so on. It was torn down not long after we lived there.

As I'd gotten a little older, Diana found me more interesting, so we grew closer. Sometime after we'd moved in together, she apologized for picking on me so much when we were little. By that time I couldn't have cared less; it was all a memory and we were living a whole new life. Eddie used to come over to our apartment and play practical jokes on Diana and me, hiding under the covers in my bedroom, pretending he was dead. And we'd neck. I knew he wanted to sleep with me, but I was still a virgin. He would tease me about that fact and sometimes get angry with me, and that made me like him more—a relationship pattern that would later play itself out in a variety of ways with a variety of men.

"I don't know what to do," I told Diana one day. "I'd really like to sleep with Eddie. What do you think?"

"I wouldn't know anyone who would do anything like that," Diana said.

I listened to her. I still admired her and valued her opinion. And after all, this was the 1950s, the repressive postwar "wait until you're married, no matter what" era, when the line between "good" girls and "bad" was very clear and usually defined by your virginity. Eddie soon broke up with me and began dating my friend Asa Maynor. But I rebounded just fine. I already had a much more important man in my life. A man named Jeff Corey.

. . .

"THE DAY YOU MET JEFF COREY WAS THE DAY YOU RUINED YOUR life," my darling mother liked to say.

My father grumbled that Jeff Corey's class was where I learned to say "fuck," a word my mother would never have used.

As for me, there was no question in my mind that the day I met Jeff Corey was the day my life began.

The Professional Actors Workshop, as Jeff's class eventually became known, was up Cherokee and off Franklin Avenue in the Hollywood Hills. I had started studying there right after graduating high school. For a while I also attended LA City College, mostly for my parents' sake. At LA City College they made me take pantomime. I didn't like it. Jeff didn't like pantomime either. No more college.

Jeff's classes were initially held in the garage/theater behind his house. At the time he was in his early forties, with deep-set eyes and dark, wavy hair that had begun to recede a little. He had been working in movies since the early 1940s and was building quite a career as a character actor in films like *My Friend Flicka, The Devil and Daniel Webster, The Killers, Brute Force,* and *Home of the Brave.* Things looked good for Jeff until he was named as a former member of the Communist Party and subpoenaed by the House Committee on Un-American Activities. After he refused to name other supposed Communists, he was blacklisted and unable to work as an actor, so he began sharing his skills with a new generation.

Norma Jean Nielsen had told me that Jeff's garage was the place to be if you wanted to get serious about acting. For one thing, he'd worked with James Dean. James Dean had died in a car crash the year after I graduated high school. We were all devastated, for as kids we totally related to his on-screen suffering, to his need to be appreciated and acknowledged. Instead he was ignored. Misunderstood. Treated like a disappointment through and through. James Dean was the embodiment of an entire generation—my generation—the expression of all our frustration at 1950s repression, the lack of communication we were raised with, and all the angst that we could no longer hide.

I continue to think of Jimmy Dean as Cal in Elia Kazan's *East of Eden*, a performance to this day I still find so heartbreaking.

"But dad . . . I gotta way to do the lettuce . . ."

Marlon Brando, that brooding, powerful, sultry chameleon, changed our art forever, by bringing Method acting to Hollywood. He was our hero, but James Dean was our spokesman, pouring all our 1950s confusion out all over the screen.

That first night I went to Jeff's I was so nervous, all baggy sweaters and jeans, plopping down in the middle of the floor and trying not to be noticed. I had the classic actor's syndrome: "Don't look at me! . . . Wait! Wait! Look at me!"

We did a scene from William Saroyan's play *Beautiful People* that night. Later Jeff asked me, "Have you ever acted before?"

Oh God. . . .

I told him about my limited experience, *Meet Me in St. Louis* and the Joan of Arc auditions. "Well, you have talent," he said. That was nice to hear, but there was something more. There was something about Jeff that immediately put me at ease. He was so sincere, so understanding. He understood that we were all searching, emoting, trying to make sense of our lives.

I remember that, after I'd been working with him in class for a while, Jeff told me during a private session, "You're just beautiful."

His remark struck me in an entirely new way. I was sure the beauty he was talking about was inside me, not surface beauty. The idea that I could be beautiful on the outside still felt strange. No matter what anyone saw on the outside, I still felt too gawky and uncomfortable in my skin to let any compliment on my appearance sink in. However, Jeff saw things in me in those classes, things that were buried. Maybe I still felt fat, but he made me feel as though I had something to offer.

Jeff's concept of beauty was one of the most compelling aspects of the way he worked. At the time "Method" was the word where acting was concerned, but Jeff didn't limit himself to one style. He gave us many tools, and it was up to us to choose the one that worked best. Most of all, to him acting was about seeing the beauty, the importance, the meaning in everything. One night he showed us photos of broken-down fences and weeds, all dilapidated and overgrown.

"See," he said, "that's beautiful."

Everyone looked at the photos, nodding. They were all so serious. I felt more truly, deeply alive in that moment, in those classes, than ever before in my life.

• • •

Jeff attracted an incredible, fascinating group of students at every level of ability. There were a lot of men, but the women were an impressive gang too. Carole Eastman was acting then, but would soon go on to write *Five Easy Pieces*. She was fiery and spunky, with such confidence. Jeff's class is where I met Luana Anders, one of the dearest friends of my life. Luana had a Doris Day look, and we bonded immediately over acting and how we just did not understand boys. When Shirley Knight—later an Oscar nominee—joined the class, Luana and I hated her because she was so pretty and could already cry on cue. Though my friend, the television producer and director Larry Arrick, used to say, "If crying is acting, my Aunt Fanny would be a star!"

But I hadn't met Larry yet, and all I knew was that I couldn't cry on stage. (In real life, however, it seemed I never stopped.) Shirley appeared to have it all together. When she invited Luana and me to her house, we were stunned by how grown-up it seemed. She had a fireplace, she had a husband, and she was knitting, while Luana and I were these doofuses in our jeans. She was only one year older than me, but she was married and could sob on stage. Clearly I had to get my act together.

But in a way I have the men in Jeff's class to thank for sticking with my studies. If I was tired and not feeling motivated to go, I would think of the cute guys in class, and that got me out the door. When I first arrived at Jeff Corey's, James Coburn, eventual Academy Award winner and star of *The Magnificent Seven* and *The Great Escape*, was there, and so was Richard Chamberlain (I would later swoon madly over him in the television series *The Thornbirds*). Irwin Kershner was a classmate who went on to direct films like *The Eyes of Laura Mars* and *The Empire Strikes Back*. I thought he looked a bit like a button salesman.

Then there was Roger Corman. Saying that Corman later became a film producer is like saying that Walt Disney dabbled in amusement parks. Roger remains one of Hollywood's most prolific producers ever as well as a writer and director. He has done everything from westerns to horror films and will be remembered for movies like *Little Shop of Horrors* and *Fall of the House of Usher*. He mentored people like Ron Howard, Francis Ford Coppola, and Martin Scorsese. Back then he was already making movies but was in the class to learn more about actors. He was funny to watch—he often kept his eyes closed while speaking or turned his back to the rest of us.

Roy Thinnes, who would go on to star in the TV series *The Invaders,* was in our class too. I had such a crush on him. Robert Blake, television's *Baretta,* was also there. Bobby was quite insightful in his way, a little angry, and oh-so talented. He had grown up in front of cameras, starring as Mickey in the *Our Gang* television series when he was just five years old. I remember working on a scene with him for two months, in which we had to embrace. The day before we were going to do it in front of the class, right in the middle of our embrace, he tore away and yelled, "Fuck 'em! We're too good for 'em. They can pay us or we're not going to do it!"

Looking back, I was probably relieved. And a part of me understood. I find it much harder to do a scene in class than to do a play in front of an audience. In class you feel much more exposed, more vulnerable. On stage you can sink into at least a little anonymity, knowing the audience is "out there" beyond the lights. In class it's up close, personal, and you're there for criticism. To this day I would be scared to death to go back to the Actor's Studio, where I later studied, and perform for that crowd of professionals.

And then there was Jack Nicholson. Jack was in Jeff's class, but I remember first connecting with him at the Gallery Bar along with Dick Chamberlain, Carole Eastman, and writer Bob (Robert) Towne. Both Carole and Bob went on to be nominated for Academy awards, Bob winning for *Chinatown*. The Gallery Bar was so intimate, like a womb, tiny and dark and a whole world unto itself. This was the place to be before the coffee house scene really took off. There were two theaters across the street as well, so it was always full of up-and-coming actors. Others would drink, but I sipped a 7-Up.

Jack's personality sucked you in the moment you met him. He was from New Jersey, but to talk to him and listen to his easy, folksy delivery, you would have thought he was from somewhere like Texas. I thought he was so cute, with his dark brown hair and bright eyes. Such a devilish grin.

That night I asked him if he wanted to go to a beach party with me. When he said yes, I went straight over to my parents' house to make fried chicken and potato salad. There was no romance—I didn't long for Jack the way I did for Eddie—but I decided after that party that we should be best friends.

And great pals we were. Once he and his then-girlfriend Georgianna—a real stunner from acting class—came with my family and me to Balboa Island. Balboa Island, south of Los Angeles in Orange County, has long been a vacation spot attracting locals and tourists alike. I loved the pier and the pavilion, eating ice creams, and riding the ferry. That was the weekend I found out that Verve Records wanted to sign me based on the demo that Lincoln and I recorded before graduating Hollywood High. Dawn got the demo into the right hands, and now it looked like I would have a real shot. I was giddy, so Jack and I were goofier than usual. Georgianna was mortified when Jack and I stood at the edge of the water yelling, "Boobs!!!" across the bay into the night air. We vowed that "boobs" would forever be our secret word. Boobs. Years down the line, if one of us wanted to know if the other still cared, we would just say, "boobs," and if the other answered, "boobs" back, we knew everything was still the same between us. That's how racy we were back then. However, I haven't tested the theory in years.

In class it was almost always impossible for me to work on scenes with Jack because I'd be laughing so hard. If we had to kiss, forget about it. I'd fall off the couch in hysterics. That's what I did when I was embarrassed, as I often was with boys. I preferred to sit in Jack's lap and tell him my problems. "You like my devil eyebrows, Sal?" he used to say during class, with a smile.

But the man who kept me coming back to those classes was Jeff, with his infectious enthusiasm. He showed us that there were so many different ways of going about your life and career as an actor. You had to make choices, but you could live life on your own terms if you worked hard and were willing to accept the consequences. Jeff had certainly done that.

I admired people who lived on their own terms, especially women. Women who had the courage to follow their own instincts, like Katharine Hepburn. Here was a woman who, after enduring some commercial failures in the midst of an otherwise remarkable career, was labeled box office poison. So she left Hollywood and returned to the stage to do *The Philadelphia Story*, written for her by her friend Philip Barry. But she bought the rights. When the play was made into a film, she cast herself in the lead role of Tracy Lord, sandwiched between Cary Grant and Jimmy Stewart. And she went on to be nominated for an Oscar.

Jeff offered a safe place for us to be ourselves—bad, sad, confused, or just giggling—and to be a part of something. That sense of belonging was becoming essential for me. The day I went to Verve Records to sign my contract with their A&R guy, famous jazz guitarist Barney Kessel, I went alone. I didn't know him; I didn't realize I would have to record with a band I'd never met. There was no Hollywood High trio—my friends weren't there with me. Maybe eighteen-year-olds today have it all together, but I was flat-out scared. Once I signed on the dotted line, I walked out the door and never followed through, never asked what we were going to record and when. I walked away from Verve and let the world of acting envelop me, let that magic take me away. There I could release all my fear; there I had encouragement. There it was safe to be me.

At Jeff's we were insulated from glitz and glamour, not thinking about Hollywood or stardom. For us, all that mattered was learning to act, to become good at our craft. But on breaks from Jeff's class in the Hollywood Hills, we would all step outside for a talk or a smoke. Some nights we could see the giant klieg lights of the movie premieres below. Looking at those lights grazing the night sky, it was as though I was back in the bathroom mirror again: *Someday . . .*

But I had a lot still to learn.

CHAPTER 2

Make Believe

AFTER ABOUT SIX MONTHS OF BREATHING AND SCENE STUDY and sitting in the middle of the floor looking like a frump, Jeff Corey took me aside one day after class. He could see how uncomfortable I was with myself, how I couldn't take a compliment. He told me in no uncertain terms that I needed to see an analyst and start to deal with some of my self-esteem issues. It was quite clear to him, he explained, that I didn't like myself.

I waited for him to finish, then began to wail like a child.

"But I don't want to hate my parents!!"

I was sure that was what would happen if I went into therapy. Who would ever want to hate Edith and Jack Kellerman?

My mother, a dispenser of treats and unconditional love, is probably responsible for the sugar addiction that I have to this day. She made three different kinds of fudge and always iced her cakes too early. She brought them to parties like that—cracked. But they were delicious. She came from the tiny town of Portland, Arkansas—one of those towns that you were leaving the minute you entered it.

She was tiny and adorable and sometimes a little plumper than she would have liked. But in her teal blue housecoat with black velvet piping, I thought she was the most beautiful woman in the world.

My mom was a piano teacher with a daughter—me—who could not learn to play, no matter who was teaching her. But I sang everywhere and all the time—grocery stores, church, alone—and I always got all the best laughs at all the recitals. My parents had met in a piano store, where my mother, then nineteen, was giving demonstrations.

My father was handsome in that man's man kind of way. He had a winning smile and was born to wear a suit, tie, and a fedora. He could be stern but he was funny. Not knowing which side of him would show up was tricky sometimes.

He'd wanted to be an actor. That lasted two minutes. When he couldn't get a job, he became a traveling salesman instead, at first for Shell Oil. Two sides of the same coin, I guess—acting and sales. My dad had no problem quitting jobs when he wasn't promoted as quickly as he thought he should have been, but he was never out of work and excelled even at jobs he didn't like that much. He bloomed where he was planted. Move on. Reinvent.

Daddy got up at six every morning to read the paper and came home at around seven each night, poured himself a drink, and read *Time* magazine before dinner. He liked to brag that he weighed 175 pounds all his life. Beyond that, he never talked about himself. Never. Not a word, except maybe about work.

Not until much later in my life did I learn both my mother and father had been abandoned by their parents. My mom had lost her father to jail. He'd shot someone in a card game on a riverboat. And my father had three fathers die by the time he was nineteen years old. Father number three drank away all the money before he passed, and Daddy had to join the Marines instead of going to college. I think that made him feel less than everyone else somehow.

My mom and dad loved each other. "Edith, you're just going to have to stick up for yourself," Dad would say about their fights.

At one point or another we all had to endure my father's disappointed nagging. For example, there was The Coffee Incident.

"Edith! This coffee is not hot!" he would say.

"Oh, dear," Mom said. "Let me get you another cup."

Then, the next day: "Edith! This coffee is not hot. Can you not make a good cup of coffee?"

"Okay, dear, I'll get another pot."

Yet another day: "Edith, if you can't make a hot cup of coffee, I'm going to have to get a divorce!"

After about three weeks of this, of my mother rushing back and forth to the kitchen fetching coffee and my father threatening divorce, my mother finally turned on her heel and said, "Well, then, Jack dear, why don't you get one?"

I was terrified. I was sure that was it for my parents. DIVORCE. I raced over to my neighbor's house.

"My parents are getting a divorce!" I cried and told them about my dad's coffee.

The next day the neighbors saw me outside and, laughing, called over the fence. "Sally, are your parents divorced yet?" They thought it was hilarious.

The neighbors knew it wasn't serious, but I didn't know which end was up sometimes in my house. Diana called Dad's outbursts "flying off the handle." I hated seeing my father act entitled and my mother placating. Daddy always apologized, but that didn't stop him from doing the same thing again.

My parents never divorced, and my fears about that eventually subsided.

• • •

I WONDER WHY GOD CHOSE ME TO SEE THE WORLD THROUGH my eyes? You knew right away I was going to be an actress.

This was the thought that popped into my head at the age of seven as I sat under the bushes in Granada Hills in the San Fernando Valley. I was in the country, often alone, except for my black cocker spaniel, Shadow. I looked up to my sister, Diana, but she didn't want me tagging along. Her full name was Diana Dean Kellerman, but my father called her "Dinky Dean." "Hi Dinky!" I'd always squeal. Oh, how I worshipped her. "Shut up, Stinky!" she'd respond. She was always trying to get rid of me, as older siblings often do to their younger, pesky brothers and sisters. She was always tackling me and snapping towels at my legs and behind while we were washing the dishes. She liked books and studying; I sang until it drove her crazy and wanted to wander, wanted to be outside.

I was happy out in the world, in the groves of the valley with my pal Shadow. I would sit and look around, knowing that what appeared before my eyes—the eyes that God had chosen for me—looked different from what it would look like to any other person anywhere else in the world. To this day I am an overwhelmingly visual person, stimulated more by images than words on a page.

Being in the country thrilled me. It still does. I lived in the real San Fernando Valley back then, not the Valley of sprawling suburbs and strip malls. It was the Valley of orange groves and pastures, of dirt roads, eucalyptus trees, and fields of flowers, and of making colorful papier-mâché creations at the old Spanish Mission. There was one store in Granada Hills, a service station with two pumps, and a Chow Dog snack shop, which was the closest thing we had to a soda fountain. When we'd get off the bus after school, we'd go to the Chow Dog. The boys in my class would pull back the lid of the freezer, take a bite from an ice cream, and put it back. I scolded them every time, but one day I was out walking by myself and it was so hot and I was so hungry that I suddenly found myself eyeing that freezer. The man who ran the shop was in the back, and I thought, *Maybe just this one time if I snuck a bite it will be okay.* As the cool ice cream bar headed toward my mouth, out came the shopkeeper. "So YOU'RE the one who's been taking all the ice cream!" he shouted. I had to run all the way home to get the ten cents I owed and—worst of all—tell my parents.

The heat will make people do all kinds of things, and the Valley was hot, hot, hot. Summers were about swimming in all the public plunges and getting our yearly haircuts.

"Time for your haircut," Mom would say.

I got used to it, but it could be disconcerting for other kids. I remember Dickie Forrest moving in across the street just before my annual lopping.

"Hey," he said, "how come you cut your hair when I was just getting to know you?"

Then there was the time when my beautiful cousin from New Orleans, Millidge Marie Haas, was getting married and asked me to be her flower girl. That called for a special haircut. So my mom sat me down, got out the shears, and cut my long, brown hair off all the way up to the middle of my ears. Then off we went to the beauty parlor for the finishing touch, something called a "permanent."

If only it had been a "temporary."

I sat down in the chair, the hairdresser snapped the long bib around my neck, and the next thing I knew I was sitting beneath a machine that looked like it was from outer space. They put what felt like a fifty-pound bucket on my head and plugged me into a wall.

When I emerged I looked like Larry from the *Three Stooges*: my hair was flat on top with fuzzy frizz sticking out to either side. What a trauma! I was completely devastated. I wanted to hurl myself off a cliff. I was six years old and wasn't sure I could go on.

My mother thought I was overreacting and tried to reassure me. "You are God's perfect child," she told me, as always.

• • •

MY MOTHER WAS A CHRISTIAN SCIENTIST, WHICH IS ONE OF the most misunderstood faiths going. There were no doctors or trips to the hospital, this was true. But there was a lot of calm and faith and joy, if my mom's example was typical.

No doctors meant that when I got sick I got Red Hots for pills and got to lay in my mom's bed and listen to *The Shadow* on the

radio. If I felt particularly bad, she would make me floating is-
lands too—little bits of meringue resting on a runny vanilla cus-
tard to soothe what ailed me. Baked custards too. And if I ever
came home from school crying, I got cinnamon toast with butter
and a cup of cocoa. Finding candy in our house was like a game.
It was stashed in the linen closet, in my father's golf bag in the
trunk of his car, even in the bottom of the dirty clothes hamper. I
thought the hunt was fun. While other kids were studying, I was
looking for candy in the laundry room.

To my mind, mom's was a spiritual, loving God. She reminded
me of this and her abundant view of the world on a daily basis:

"You are God's perfect child."

"Supply is unlimited."

"The expectancy of good."

"Fear has no power, only what we give it."

But one of her sayings scared me a little.

"Ingratitude is the back door through which all our blessings
escape."

God forbid I had an ungrateful thought. I worried that every
time I complained I was shooing my blessings away.

Perhaps the one that has given me the most comfort is "Everything we need is within us."

I think of books today and various movements that rely on
visualization or embracing gratitude and trusting that all will be
revealed in the best possible way, and all I can think is that my
mom was ahead of her time. She had her faith in God tested on
more than one occasion, but she never, ever complained.

"I sure wish I was taller" was about the only thing even close
to a complaint that I ever heard from her lips.

• • •

SOMETIME AROUND FIFTH GRADE WE MOVED TO SAN FER-
nando proper, to a lovely little house on Brand Boulevard two
blocks in from Laurel Canyon. That's where I trained Shadow to
jump the fence. I was so proud (my father not so much). Shadow

and I would wander around looking for adventures together. One day, while we were out walking, I saw a huge expanse of dirt in the distance. I got a little closer. They were houses, but strangely, they were all being built at the same time. They looked exactly alike. *Oh no*, I thought, looking at the changing Valley, *I hope it doesn't get too crowded.*

I swam like a fish throughout junior high and even won first place in All-Valley butterfly as well as third in All-City medley. But things started to change socially, and my self-image started to take a hit. I was growing—fast—and suddenly looking for reasons to feel good about myself. One of the most frustrating things about being so tall so young was that there was very little I could wear in my size that was cute. There were no clothes for big girls, for people who didn't look like my little five-foot-two mom, all high heels and petite femininity. But feeling big made me ready to take anything that was said to me the wrong way. When one of the kids in my seventh-grade class told me I had a crooked smile, at first it hurt my feelings.

"No," my friend explained. "It's sexy."

Sexy? What was that, exactly? I wasn't entirely sure, but I could tell by the way he said the word that I definitely wanted to be it. So when it was time for school pictures, I tried to smile just as crooked as I could. The day we took the pictures home I showed my father the best shot.

"That's disgusting," he said, and he tore it to pieces in front of me.

He wanted my older sister, Diana, and me to be more like our mother: to wear dresses, to be more, well, demure. So the two of us occasionally found ourselves dressed in matching pinafores. He also wanted us to do well in school. Diana was a bookworm, but school was never my thing, outside of drama, choir, gym, and recess. I preferred playing in George Pupitch's haystack to doing my homework. George called me "moo moo clarabell jersey bounce labatroite" after all his neighboring cows because I was taller than all the neighboring cows—and most of the boys. But once I returned from haystacks and walks with Shadow, my father was always checking in on me, hovering over me and my books.

"Think!" he'd snap, when all I wanted to do was nap. I couldn't manage to read to save my life. I'd look ahead a few pages so that if my dad quizzed me, I would have an answer. "Tom Sawyer was just getting some kids to paint a fence," I'd tell my father.

"Okay . . . very good," he'd say. And the minute he was out the door I'd be asleep.

I earned Cs, Ds, and Fs. I needed—still do—people to make things interesting for me. Sitting in a classroom with a teacher verbally instructing me put me to sleep. I just couldn't take it in. Not until I had kids of my own would I discover I had a life-long learning disability, the kind that wasn't acknowledged—let alone diagnosed or medicated—in the 1950s. If you did poorly, you weren't working hard enough, plain and simple. Even later, after millions of classes, when actors or teachers would give me books or lecture about the "spine of the character," the words and lessons never sunk in. I need to *be*. I need to *do*.

. . .

STILL, I MANAGED TO KEEP SCHOOL INTERESTING. IN ELEMEN-tary school I'd started a Cowgirl Club. We ran around slapping our legs, pretending to be riding horses. I was a huge fan of Betty Hutton and used to paint freckles on my nose and put on my roller skates and sing songs from *Annie Get Your Gun*. Another highlight of my youth was joining the Bathroom Club. To belong, you had to be willing to go to the bathroom in the orange groves. I was the only girl in the club. In middle school clubs got a little clique-ier. Girls were invited to join, girls were kicked out. None of it made a whole lot of sense to me.

When I was invited to join the Girls Club at San Fernando Junior High, my best friend, Sherry, didn't want me to and was a little possessive of my attention. Sherry and I had known each other for years, and she didn't like me to have other friends.

When we were younger we would take snails from the garden, put them in a jar, salt them, and watch them shrivel and die. (We hadn't heard about animal cruelty.) When we moved on to having sleepovers, Sherry told me how to masturbate. But then Sherry joined the Girls Club before me—the same one she'd insisted I not join—and kicked out the girl who had invited me to join. Then I insisted we bring her back, and they did. Then they all kicked me out. I had no idea know why, but something occurred to me: I could get myself a whole new gang. And I did.

I was voted class clown in the ninth grade and decided to audition for the *Follies* with Sherry. I created our musical act: I was the star, the director, and the choreographer. I decided it would be a little bit Fred Astaire and Ginger Rogers, a little bit like *Show Boat*, with Ava Gardner, and that there'd be roller skates involved. Singing was nothing without a little extra something, and roller skates added real panache.

My sister told me that, on skates, I looked like an elephant on a teacup. Before, when I was younger, I was too skinny; now I was an elephant. Diana had always teased me when I would gab or sing. "Shut up, big lips, with your stupid voice!" she'd say. "Big lips" always made me cry. But she was so smart and so bookish and seemed to have the answer to everything. I idolized her. I thought she looked just like Shirley MacLaine. Was she right about my *Follies* routine? I didn't care. Nothing ever stopped me from performing.

Sherry and I rehearsed and auditioned our show to be a part of the Follies. I was stunned when we our act didn't make the cut. It was my first real performance rejection—but certainly not the last. I retired to my room and stood in front of the mirror. I looked deep into my own eyes, smiling a crooked smile.

Someday . . . Someday . . .

By the time I was in junior high, acting and singing were already inseparable for me. I wanted to be a movie star, and I wanted to have a huge wedding so everyone could come and see how pretty I looked. I wanted to sing. Unfortunately, I kept getting plumper as I worked my way through junior high, so admitting out loud I wanted to act began to seem like more of a stretch. I didn't think I looked like the actresses I admired. I didn't look like Doris Day. So I kept my desire a secret.

With the onset of my extra pounds, our mealtimes went from the routine teasing of my mom to an ongoing interrogation from my father. He analyzed every bite that made its way from my plate to my mouth.

"Sit up straight. Do you want to eat in the garage? That's too much salt! That's too much sugar!"

He became the warden of the prison I'd made, burying myself under the weight of Twinkies and candy bars until I was ready to come out.

There was little that my mother could do but put her usual positive spin on my weight gain. "Well, darling," she used to say, "you're so well proportioned."

Oh, Mom. To this day whenever a script hands me a "dear," I always wish it were a "darling."

My weight gain was partly due to puberty and shooting skyward. But in therapy I realized that there was also probably some fallout from the unwanted attention I received from the father of a friend, "Jennifer," whenever I spent the night at her house.

The first time he climbed into bed with me I was around ten or eleven years old. Jennifer and I came in from outside, covered in adobe mud. We cleaned up and crawled into Jennifer's twin beds. Jennifer's father came in to say good night and then, instead of leaving, got into bed with me. I didn't know what to do. I just froze.

Maybe it was because I didn't cry out that he kept pushing it. He kept after me, holding me and touching my chest, eventually putting his hand between my legs. He would stroll around the house naked with a huge erection while I was there. I remember wondering how it was that men ever got their pants on. Once he took Jennifer and me for a drive and parked somewhere in the woods. He began to tell us dirty stories, things I'd never heard before or even understood. Then he said, "You girls won't be virgins when you get married." Jennifer and I started sobbing. With every advance, I didn't know what to say. Only once did he ever put my hand on his penis. And that was when I finally managed to speak. "Don't you ever touch me again," I said, and that was all it took. However, it took me a long time to work up the courage to do it.

I didn't dare tell my parents. I never told anyone—except Jennifer. When I did, she just glared at me, furious, and said, "So?"

. . .

IT TOOK ME YEARS TO UNDERSTAND THAT I HAD FINE PARENTS who simply reflected their own lifetime of pain, their own secrets. But they never, ever complained. They lived. They had fun. Still, I regarded them as products of the Victorian era. There was a right way to do things and a wrong way. There were rules, and people lived their lives according to those rules, especially proper young women. There was a lot that went unsaid in our house, things I would have liked to have known about. The foremost of these was the story of my younger sister.

My mother waved down to Diana and me from the hospital window when the baby was born. We weren't allowed to go up to see her for ourselves. Those were the days when doctors and nurses swept in to take your child the moment it was out of your body. A hospital room with a newborn was not the place for children.

When my parents brought Victoria home, I thought she was the most adorable thing I had ever seen. At first she just lay there in her crib, staring off. Then, after a few months, she learned to giggle and would make eye contact. She was about eight months old when my mother left for a weekend to attend a spiritual conference. She had never left us before. Because she had to leave town, she arranged for a housekeeper to come stay to take care of Diana, me, and little Victoria.

I remember the housekeeper standing at our old-fashioned

stove the first night my mother was gone. The housekeeper was talking to me as she was stirring supper on the stove. I liked watching her cook. It was kind of mesmerizing.

She told me about a friend of hers who was staying with a family when their baby died. Then she added, "I just don't know what I would do if that happened to me."

That sounded horrible to me. She stopped talking and kept on stirring. I watched her spoon go around and around. Was this an omen?

Our house had railroad bedrooms—you had to pass through Diana's and my bedroom to get to Victoria's. So the next morning there was no way Diana and I would not know what was happening.

The housekeeper came running through our room on her way out into the hall, screaming, "The baby's dead!!! The baby's dead!!! The baby!"

I froze. My father was next, flying into our room from the hall, racing in to see Vicky.

He staggered back out of Vicky's room, saying, "Girls, don't go in there. Stay where you are!"

As soon as he was out in the hall, I snuck into Vicky's room. She was just lying there, a little bit of saliva at the corner of her mouth, her eyes still open. I ran into the bathroom with Diana before my father caught me. We could still hear the hysterical cries of the housekeeper. I was furious. I was sure it was somehow her fault.

"Let me out of here!" I yelled at Diana. "I'm gonna kill her! Let me out! LET ME OUT!"

Diana was so kind; she tried to calm me down. All of a sudden my dad swooped in and took us down the street to the home of the Greens, our close family friends. Then he left without saying when he'd be back. All we knew was that he was going to see my mother.

I loved the Greens and was comfortable there. Lori Ann, one of my good friends, was two years younger than I was and had two brothers, one my age and one older. Their mom, Jean, an attractive blond woman, was my mom's best friend and also a Christian Scientist. She drove a fancy Lincoln with a tire on the back. She'd pull up to our house and give a honk, and then she and my mother would go for lunch. Mrs. Green was funny and kind and used to braid my hair and pull on it like I was one of her own kids. One Sunday, while walking home from Sunday school with my good friend Lori Ann, we found some pamphlets lying on the sidewalk and got the wonderful idea to go door to door and sell them for ten cents each! When we got back to the Green's house, Mrs. Green was amused.

"How wonderful, girls," she said. "But these are pamphlets for the Catholic Church."

But even kind Mrs. Green could not tell me when I would see my parents again. I went to school and tried not to think about it. Then one day our car appeared at the curb. Both my mother and father were in it. They packed up our things, making no mention of Vicky. When we got home, everything to do with my baby sister was gone. There was no crib. There were no toys. No photos. Nothing. There was no sign she had ever existed at all.

From that moment forward, my family acted as if nothing had happened. I don't know if my ability to pick myself up and start over again came from that experience, or if my willingness to accept new realities or create my own without much of hiccup stemmed from that. But I do know that it was only during the writing of this book that I realized I have never, ever, seen a photo of Vicky or heard her name mentioned since she left us.

One day, a couple of weeks after Vicky died, I said to Mom, "Didn't you love Vicky?"

My mother gasped and turned away and said in a broken voice, "Of course, dear. Why?"

"Because you never cried."

She said, her voice breaking, "I was just trying to protect you girls."

I recently talked to Diana, and we both admitted that we felt so sad that our family never said anything about the loss of our sister, and we felt so bad for our mother's feeling that she couldn't discuss it because she had to protect her daughters.

· · ·

So maybe therapy wasn't such a bad idea after all. I trusted Jeff Corey; I looked up to him. On his advice, I began a lifetime of therapy. At the very least, I thought the therapist—a lovely man at the university—could help me lose weight and then I would feel better about myself. That's how it always works, right? So I went because I thought I was fat and didn't want to be fat anymore. But the very thing that I did not want to happen— hating my parents—did.

As soon as I started seeing the therapist, I was blaming my mom and dad for everything. I rebelled against Christian Science. *If God is so great, then how come I'm fat, don't have a boyfriend, and I'm not a movie star?* I'd rail. I was having tantrums and shouting and wanting them not to have Victorian values and wanting my mother not to be so proper and wanting my dad not to be tight and jiggle the change in his pocket and be stern and severe and judgmental. He didn't want me to be in a pair of jeans; he wanted me to be in a dress. But I was a rebel, so he had a hard time liking me. And it seemed as if he didn't like me unless I was in a dress. But he wanted to like me. I believe he really wanted to like me.

Woven into my memory was another trauma. One day, while we were still living in San Fernando, my mom had said, "Dear, we're moving tomorrow and you can't take your dog Shadow."

I almost died. The very next day we drove to the vet. Shadow was shaking all the way there, and I was sobbing. When Mom learned that we couldn't just leave him at the vet's and not come back for him, we drove home and left him with a neighbor, who said she'd take care of him. Shadow apparently spent his last days walking the route with the postman. I never saw Shadow again, but I dreamed about him for years.

On the day we moved to "town"—Los Angeles—in the middle of my sophomore year of high school, I was sure my mother had ruined my life. Los Angeles was big, busy, and full of distraction—everything our little Valley was not. I remember once saying, "Mom, where's the town?" It seemed to be everywhere and nowhere at once.

I'd always wanted to be an actress even if it took me a while to admit it. I loved to watch TV with my family—Edward R. Murrow's *See It Now*, Jack Benny, Groucho Marx, Jackie Gleason, *Dragnet*, and, the queen of them all, *I Love Lucy*. I worshipped Lucille Ball. But I loved my Valley, and Los Angeles never figured in my dreams. In my mind Hollywood had nothing to do with becoming an actress.

Mom was happy about the move, though. She loved being out of the Valley and closer to my sister, who was attending UCLA. She also believed that she had all the answers. There was one right way to live life, and she was going to teach me—or die trying. She would not let LA ruin me.

CHAPTER 3

Check, Please

MY MOTHER ONCE TOLD ME THAT SHE TRULY BELIEVED I HAD decided to become an actress just so that I could become a waitress. That cracked me up.

But the truth was that I needed work. I needed money to pay for acting classes with Jeff Corey. So during my early years in Hollywood, when I lived in and around Sunset Boulevard, I spent much of that time dipping down for the cups and dishes at Chez Paulette.

Before Chez Paulette I had had two other brief and failed attempts at work in the office world. At one job I was a filing clerk at Capitol Records. I could barely read, so filing was not my specialty. I threw up every morning out of fear that I'd be found out (and I was). And for a while I was an elevator operator at Colter's, a store on Miracle Mile. I lasted two days because I got carsick going up and down all day.

Like most actors, I spent my share of time on the unemployment line. That was where my friend David Bennett from acting class would often find me, yank me out of line, and force me to go out on auditions. But then I found my true actress's calling and began waiting tables.

It was the late 1950s. Los Angeles was beautiful then—all blue skies and puffy white clouds and no traffic or paparazzi. Chez Paulette, a coffeehouse, was on Sunset Boulevard about a block or so east of La Cienega, across from Dino's restaurant, which was owned by Rat Packer Dean Martin. That's where the television show *77 Sunset Strip* took place, featuring my now ex-boyfriend Eddie Byrnes. At first the hip coffeehouse was a place called the Unicorn on Sunset and started by a great guy named Herby Cohen. My best friend, Luana, and I hung out there every night listening to live folk music. Chez Paulette opened later; it was a place where people came to eat and talk.

Chez Paulette was long and narrow, with six or seven tables on the outside patio and maybe ten or so round tables inside. The place was packed every night. There was always flamenco music playing on the stereo, wafting out the doors onto Sunset Boulevard, the center of all things. However, this music did nothing to dissuade me from singing whenever I felt like it as I flitted from table to table.

My boss at Chez Paulette was Max Lewin. He was short, had a very obvious comb-over, and walked with a limp. But despite all that, he carried himself as though he were Napoleon. Max and his family were Polish—I absolutely adored his accent! He could be gruff and bossy at times but protective at others. His parents did all the cooking in the back; they were very sweet but didn't say much. Their most popular dessert was the Sachertorte, an Austrian chocolate cake that had a layer of apricot jam, a dish that first became famous at the Hotel Sacher in Vienna. When someone asked me what we had for dessert, I'd say, "*they* have soccer tortas."

One of the mainstays of Chez Paulette was Barry Feinstein. Barry, who was from New York, worked behind the counter, where he manned the cappuccino machine and prepared all the ice cream dishes, coffees, and hot apple cider. Also in charge of prep work, he was usually the first one to show up and the first one to leave. Whenever I arrived early to set up tables, Barry would already be there, grumbling as he sliced and chopped oranges and lemons for the hot cider. I would look at him and think, *What a man.* He didn't have but a few wisps of curls on his balding head, and those that were there he wore very close cropped. He was a little stocky—manly, I thought—and he always looked unshaven.

Barry was a photographer who did a lot of work for record companies. He showed me some of his pictures, which were stunning. He eventually became incredibly successful, shooting album covers for people like Bob Dylan and George Harrison, as well as for my hero Janis Joplin's 1971 album *Pearl.* Though he always said that one day he'd photograph me, he never did.

The closest thing I ever got to a compliment from Barry was "Hey, Sally, you look sorta good tonight." Gee, thanks. But usually when I came in to work, Barry would greet me with "Oh God, kiss me, sit on my face." Another one of his favorite sayings was "I gotta get out of this fuckin' town." Sometimes, when the place was packed, I'd run up to the counter and say, "Two hot ciders on the double, Barry!" Barry would grab my hand, shove it in the hot cider, and say, "Repeat after me: shit-fuck-tits-piss-balls-suck-cunt-lick-chew." I would say "No, I won't! Let go of my hand!" He would repeat the litany while Max, my boss, would be yelling "Sally, get the hot cider!" He knew I was incredibly naive and inexperienced, so he loved to tease me. He was so outrageous, such a little dickens. As for a country girl like me, well, it all felt rebellious and like too much fun.

Beyond that, we hardly spoke a word to each other. Though Barry may have always acted a little grumpy, he had a great laugh that cut through his tough, crabby exterior.

An expert at waiting tables I was not, but what I lacked in expertise I made up for in enthusiasm. I loved the physicality of waitressing—swooping in and dipping down to pick up the cups, drop off dishes, and then dashing away to do it all over again. I wore my old wool skirt with the crinoline underneath and kept my hair pulled back.

Another perk of the job, as far as I was concerned, was getting to talk to everybody. It was better than going to a party—I was invited to every table. Sometimes I'd sit down and visit with one of my pals until Max barked in his Polish accent: "Sally, when you finish talking to your friend, do you mind waiting on the tables?"

Chez Paulette was my home away from home, but I did have a place of my own. Shortly after getting fired from Capitol Records, Diana took a job in Washington, DC, with the State Department, and I moved in with Virginia Aldridge. We were an odd pair. Virginia was a dancer on the television program Dick Sinclair's *Polka Parade*; she would go on to become a writer and work a lot in TV. She always helped me—drove me to work, loaned me five bucks if I needed it. Very sweet. I, however, felt like a schlub. I took twin beds from my parents' house, then drew a diagram of how our apartment should look. Virginia and I used the box springs for our two couches and the mattresses for our beds. So much for my decorating career.

At the time I was occasionally teaching at the Crystal Scarborough swim school, and I also got a job wrapping packages at Bullock's department store on Wilshire near Western Avenue, where I'd once driven with my mom all the way from San Fernando to buy my one good sweater. I was terrible at wrapping; to this day it's no mystery which presents under the tree yours truly wrapped.

Beyond that, I would lie on the floor in my apartment, lamenting my lot in life and the fact I wasn't getting real acting jobs; occasionally my mother would drop by with a little money and a roast. I would still call or visit home, sometimes just to tell my mother how nothing was working out the way I'd planned or how I was fat. My mother would get off the phone in such a state, wondering what she could do to help. Then my dad, not buying a bit of it, would step in.

Never one for whiners, my dad would say, "Edith! She's fine! Now that she's just called and unloaded on you, she's probably out having a great time."

Dad was right. I was having a great time. I've always made sure to suffer—but I never let that stop me from having fun.

. . .

EVEN ON A WAITRESS'S SALARY, I COULD AFFORD TO LIVE RIGHT in the middle of it all, just steps from Sunset Boulevard. And I could afford acting classes to boot. Working at Chez Paulette was my first big star turn—mingling with the greats. At that point I was waiting on more movie stars than I would work with over my entire career.

Carroll Righter, "Astrologer to the Stars," came in the first night I worked at the Chez. He called out to me: "Waiter!" thinking I was a man because of my height. Psychic? Maybe not. But Max told me I had to be nice to him. I usually found even the grouchy customers fun. The surlier, the better.

"Can I have some salt?" one regular asked me as I put down his hamburger. And I scooted off to retrieve it.

I returned, salt in hand, and went about my business. A few moments later he called me over again.

"Can I have some mustard?"

Of course. I fetched the mustard and brought it over. Within moments he called me over once more.

"Can I have some pepper?" he asked.

"How about asking for it all at once?"

"Look, lady," he said. "It's not my fault you're a waitress."

Will Sage was an older actor who came in regularly and always left me a ten-cent tip. "Buy yourself a new hat," Will would say. A nickel was the norm among customers. Occasionally a diner at Chez Paulette would be in a good mood and leave a quarter. One time an older man left me a whole dollar, and I chased him down the street, yelling, "Sir! Sir! You left your money!"

Will was so kind. He'd stop by my apartment, which was always unlocked in those days, and fix little things for us. He always left a note that said, "The bunny was here." For the handyman work, I should have been tipping him.

You never knew who else would stop by at Chez Paulette. John Cassavetes, John Barrymore Jr., other producers and directors. There may have been a couple of famous Hollywood women that I waited on, but I mostly remember the men.

Steve McQueen would stop by with his very pregnant wife, Neile, dropping her off so she could relax and stay off her feet while he took off on his motorcycle.

The first time I saw Warren Beatty he was with his agent Paul Brandon. Warren asked Paul to find out if I would go out with him. Paul asked. I looked at Warren and thought, "Aw, he's just a kid my age."

"Absolutely not," I said.

At the time Warren asked me out, I liked an actor named Harry Guardino, who was older, dark, and Italian. He used to come into Chez Paulette all the time. One night a customer said to me, "You're really big."

Harry leapt to my defense: "No, she's not. She's a woman and beautiful!"

That's all it took. I had an official crush. Unfortunately, Harry was married. The next year Warren Beatty was being celebrated as the handsomest guy in town and starring in Elia Kazan's *Splendor in the Grass*. But then I've never been known for my foresight.

• • •

AT THAT POINT I WAS IN THERAPY. I STILL REMEMBER THE first question my therapist asked me: *Do you masturbate?* I cried for the whole hour, I was so ashamed. But once I got over that—while continuing to pray for forgiveness every time I masturbated—I spent my first half year or so of therapy trying to get over my mad, desperate love for Marlon Brando. Then one night, as we were closing up and I was wiping down the tables, Max came rushing over.

"We're OPEN!" he said in an excited whisper.

I looked up, and in walked Marlon with a tall blond man I'd never seen before. I froze, then quickly thawed myself out and got back to wiping off the tables on the patio.

The last time I'd bumped into Marlon, I was with Virginia. That had been a short while after my infamous first car ride with him. That night he'd invited Virginia and me up to his house along with a couple of his friends: Christian Marquand, the French actor many will remember from *Lord Jim* and *Apocalypse Now*, and Roger Vadim, who would go on to write *Barbarella* and marry its star, Jane Fonda. At this point Vadim may have been coming out of his marriage to Brigitte Bardot.

We had all gone to Marlon's place on Mulholland, where he played the bongos for us. At the end of the night he instructed Virginia and me to drop off Christian and Vadim. Instead of taking the guys straight home, we stopped at the Sea Witch for a snack and then went back our place on Havenhurst. Christian and I hung out in the living room, necking on my box spring, while Virginia was in the bedroom with Vadim. Nobody got laid, or "lost our snowflakes," as we liked to put it. As morning dawned, we drove the guys back to the Beverly Hilton in Virginia's Plymouth, which had ratty lining that hung down in all our faces. The guys got out of the car and said they'd call the next day.

Of course they didn't.

Despondent after waiting all day by the phone, we finally gave up and decided go to see . . . *And God Created Woman*, written and directed by Vadim and starring Bardot and Christian. That just made us sicker than we were before; Christian was so gorgeous and Vadim so obviously talented. We went to drown our sorrows at Cosmo Alley. As we arrived—wearing the same clothes we'd had on the night before—who should we see come strolling out the door but Marlon, Vadim, and Christian?

Marlon said, "Look, boys! Your girls are here!"

Then he said good-bye and abruptly walked off, leaving his friends behind.

Vadim looked at me and said, "I'm very disappointed in you, Sally."

"He's not really leaving, is he?" Christian asked, referring to Marlon.

"I think he is," I said.

Looking puzzled and awkward, Vadim and Christian started chasing after Marlon, yelling, "Marlon, come back, come back, don't leave us!"

Virginia and I just looked at each other.

Afterward, whenever we thought of that night, Virginia and I would blame our disappointment on the lining of our Plymouth. "They would have loved us if we hadn't driven them home in the old Plymouth," we'd always joke.

That had been a few months before. And now here was Marlon again. Max barked at me to bring him and his friend their menus. Fine. I dropped them off and made a beeline for the other end of the room. I kept wiping the same clean tables over and over again, but then wiped myself into a corner right next to Marlon's table.

"Sally," he mumbled in his cool, raspy voice. "Don't you remember me, or are you playing it cool?"

I whirled toward him, just as I had the first night I'd met him.

"I'm playing it cool because every minute I've ever spent with you was the worst minute of my life!"

He just smiled.

"Would you like to come up to the house?

"Yes, I would," I said.

I took off my apron. The three of us got into Marlon's car, with me in the middle, frozen again, just as I had been at Cosmo Alley. When we arrived at his house, Marlon ran quickly inside, saying he needed to go to the bathroom. I stood alone in the dark with the other man.

"It must be wonderful to be so quiet and self-contained," he said.

I could definitely never keep up that act. I was tempted to flee before the real me showed up and started talking a mile a minute.

Marlon showed the three of us up to his bedroom, where I was certain he was trying to set me up with his friend. I don't remember what we were talking about, but at one point I got a little teary. Marlon reached over and touched my leg, trying to comfort me, and I said, testily, "Don't touch me, because you'll never touch me as much as I want you to."

I looked up to see that the blond man was gone. I was alone in bed with my hero.

I spent the night fighting him off, all because I wanted to be special. I didn't want to be one of many. He was *my* hero. I always felt he would understand me if he really got to know me. I was special, all right: Marlon hated me. The next morning I awoke to slamming doors and drawers. Marlon was huffing and puffing and stomping around.

I sat straight up in bed and said, "Hey! You can't be mad at me because I didn't sleep with you." A mistake I wouldn't make in my next life.

I left, having said no to Marlon once again. I didn't see him at the Chez after that.

I think back to those days at the restaurant and realize now that they were a snapshot of unspoiled, classic Hollywood. Imagine Marlon Brando and Steve McQueen sitting undisturbed as they ate their food, not surrounded by cameras or reporters or iPhones. Steve was already a big name, and Marlon was a legend, having done *Viva Zapata, The Men, Guys and Dolls, Streetcar Named Desire,* and *The Wild One,* to name just a few of his films. He had been nominated for five Oscars and won one, for *On the Waterfront.* And there he sat at one of our tables, not bothered by a soul. Can you imagine George Clooney and Brad Pitt sitting down for a hot apple cider on Sunset Boulevard today, being left alone, in peace? It was another world. The actors we admired were larger than life and yet within reach.

. . .

OF COURSE, MY FRIENDS CAME INTO CHEZ PAULETTE AS WELL. Everyone hung out there: Jack, Luana, Carole Eastman, my friend piano player–singer-songwriter Morgan Ames, and the rest of our class. Jack, Luana, and Sandra Knight (who later married Jack), had been "runners" at MGM, teenagers taking scripts and notes from one building to another. Luana and I were thick as thieves. I was still rooming with Virginia, and though we hung out occasionally, we didn't have a lot in common because Luana and I weren't girlie girls like her. We looked down on perfect hair and makeup. Somewhere between Beatniks and hippies in our shirts and messy jeans, we thought ourselves cool and soulful and the ones with the real goods.

Luana had grown up in foster care, so trust wasn't something that came easily to her. But she was such a great listener and so giving that everyone adored her. I'd mention something in passing that I liked—a purse, a top—and it would show up hanging from the doorknob of my apartment the next day. Virginia wanted to be friends with Luana, but Luana wasn't interested. "Is Sally here?" is about all she'd say to Virginia, and then Luana and I would go sit in my little walk-in closet—the only real private place in the apartment because I shared a bedroom with Virginia—and giggle.

Morgan Ames was another great pal, with lacy plastic eyeglass frames and a bad perm until Luana and I helped her get rid of both. She played piano and was a struggling musician at the time, and we had been introduced because a mutual friend, Bud Dashiell, of the folk duo Bud and Travis, knew I wanted to sing and thought Morgan and I would make a perfect duo. I don't know who was the worse performer back then, her or me. Morgan was the one who'd coined the phrase "snowflake" as code for our virginity, which was the topic of the day.

After long nights waiting tables, I'd get to bed around 2 or 3 A.M., so I'd sleep in. In the mornings I would meet Luana or Morgan for breakfast at Schwab's, two blocks away from my apartment on Havenhurst. Schwab's had everything: it was a soda fountain, a pharmacy, and a place where, anytime of the day, you could see someone you knew—mostly out-of-work actors. Plus, Schwab's had great soup.

Next to Schwab's, on the corner of Sunset and Crescent Heights, was Googie's Coffeehouse, a big spot for after-hours hamburgers. Its design was out of this world. John Lautner, a famed architect, had designed it with a real midcentury, space-age, atomic feel, with sharp angles, angled rooftops, and starbursts—a classic, funky, 1950s Los Angeles look that would define an entire architectural style known today as "Googie." Sadly, Googie's and Schwab's are long gone. Today the space is a shopping behemoth sporting a Trader Joe's, Veggie Grill, Crunch Gym, and Rockin' Sushi.

The Sea Witch was another of our favorite spots for a sandwich and a malt. My friend Burt Shonberg, a vibrant and eccentric artist, lived in a tiny room above Sunset Boulevard, not too far from the Witch, and he painted murals on its interior walls in exchange for free food. He did that all over Hollywood—art for food! But the time always came when the coffeehouses would change hands or close up for good, and Burt would watch his beautiful work being painted over, often in a drab, lifeless white, as the space prepared for its next inhabitant.

On my twenty-first birthday Burt made a painting for me titled, "Something Greeen for Sally," featuring a psychedelic alien and my then-address, 1331 Havenhurst, down in the corner. Green was my favorite color. I still have the painting hanging in my office. Just this year I was interviewed for a documentary about Burt. He developed quite a following over the course of his life—Ringo Starr purchased several of his paintings—but I often wonder how many walls along Sunset have Burt's magic buried beneath layers of paint.

After I got off shift, if I was still up for it, I'd go with Barry to the neon-lit Knife and Fork and have some chocolate ice cream with bananas. Otherwise, I'd go back to my apartment and have people over there. Or I might—as I did on one particularly bizarre night—find myself getting a freakish lesson in human sexuality from a man with a bath towel wrapped around his head.

On the surface Mr. Blank—who I'd always refer to as Towel Head after my first "lesson"—seemed like a perfectly normal guy when first he showed up at Chez Paulette. One evening he walked into the Chez with Anna Kashfi, Marlon Brando's first wife. I was so excited. She'd been married to Marlon. Anyone who was close to Marlon I found fascinating.

"Can I have some honey, honey?" Mr. "Blank" said to me after I had brought over some tea. I brought him his honey, wondering how he knew Marlon and Anna, and the three of us made some small talk. Mr. Blank mentioned to me that he painted, and that's really all I remember about our introduction.

But that wasn't the last of him. Several nights later, as Max and I were closing up, the phone rang. It was around 1 or 2 A.M., and Max told me I had a call. It was Mr. Blank. Did I remember him from the other night? Sure, I did. Well, would I like to come over and see some of his paintings?

It was after one in the morning, but I was young, virginal, and a little thick around the waist—not to mention the head, when it came to men—far from experienced, to say the least. The old line, "Hey, honey, wanna come up and see my etchings?" was lost on me. Something felt strange about it, but I have never been good at saying no. I rarely had the confidence to speak my mind or turn anyone down. So I pawned off the decision on the only person nearby that I could ask for advice: Max "Napoleon" Lewin.

I put my hand over the phone and turned to Max in a tizzy. I explained my situation and asked him what he thought. Should I go over to see the man's paintings? What did Max think of Mr. Blank?

Max, in all his wisdom, answered, "I would trust him with my life."

I may have been inexperienced— people like Barry were constantly teasing me for being uptight and naive—but I always had a healthy curiosity. Because I had Max's blessing, I thought I should risk the adventure. I got back on the phone and said I would be on my way.

"I hope you don't mind that I have my robe on," Mr. Blank said.

"That's fine," I answered. "As long as you don't take it off."

When I arrived at the apartment, Mr. Blank did, indeed, answer the door in his robe.

He had a nice apartment—bigger than mine, certainly—and he walked me over to the living room, where there were two couches. I perched on one, he sat on the other. After a little small talk, he steered the conversation toward the topic of nudist colonies.

"People should feel free to sit with each other naked," he began.

Uh-huh . . . okay. I wondered why he was telling me this, but I just sat and listened innocently. I didn't know about nudist colonies.

Then, suddenly, he stood and excused himself, disappearing down the hall. I naturally assumed that he was going to get his paintings.

So I waited. And waited.

When he did finally return, he was empty handed. He was still wearing the robe, but now he had a bath towel hanging around his neck too.

I asked him what the towel was for.

"It's funny that you noticed that," he said, as if it were the most insightful question. "I really think men and women should feel free with their bodies."

I thought he was going to sit down and return to the nudist colony discussion. Instead, he continued, "For instance, if I should whip off my robe, you should be perfectly comfortable . . ."

With that, he dropped his robe, sweeping the towel up around his head and face like a mummy. He performed both actions in one giant swoop—the robe hitting the floor and the towel going up around his head—as though his movements had been carefully rehearsed or he'd done them a thousand times before. A little sliver of eyeball was all I could see of his face.

"This won't do any good," I said, turning away. "Because I'm not going to look. Besides, you can see me."

Out of the corner of my eye I saw him adjust the towel so that his eyes were now completely covered.

I peeked. I had to. There he stood, completely naked, with a huge erection.

Then he began talking—lecturing me, really.

"It's important for you to understand that a man has plenty of control even if he has an erection," he said, his voice quivering and his breath becoming heavier. "I mean, a man can just stand there with an erection. Don't let them fool you. Don't ever let them tell you that you have to give in, claiming they can't control themselves. A man can hold it for a long time. Because a girl like you—and I'm trying to help you here because I know you're a virgin—it's really very important that you understand these kinds of things."

As he kept talking, I felt myself shift into classroom mode as though I were sitting in school, in front of a blackboard. I wasn't scared; I was mesmerized. I told him I couldn't wait to tell my analyst what I was learning. He said in a wobbling voice, "Well, be sure to tell him, a friend was just trying to help you."

"I'll show you in a minute what a man likes to do and what he likes a woman to do," he went on, then carefully made his way back to the couch across from me. He lay down, put his hand on his erection—the towel still on his head, of course—and began to stroke himself. As he did, he gave me a play-by-play account of what he was doing to himself.

After a short time he reached over and took my hand and placed it over his. He held it there and explained in detail what was about to happen next and that I shouldn't be alarmed. But I was bit anxious. This was only the second time in my life I had ever touched a man's penis; the first was Jennifer's father.

Then Towel Head ejaculated, and the lesson appeared to be over.

I stood up and prepared to leave.

"Gee, thanks," I said, making my way toward the door. "I can't wait to tell my analyst about this."

"Oh well, remember when you do, you just tell him that a friend was trying to help you," he answered.

"Oh, I sure will," I said.

I meant it sincerely. I know it sounds crazy, but I was so grateful that he would take the time to teach me, to show me how it all worked.

Then, as I moved past him to exit into the hall, I actually shook his hand. Then he reached out and touched my boobs. I kept right on walking and went to my car.

Driving home, I was excited, elated, and wired from the whole strange experience. Then suddenly, it struck me, "Oh my God, that was horrible. What have I done?!"

When I got home, I went into Virginia's room, woke her up, and told her the whole bizarre tale. She found it amusing more than anything and wasn't all that fazed. But she was distracted. She had news of her own that she wanted to share with me.

"I lost my snowflake last night!" she exclaimed.

So there it was. I got the pervert and Virginia got laid.

The next night I went to work, dreading the possibility that Mr. Blank might come in. How would I act? What would I say? But Towel Head was a no-show. Months later, when he did return, we both pretended that nothing had ever happened.

I never did see his paintings.

CHAPTER 4

Loss and Longing

ONE PERSON WHO TOOK MY DISTRESS OVER THE TOWEL HEAD incident seriously was Tom Pittman. A fine actor, Tom was going to be the next James Dean, or so people thought. He was around the same size as James Dean, with the same soulful intensity, that same brooding look. Tom, who was about five years older than me, was a kindred spirit. I looked up to him and hung on his every word. He was kind and spiritual, believing strongly in things like God and hope. He cared for me, touched my heart, and was one of the most important people in my young life.

I'd met Tom through mutual friends shortly after my family moved to Los Angeles. He would come over to visit when we were living in Park LaBrea. The first time he had a proper role on live television, on *Playhouse 90,* he came over to watch it with my parents and me. He was never too fond of his own image. The moment Tom saw himself appear on screen, he gave a little groan and crawled under the coffee table. My dad didn't like that at all. He didn't have to say anything; I could tell by looking at him that he didn't approve of Tom's reaction to seeing himself on TV. I only hoped that Tom didn't notice.

My father didn't like anyone who didn't like themselves. Later he would get angry with me for doing the same thing. Whenever he'd tell me he was going to tune in to see some bit part I had on TV, I used to say, "Oh, no! It's nothing. Please don't watch! Don't tell anyone."

"Fine. If that's how you want it," he'd snap. "And we'll tell all of our friends not to watch you either."

"Don't do that, Daddy!" I'd plead, reversing my position. I did want to be seen; I just didn't want to know about it.

The day after my night with Towel Head, Tom had picked me up to go to a friend's pool party. On the way I told him the whole story, start to finish, paintings to penis. Then I looked at Tom and said, "What must that man think of me?"

Tom answered, "Sally, if I were that guy, I'd be a lot more worried about what you thought of him."

Tom tried to get the guy's name out of me, but I refused to give it up. Later, to egg me on, he ran around at the pool party snatching beach towels and wrapping them around people's heads. Tom always knew how to make me laugh.

Tom never became a boyfriend. We would kiss and hug and snuggle, and I thought he was the greatest, but the minute I felt like it was going to turn serious I turned to stone. I didn't know how to react. I liked him so much but still felt so insecure, so uncomfortable with that kind of attention. He never let any of that get in the way of our friendship, though, and I felt more comfortable around him than anyone else, except for maybe Luana.

He'd call me up and say, "Come on to Will Wright's—I want to take your picture." Tom loved taking pictures, and we adored Will Wright's, a place that served some of the best desserts around. Mopey me, I would usually answer, "I can't go. I'm too fat and I have a pimple." But Tom put up with me being a sad sack.

I'll always remember the day he rang me up and said, "Meet me at the Laurel Canyon General Country Store." (It's still there—different owners, different name.) "I have something really important to talk to you about." When I finally saw him, he was deadly serious.

"Don't smoke grass, Sally," he said. "You're going to be a singer."

That was his big message. I don't know what prompted his concern. After all, I was still so painfully square. Maybe he was seeing more people he knew doing drugs. He knew I had seen that too, especially in jazz. Grass, heroin. I was around those scenes, but I was just looking. It was so different from the world I'd grown up in. But it was the music that I loved. Maybe he wanted to protect me. But what came through loud and clear was that he cared, even if he had no reason to worry. At twenty-one, I didn't smoke grass, drink, or make love. Not yet, anyway.

• • •

TOMMY HAD BEEN MISSING A LITTLE WHILE WHEN I FIRST heard about it. Someone called me up to say that Tom hadn't been seen since Halloween. He had gone to a party in Benedict Canyon, and no one had heard from him since he left. Soon after, the police called, referencing Tom, and asked me to meet them at the Renaissance, a club at the corner of Sunset and Olive, where the House of Blues is now. I knew the spot—I had gone to see Stan Getz play there. I didn't give it a second thought that they didn't ask me to come down to the station; I had never met with the police before, and all I knew was that I wanted to do whatever I could to help Tom.

The meeting started off pleasant enough. There were two men, and the questions at first were very general. How did I know Tom, when was the last time I'd seen Tom—that sort of thing. It felt more like a conversation than an interrogation. At the time Tom was working on the film *Verboten* with Samuel Fuller, a well-respected director. One of the men mentioned this and said that they thought perhaps Tom's disappearance was merely a publicity stunt. I disagreed; Tom would never pull something like that.

"So where do you think he might be?" they asked.

"He's probably in Mexico sitting on the beach with Sheree North," I said. Sheree was a wonderful actress and Tom's good friend.

"Well, we just want to be sure," they said. The meeting came to a close shortly after that, and I went home.

I didn't want to think about anything bad happening to Tom. He was always off on some adventure. Mexico. He was definitely in Mexico.

I was a little worried now but thought there must have been a simple answer. I told Luana but not anyone else that I remember. I was sure I'd hear from Tom. I soon got another call from the police. Could they please meet with me once more, they asked. This time they wanted to meet at Googie's.

This meeting felt very different from the get-go. The same two men, only this time they were playing Good Cop–Bad Cop. First they asked me if I knew whether Tom smoked marijuana. Even though most everyone I knew did smoke, it still wasn't the kind of thing you discussed openly. Smoking grass was not tolerated in any way in the 1950s and was definitely the kind of activity you pulled the shades down for, still something that sent you running to the toilet if the police were called to quiet down your party.

Now I was uncomfortable. No matter what I knew, I didn't want to say anything. I fidgeted. I said I didn't know. I felt like I was in an episode of *Dragnet*.

Now the other guy—the one I kept thinking about as the "Good Cop"—said his name was Bob Bice.

"I was Tom's best friend," he said.

Huh? I'd never heard of this guy from Tom or anyone else. What was going on?

Then all of a sudden, Bad Cop turned on me.

"Because of you, young lady, he's probably lying dead somewhere in a ditch!"

I felt my throat tighten, and I felt sick.

"What kind of monkey does he have on his back?!" Bad Cop yelled.

"Sure, he gets high, who doesn't?!" I cried. "But he doesn't have any monkey on his back."

They finally left me. I was scared. There was no way Tom could have been involved in anything bad. Not Tom.

The next thing I heard about Tom was that they had found him. He was dead.

I was heartbroken.

By the time the police found him, Tom had been missing about nineteen days. The day after my second meeting at Googie's, they finally took the helicopters up to scour the canyon to see what they could find. An officer found a damaged guardrail on one of the many sharp curves in Benedict Canyon, and there, partially hidden by the brush at the bottom of a 150-foot ravine, was Tom's Porsche Spyder. His body was thrown halfway out of his car, crushed by the steering column. A guardrail was sticking through the windshield. The police found grass in his car.

· · ·

I SAW BOB BICE ONCE MORE AFTER THE MEETING AT GOOGIE'S. He asked me to come to what he called his office, somewhere in the Valley. There he told me more about his close friendship with Tom and that he had also been listening in on Tom's phone calls. He told me things that Tom had supposedly said about me, about how much I meant to him and how much he cared about me.

"I know every time he tried to get close to you," Bob added, "you hurt him."

I didn't know how to respond. Then Bob said Tom was gay and that he was having an affair with photographer Bill Claxton, and that Tom was addicted to heroin. I refused to believe any of it. As far as I knew, Bill was dating Peggy Moffitt, lovely Peggy, a beautiful, wide-eyed, fair-skinned model. Bill and Peggy were both friends of Tom's.

If Tom had been gay or a heroin addict, I was sure I would have known, I thought. I would have been able to tell. Tom surely would have told me—we didn't keep secrets. Were these two men just lying to me? Trying to scare me into telling them something bad about Tom? Was it possible that Tom had been in trouble and I really didn't know?

Now, because of the way Tom felt about me, this Bob Bice said Tom wanted him to take care of me. It all sounded crazy. I left and hoped I'd never see him again.

Everyone from the Sunset Boulevard crowd was at the funeral. Sam Fuller, Tom's director on *Verboten,* got up to speak. "Some people say death is a blessing," he began. "In this case it isn't."

News of Tom's death made the papers across the country. "Rising Actor Meets Fate of James Dean," the *Milwaukee Journal* stated. The paper called him "moody" and wrote of his love of "souped-up" cars. The article talked about how everyone thought he was going to be the Next Big Thing.

Not long after the funeral, Tom's father, a small unimposing Norwegian man, came into Chez Paulette. He walked up and introduced himself to me.

"I know Tommy loved you very much," he said. I didn't know what to say. Tom's father had been a radio and television actor, but as far as I could tell, the two were never close. But Tom's father believed that if the police had chosen to spend the money and the time, Tom would have been found much sooner and would have survived.

I was at my parents' house the day that the subpoena arrived in the mail. It turns out that Tom's father was suing the Los Angeles Police Department for not acting sooner on his missing-persons report. I was in knots. I knew they were going to bring up the drug issue again. In those days marijuana use was a serious offense.

My friend Morgan came with me to the courthouse, along with Burt Shonberg, the painter from Chez Paulette. I sat and listened as officers and others gave their testimony about when this or that happened. They talked about the night Tom died and how they had found marijuana in his car.

When I was called to the stand, I stood, shaking, and made my way to the front of the courtroom.

"Is it true you knew Tom Pittman was smoking grass?"

Scared to death, I lied: "No, I didn't."

That's it. I thought to myself. It's over. I'm going right to jail.

Next they called Bob Bice to the stand. It had begun to sink in that he wasn't who he said he was. I still didn't believe he was Tom's friend.

"And when did you first hear about Tom Pittman smoking grass?" they asked Bice.

"From Sally Kellerman," he answered.

Shit! I thought. They called me back to the stand and asked me the same question. Again, I denied knowing anything about Tom smoking grass. I was sure I would be hauled off in irons.

I wasn't, but the worst wasn't over. My name and picture landed in the paper, where I was described as a "part-time waitress and actress." At least that part was accurate, but the rumors that soon followed were not. People started saying that I had ratted Tom out, spilled information about his life to the police. Some people stopped talking to me. I didn't find out until many years later that Alan Putterman, a regular at the Chez Paulette, had told everyone that I had stabbed Tom in the back. My true friends—Luana, Jack, Morgan—never changed toward me. And Burt Shonberg, the painter, was always so friendly no matter what anyone said. He was never one to go along with the crowd.

It was an incredibly painful time for me. Tom's death epitomized those "rebel" years in Hollywood: the disdain the straight culture had for drugs, sex, and what so many of our parents and authority figures considered the so-called "fast" life. Not only had I lost one of my best friends, but I had become persona non grata in many people's eyes. I hated that people saw me as some sort of stoolie.

"He told me to take care of you," Bob had said that day we met. I didn't want to be taken care of—at least not by Bob, whom I soon learned was an actor, just like the rest of us. The next time I saw him was as a bus driver in a Greyhound commercial. What his relationship with Tommy really was, I'll never know.

· · ·

Tom's death indirectly brought on another difficult loss. My friend Luana had been my heart and soul. I used to tell her that I loved her so much that I worried I was a lesbian and questioned whether she loved me as much as I loved her.

"It took you until Tommy died for you to realize how much he loved you," she told me. "Are you going to take that long to know that I love you?"

She left a note on my apartment door, the same apartment where we would hide in the closet to rehash the day's adventures: *I don't know how many other ways to prove I love you, so I'm going away.*

I thought my little heart would break.

She wasn't gone altogether; she had work in other parts of the country and was leaving town. I knew we were still dear friends. But everything was different when Luana wasn't there. She was my confidante, my best friend.

Losing first Tom and then Luana—I was heartbroken. Thank God for the friends who kept me entertained and dragged me out of bed to auditions. Therapy would not have been enough to keep depression at bay. I went to class, where I felt safe. Even when other actors moved on from Jeff's, I stayed.

Tom was so young, so lovely, and his career was just taking off. Not since Vicky died had the death of someone close to me been so shocking and devastating, something that made me question the order of things in the world. Wasn't he God's perfect child? I certainly thought so.

Back at home my father seemed to ignore the tragic aspects of the news story featuring my testimony in court. He cut my picture out of the local paper, framing it and placing it on his dresser. One day, not long after the picture ran, I was walking into my parents' house as the housekeeper was leaving. She ran up to me, beaming and very excited.

"Oh! I saw your picture in the paper!" she said. "What were you singing?"

CHAPTER 5

Pushing the Limits

GOING TO AUDITIONS FINALLY STARTED TO PAY OFF. I SCORED
a bit part in a film as a corpse and another as a prostitute in *Machine Gun Kelly*, directed by my friend Roger Corman. It became
clear to me that, to feel less depressed, I needed better jobs and I
needed to get laid. Both started to happen in the 1960s. In both
realms the results were mixed.

Bob Sampson was one of the guys who kept me from sleeping
all day. I adored Bob, and he always knew how to enjoy himself.
He went on to do a ton of television, including *Twilight Zone* and
movies like *Dark Side of the Moon*. To me, he was not only a partner in crime but also my first accompanist outside of high school.
I still sang every chance I got and would occasionally get up the
chutzpah to sing a tune in a piano bar during an open mic. But I
wasn't ready to venture out as a solo act. I liked my acting cocoon,
where I could practice my work in front of other performers. Still,
I loved when Bob would come over and play the piano for me. He
played everything in the key of C and never fussed if I kept him
waiting for two hours while I combed my hair. We would sing and
play a while, and then we would head out for adventure.

Music was in the clubs, acting was in the classes, and fun was
in the coffeehouses, at the beach, and on Olvera Street in down-

town LA—if only I could get up and out to see it. Bob and I went to the movies at the Apollo and ate too much popcorn. We rode bicycles built for two in Griffith Park and huddled in sleeping bags on Venice Beach at night. If you tried that today, you'd have your throat slit. But back then we were the only ones there! We had Los Angeles all to ourselves. We goofed around in the train station, wandered down Olvera Street—then blissfully free of tourists— looking at sombreros and eating the best taquitos in the world.

I still saw Morgan Ames, of course. We often hung out in after-hours jazz clubs. If my poor mother only knew. I also spent time with Greta Chi, the tall, beautiful Eurasian actress who was my new roommate. I don't remember how Greta and I found each other, but we had a wonderful apartment on Sweetzer in a Spanish-style building. It was a two bedroom with its own balcony, which we shared with another darling woman, an actress named Diana Spencer.

I saw my parents as well, sometimes going over for a meal. My sister Diana was back in Los Angeles now after working in both Washington, DC, and Paris. She was living near the beach with her husband, Ian Graham, whom she'd met while working at the Rand Corporation. Ian was quiet and older than Diana but seemed kind and shared her love of travel. They went to Europe; they played paddle tennis.

Diana's marriage was a bit of a surprise, not because her husband was older but because she had confided something she was struggling with: her attraction to and affairs with other women. I was so touched she thought to share something so personal with me. I don't know whether she had told my mother. If she had, Mom never said a word.

It is hard enough being gay in *this* day and age, but in the 1950s and 1960s there was little or no tolerance of homosexuality. Back then people viewed it, at best, as a mental illness or, worse, as a dangerous perversion. Sodomy laws in most states made homosexuals subject to harassment and arrest. No one entertained the possibility that someone could be born gay, which is what I believe.

So most gay people did what Diana did: married members of the opposite sex and tried to live "normal" lives, all the while pushing their feelings deep down inside, as far as they could, in the hope they would simply disappear.

Diana and I had grown closer over the years. She had written me a letter once, while she was working overseas, apologizing for not being more supportive when I went to her wondering if I should have my first sexual experience with Eddie Byrnes. She didn't have to do that, so I wonder now if her own struggles were surfacing then. We had grown closer still since her wedding. I remember that when I visited her and Ian's apartment, she would ask me things like how to walk in heels and how to move around in dresses. She wanted things to work out with Ian, and I wanted to support whatever choice she was making. We had come a long way as sisters, "Dinky and Stinky," and as friends.

• • •

WORK IMPROVED IN FITS AND STARTS. A COUPLE YEARS EARlier I'd made my stage debut in Henrik Ibsen's *Enemy of the People*. (Not to put down my first film role in *Reform School Girl*, in which I'd acted alongside my darling Luana and my first boyfriend, Eddie Byrnes—well, maybe not alongside, as I had two lines, whereas Luana was one of the leads. I was big and butch, and when I came on screen, everyone laughed.) I believed then—and still do—that plays are critical for helping an actress grow. The film's director, John Marley, hired me for *Enemy* right out of Chez Paulette. That, and the fact I'd been studying acting for years and now felt ready, had emboldened me to try to get an agent.

Today so many of the kids coming to LA get an agent immediately and then see what work they can land. But back then it was different—learning to act was your first priority. Only if you worked and studied and got proficient at the craft would you have a long career. Not that you can't get lucky and land a reality show these days, but chances are that won't sustain you in the long run.

Luana advised me to lie when I starting talking to agents, telling them that I had done summer stock. So I went to the Paul Kohner Agency for a meeting and coolly mentioned that I had done "summer stock." Naturally, the agent I was meeting with asked me which summer stock I had done. Unfortunately, I hadn't thought about what summer stock I was going to be lying about. Luckily for me, he got an important phone call and ended the meeting abruptly. Needless to say, I didn't sign with Paul Kohner.

Enemy, which we performed at the Civic Playhouse on La Cienega, had won me my first real review: *Although her fresh beauty was a delight to the eyes, her wooden portrayal left so much to be desired that she should get out of the business.*

Fantastic. This, of course, was the opposite of what I'd always thought: that I was talented but unattractive. Yet somehow this review—and not my imaginary summer stock experience—finally landed me an agent. Progress!

That didn't mean I got any better at auditions. In an effort to land a bit part on some television series looking for a "sexy" girl, I went to an audition on the Warner Brothers lot with a head full of teased hair and a bra stuffed full of toilet paper. Standing around, waiting for my turn to go in, I was tucking and poking at my tissue boobs. Yeah, baby, sexy!

The director took one look at me and said, "Not only are you not sexy, but you're like a cowering little mouse, and I can see your toilet paper."

Totally deflated, I left. On my way out I ran into writer and producer Jerry Davis, who worked on shows like *Bewitched* and *The Odd Couple.*

"What's a pretty girl like you doing wandering around, lost?" he asked.

I told him my sad story, and he walked me into Bill Orr's office. Bill was head of Warner's television department and married to Joy Page, studio head Jack Warner's stepdaughter. All of a sudden I was cast in an episode of *Surfside 6*, starring Troy Donahue. Jerry, Bill, and I became fast friends. Then one day Bill called me at home with a proposition.

"There's a man I know," he began, "who would like to get you an apartment . . ." That sounded great.

"He would make sure you always worked," Bill went on. That's when what he meant dawned on me.

"How could you think I was that kind of girl?!" I sobbed.

Bill felt terrible. "Alright, alright. It's okay. I'm sorry, don't worry."

Now, if somebody called with the same offer today. . . . Just kidding.

. . .

I MAY STILL HAVE BEEN NAIVE, YES, BUT AT LEAST I'D LOST MY virginity. It was the 1960s: free love and no AIDS. Someone once told me, "If you're still a virgin by the time you're twenty-two, you'll be frigid." So I went right out at twenty-one-and-a-half to find someone who liked me better than I liked him and who wouldn't tell anyone.

I don't remember even the name of the man who took my "snowflake," as Morgan would say. He was very nice, but I felt sick to my stomach just thinking about the whole episode. I still feel bad that I never returned any of his calls. The experience was short lived and didn't exactly produce fireworks. Even so, after I lost my snowflake, my buddy Bob Sampson and I made love once a year, whether we needed it or not. Good old Bob.

Then, along came Bill Duffy.

"If there's anybody in the world I want to look like, it's Bill Duffy," Jack used to say about his friend Bill, also an actor. Bill was handsome, that's for sure. I had been spending a lot of time with Jack and Bill and the wonderful actor Dick Bradford, who was in movies like *The Legend of Billy Jean* and *More American Graffiti*. He was also a painter. The three of them shared a house. Some nights Bill's cousin Kenny would come over and play guitar or bass, and I'd sit in the middle of the floor and practice singing in front of them. Kenny even helped me make demos, which ended up getting stuffed in a drawer, waiting for the day when I was ready to do something with them. Then Jack and I would argue about serious matters of the day, like who had the best Mexican food, El Cholo or El Coyote.

Bill and I soon began an affair. One evening while we were sitting in a car, he asked me if I wanted to be his girlfriend. There was something so cute and romantic about the way he asked that I had to say yes.

We had an amazing sexual connection. I finally got what making love was all about, and we went at it like rabbits, nonstop, wherever and whenever we could. With Bill I discovered orgasms. After making love all night, we'd go to Norm's and have spaghetti for breakfast to refuel before getting started up again.

Then, as often happens when you're a naive, generally inexperienced woman in her early twenties with no sex education, I got pregnant.

The only people who knew were Luana, Morgan, Jack, Bob Sampson, and my sister Diana and her husband, Ian. I was terrified. I didn't know what to do. At first I thought I would keep the child. I started learning to cook and got in touch with my inner homemaker by recovering a couch in orange burlap. "You'll only want the baby when it laughs," my therapist said. "You won't want him when he cries."

Bill wanted to get married. I wasn't really in love with him. Where would we live? With Jack? So Bill and I had a big fight. I was working on *Surfside 6* at the time and was invited to spend the weekend on the beach in Venice with some of the cast and crew. When I returned home Sunday evening, sunburned and pregnant, I saw Jack and Dick going up the steps to my apartment.

Uh-oh, I thought. *Bill.*

When I entered the apartment, he was lying on my couch, drunk. "Hi, honey," I said.

"Fuck you, honey," he replied, jumping up from the couch and smashing over his knee a painting Jack had given me. Glass flew. Bleeding now, Bill was staggering around, saying that he would go to the police if I got an abortion. While Jack and Dick chased Bill out of the house, I huddled in a corner. Bill's bloody hand-prints covered the railing along the stairs leading down to the street. Tired, weepy, and nauseated, I began to clean up.

A few minutes later the phone rang. It was Jack.

"Sal, I don't mean to be an alarmist," he said, "but you need to get out of there for awhile. I think Bill's coming."

I hung up the phone and panicked. What should I do? Where could I go? The phone rang again.

"Jack?"

No. It was George Peppard, whom I'd met through my friend Suzanne Pleshette.

"I'm in town," he announced. "I'm at the Chateau Marmont. Why don't you come over?"

I thought for a second. I was swollen and sunburned, and I needed a place to stay. I drove over to the Chateau Marmont.

George tried to hit on me. I couldn't tell him that I was pregnant or why I'd come over, if not to sleep with him. So it was a seamy and weird night. Not his fault. The next day he sent me flowers.

I had to make a decision. The truth was that I wasn't prepared to have a baby. I could barely take care of myself. I was struggling to pay the rent, even with two roommates. My therapist told me he "knew a guy" over in Glendale who could take care of me. Bill offered some money when he sobered up. I told him he could keep it. Bob Sampson offered to marry me, which was sweet but, as we both knew, not a smart option. He loaned me the money I needed to get the procedure.

Jack and Morgan drove me to Glendale and stayed with me. When we arrived at the house—it wasn't an office at all—the doctor wasn't there. I was taken into one of the bedrooms and given something to "help me relax." When I woke up, the proce-dure was over.

Jack and Morgan took me to Du-Par's for breakfast and then

back to my apartment. Diana and Ian stopped by with a home-made brown betty. I appreciated that so much—both the cake and Diana's support. We were all struggling in our own ways to break free of the restrictions of the 1950s and find our way in a rapidly changing world where the rules governing women's be-havior were changing...but not *that* much. Diana didn't judge me. There was no criticism, only caring.

Within a few days I began to experience an excruciating pain in my leg. I went to see my mom. Several years earlier, when I was around eighteen, was the first time I convinced my mother to take me to the doctor. That time it was for diet pills, dexamyl spansules, which made me feel like Felix the Cat on the inside. They burnt out my nervous system and eventually became a pop-ular street drug. That experience had not sold my Christian Sci-entist mother on the wonders of Western medicine. But this time around she could tell something was really wrong, so she brought me to a doctor, who me rushed to the hospital. My fallopian tubes were dangerously inflamed; I spent ten days in the hospital hooked up to an IV. Serious infections like mine were what hap-pened back then to women without options. That's why I become so enraged today when people continue to try to keep young women uneducated and leave them with nowhere safe to turn.

Once I landed in the hospital, there was no hiding what had happened from my parents. They both knew what I had done. My mom told me that my dad cried when she told him about the abortion, sobbing, "Why didn't she know she could come to us? Didn't she know we would have helped?" What a difference from the angry, stern father I had come to expect, the one who hated my braless outfits and torn jeans and rebellious nature. He was heartbroken.

Now I realize that I probably could have gone to them for help. My parents, bless them, no matter how they felt about my choice of career, saw just about everything I ever did. Set dressing as a dead body? They were there. One line in a play at the Pico Play-house? They got tickets. And who can forget my riveting delivery of the words, "You may go right in," on the live television program *Playhouse 90*? Not only did my parents tune in; they also told all their friends to do the same. I was mortified. What a jerk I could be, not appreciating how my parents supported me. So they wanted a lady. So my dad didn't want a crybaby. Who could blame him? And despite his stern nature, he was encouraging, even if I couldn't hear it. That above all is clear in this letter he later sent me, which I came across while writing this book.

> January 8, 1963
>
> Darling,
>
> The enclosed check does not give me the right to offer advice, but being your father I just naturally use my dictatorial powers and suggest that:
>
> 1. You think positive.
> 2. See people in your profession.
> 3. To talk [to people in your profession].
> 4. Practice acting by yourself if necessary, before the mirror.
> 5. Ditto #4.
> 6. Ditto #4.
> 7. Realize the truth—that you are a fine actress.
> 8. Have faith and trust in God.
> 9. And—Help yourself by asking for work! Don't be afraid to ask. You have ability to offer and the world needs entertainment more than ever, what with all the discontent around the globe.
> 10. Above all—don't worry, you always have mother and me.

Dad left out one of his favorite lines: *Did you tell them that you get all your talent from me, Sal?*

I was blown away when I found this letter. I didn't remember ever receiving it. I'd been too self-centered to realize that despite my dad's quick temper and my mom's picky ways, they not only cared about me but also wanted for me what I wanted for myself.

In the early 1960s my father worked in downtown Los Angeles as the vice president of a small crude oil company. He knew that neighborhood was one of my hangouts and would often ask me to go to lunch with him and meet the people in his office. But I never did. I was sure he would hate what I was wearing, so I always begged off and made excuses. I'm so sorry, Dad—and grateful.

· · ·

AFTER THE WHOLE ORDEAL BILL AND I MADE LOVE ONE LAST time, as a goodbye. In the wake of the abortion and our breakup, I was depressed. I resumed my sad-sack routine of lying around, going to the unemployment office and acting class, waiting tables, and eating Oreos.

Thank God for David Bennett, Bob Sampson, and Roy Thinnes, who got me out of bed and off to auditions. David and I were spending so much time together that I had begun to call him my cousin. We had met at Jeff Corey's, and at first I thought he was the most obnoxious guy on earth. He would say things like, "You're going to be a star," which I hated because I was sure if he said it out loud, no one would believe him and it would never happen. One of the first times we went to the movies together David showed up at the Egyptian Theatre on Hollywood Boulevard wearing a white Bombay suit and a bad toupee. I couldn't bear those white suits and hairpieces, but I couldn't imagine life without David, either. My father loved him because he looked after me so well. Later, when David moved to New York City, I remember my dad saying, "That's great," but asking him, "Who will take care of Sally?"

One day, early in 1962, David and Roy tried to get me to audition for *The Marriage-Go-Round* at the Pasadena Playhouse with Don Porter and Marsha Hunt.

"Get in the car," they insisted.

"I'm not sexy. I'm not going," I wailed.

But off I went. A week or so later, while I was lying in bed, the phone rang.

"I'm sorry," the voice said, "but you didn't get the part."

Figures, I thought, and rolled back over to go back to sleep. Then the phone rang again.

"I was wrong. You've got the part."

I can only assume that their first choice had passed.

After the run in Pasadena I got to perform with Ozzie and Harriet Nelson in the Kenley Players presentation of *The Marriage-Go-Round* in Columbus, Ohio. But that meant I had to pull out of a play called *Camino Real,* which was being done at Company of Angels with Leonard Nimoy directing. Leonard and Dick Chamberlain and Vic Morrow helped start the now-famous theater as a place where actors could work and rehearse without the pressure of commercial success. It was founded in 1959 in a parking lot at Vine and Waring, behind a restaurant. I hammered in maybe two nails and would sometimes work as an usher at Angels if a friend was doing a play there. Today it is the oldest repertory theater in Los Angeles.

When I got back from Ohio, they were still rehearsing and trying to get the play off the ground, struggling with annoying bureaucracy and things like permits. Leonard was the one who really made the Angels fly. I remember him taking me aside one night after I'd shown up late for rehearsal—again.

As we stood in the parking lot, I could see that Leonard was frustrated.

"Why is it that you talented people are always coming late?" he asked.

Talented?

I missed the part about being late. I was just thrilled that he said I was talented!

Camino Real didn't get off the ground, but in 1962 Michael Shurtleff's *Call Me by My Rightful Name* did. I was cast in it opposite my lovely Bob Sampson and directed by my good friend Tom Selden. There's nothing like a play. Throughout my career I have tried to do them as often as I could, just to humiliate myself. This one, though I least expected it to, launched my career.

At the time I was still waiting tables at the Chez. Joe Stefano, who had written Hitchcock's *Psycho* and was producing and writing *The Outer Limits* for television, had seen me in *Enemy of the People*. Luckily for me, he bothered to see me again in *Call Me by My Rightful Name*.

"I can't believe the growth!" Joe said to me after the show, as I was standing in the parking lot with Bob. "I may be doing a TV series, and if I do, I'm going to find a part for you."

As he drove away, I turned to Bob Sampson and said, "I'll be in the restaurant for the rest of my life."

Six months later a script showed up at my apartment with a note: *The part is Ingrid, the magic is yours.*

Now, thanks to Joe, after eight years of studying and waitressing and doing gigs like playing a Swedish blind date wearing big, tall antlers, on *The Fred MacMurray Show*, I finally had a real part: Ingrid, the nurse in an episode of the TV series *The Outer Limits* called, "The Human Factor."

"There is nothing wrong with your television set . . ." the oscilloscope voice announced at the beginning of every *Outer Limits*. It was so otherworldly and creepy and fun.

On the first day of shooting Joe was there, paying close attention. He turned to the director and said, "Does she understand her motivation?" The director said yes. He then turned to Conrad Hall and William Fraker, two incredibly talented cinematographers—both handsome, both bearded—and told them, "Make her look like a movie star!" That was Joe Stefano—a product of Old Hollywood. Connie and Bill handed me a muskrat collar and a cigarette, lit me, and that was it. A star was born.

I felt great until I saw a rough cut of that episode. Then I jumped in my car, hit the gas, and drove one hundred miles per hour to the television set of *Combat*, which Vic Morrow was filming. We went to his trailer and I sobbed, "I'm not just ugly, I'm untalented!" Vic was a darling. He comforted me and sent me on my way.

To highlight that first episode, Joe took out an ad in *Variety*. It included a note to me for all to see: *Your shining moments in "The Human Factor" reveal your own very special glamour—the kind we think of when we think of a classic "movie star"—and will, we believe, create an exciting and new image in the minds of all those who already know you to be a skilled and genuine actress.*

At the time Jerry Bick, my agent and friend, had already dumped me as a client. I begged him just to keep me on his roster so if someone did happen to call, I'd get the message. The day the *Outer Limits* episode aired, Jerry was on the Universal lot. One of his colleagues walked up and said, "Hey, Jerry, I saw your client on TV last night. Guess she'll be moving to William Morris today."

And that's just what happened. I've never stopped working from that day forth. Joe Stefano started my career in television, and I'll never be able to thank him fully.

Joe not only cast me again, but he also wrote an episode of *Outer Limits*, "The Bellero Shield," with me in mind. Martin Landau was cast as my husband, and Broadway legend Chita Rivera played my barefoot housekeeper. This time I was a conniving and ambitious housewife in a housecoat with a mink collar. I killed the most adorable alien you've ever seen and then ended up trapped in a big glass bubble. Chita taught me how to scream. At the end of that episode the bubble—my barrier to freedom—was removed, but I didn't believe it. I had created my own bubble, my own prison. I stood there, trapped, in a prison of my own creation.

* * *

ONCE I SIGNED AT WILLIAM MORRIS, I DECIDED TO AUDITION for the Actor's Studio. It had been around since the late 1940s and was notoriously difficult to get into. But I needed to keep studying, and I wanted to raise my game. I had been working on a scene with my dear friend Elizabeth Hush for about two months. In the scene we were both supposed to be drunk, though neither of us really drank. But the night of the audition Liz (I've decided to blame this on Liz) said, "Hey, why don't we have a drink?" And

so we did. We got into the Actor's Studio under false pretenses—
we were actually drunk, not just playing drunks. In fact, I've have
never been so sick in all my life. I weaved home in the car and
spent the next two hours throwing up in the bathroom. But hey,
we got in!

I worked at the Actor's Studio, feeling so fat that I wore muu-
muus and tried anything to lose weight. Hollywood was—is—
very unforgiving when it comes to appearances, and there's
nothing like being on stage or on screen to really bring out your
insecurities. (Most of all, *I* was unforgiving. People of all sizes
work in Hollywood—I just wanted to be one of the thin ones.)
So everyone was getting into amphetamines, food combining—
whatever they heard would work. I took some sort of shots that
contained apples. I went on fruit fasts. You couldn't just eat figs—
they had to be Kadota figs from the Third Street Farmer's Market.
I went with Roy Thinnes (on whom I still had a terrible crush at
the time) to get some sort of magical shots—I had *no* idea what
was in them—that were supposed to allow me to eat whatever I
wanted. I injected pregnant women's urine. People now ask if I
was ever anorexic. The answer is no—I wasn't that disciplined.

Luana got into the Actor's Studio too. She had started working
a lot in films and had starred in one produced by Roger Corman
called *Dementia 13*, written and directed in 1963 by a little-known,
up-and-coming writer-director named Francis Ford Coppola.

Jack had moved on to Marty Landau's acting class, but we still
hung out. Our group consisted of me and Luana, Jack, and Sandra
Knight—she and Jack were serious now. Shortly after *The Outer
Limits* I ran into Jack's friend, Stuart Cohen, at the Daisy, a popular place to dance.

"I'm going to be your manager," Stuart said to me.

"Oh, you are?" I laughed and started dancing away in the other
direction.

Stuart started calling me five times a day. I'd answer the phone,
and he'd say, "So?"

I'd say, "What do you mean, 'So'? You called me."

But he was irresistible.

Stuart insisted he wouldn't take any money from me until he got me in the movies. I liked that part of the proposition, so we decided to work together. He soon began to change the way I looked at things.

One of the first auditions Stuart got for me was for a musical in Sacramento. When he arrived to take me, I told him in tears that I was sick of my one Chanel audition suit. I couldn't bear to put it on again.

"Have you seen your *punim*?" he asked. (That's Yiddish for face.) "Go put your jeans on and that yellow shirt you can practically see through."

Talk about freedom! As far as I knew at that time, nobody ever wore jeans to an audition. Then Stuart said, "And besides, you'll be so good that you'll get the part—then have to buy your way out of your contract 'cause you'll end up being too busy to do it."

As it turned out, Stuart did change the course of my career more than I could have imagined. I got so lucky when I crossed paths with him. I loved him so much.

In addition to Stuart, two other very important people entered my life around this time.

I met Larry Kert through my friend Bob Sampson shortly after *Outer Limits*. Larry was the original "Tony" in the Broadway production of *West Side Story* and also toured with the production. Bob and I drove all over the country to hear Larry sing, all of us camped out in sleeping bags on the floor in someone's apartment. When Larry sang, "Maria," it melted me every time.

When Larry got back to town, we spent a lot of time together. One night we went to see the movie *The Servant*, starring Dirk Bogarde and James Fox, at the Oriental Theatre on Sunset Boulevard. (That's the same theater where I first saw Marlon in those white pants. Today the theater is a Guitar Center—very depressing.)

I found the movie, about a British manservant who ends up controlling and switching places with his "master," very decadent and stimulating—so much so that when I got out of the theater,

I thought, "I gotta get laid or do something." Larry was so much fun to be with, so wild and irreverent, but he was gay. What was a girl to do?

So we went up to Anjanette Comer and Alex Cord's house. They were both great actors and great friends, and that night I smoked grass for the second time in my life. The first time I ever really got high had been at Jack's house, with Alejandro Rey, the Argentinean actor then making a name for himself on *Flying Nun*. All of a sudden, after we'd all had our fair share of herb, Alejandro started talking about going to the police to tell them what he had done. I looked around. None of us understood what the heck he was talking about. He couldn't be serious, could he? Then he said, "I hear the sounds of the hind legs of a horse hitting in the night . . ." Only when Alejandro said "hitting," it sounded like "heating." So there I was, stoned, and Alejandro was carrying on about the hind legs of a horse heating in the night. Luckily he didn't turn himself in to the cops for smoking pot, but he did take Jack's record collection. All in all, it was a strange evening. I couldn't wait to be sober.

My second time smoking pot, with Larry, was so much fun, so freeing. I hopped on the back of his motorcycle, and we flew into a rainy LA night, without a care in the world. I yelled in his ear, "We could be killed!" He yelled back, "I know!" I soon began smoking a lot more grass. I had a right to come home and relax my mind after a hard day's work, I thought.

Larry knew the actor Robert Walker, and most Sundays we'd drive out to Malibu to hang out. Bobby and his wife, Ellie, were renting a little place from Rod Steiger. We would swim, smoke grass, and eat delicious meals that Ellie cooked for everyone. Next door lived Jane Fonda, who was, at that time, with Roger Vadim. My memory of Jane during that period was of her running around, cooing in French, and looking just as she did in *Barbarella* with her flowing hair, big doe eyes, and killer figure, while I looked like Lynn Redgrave in *Georgy Girl*—a little gawky, a little rough around the edges.

Malibu was more of a place than a label back then. It was mellow, relaxing. You didn't go there to be seen; you went there to see your friends. That said, you still never knew whom you were going to run into on the beach. Some days it was Dennis Hopper or his wife, Brooke, with their young daughter, Marin. Other times it was Peter Fonda or Dan Melnick of MGM, Terry Malick, Terry Southern—all the Terry's. And one very special day it was Jennifer Jones.

Jennifer was Bobby's mother, she was the personification of Hollywood glamour. She had won the Academy Award for her lead role in *The Song of Bernadette*. After splitting from Bobby's father, she had married David O. Selznick, the producer best known for *Gone with the Wind*. Selznick had launched the careers of many great stars of the Old Hollywood era, including Jennifer herself.

Jennifer came by for a visit one afternoon, and I'll never forget the sight of her. There I was, lying on the beach in my sloppy pink bikini, and there was Jennifer, walking by in an elegant caftan and a large picture hat, looking just like the 1940s movie star that she was. I was immediately star struck. We exchanged a few words, and off she went. A few days later the phone rang, and it was Jennifer inviting me to dinner at her house. The night of the dinner I got held up shooting *Slattery's People,* directed by my close friend Mark Rydell and starring Richard Crenna. But when I finally got to her house, Jennifer was perfectly gracious. "Sally, darling," she said, "I'd like you to meet some friends of mine . . ."

She led me into a dimly lit room filled with orchids—Jennifer's version of a kasbah. Sitting at a long dining room table, soaked in candlelight, were Ingrid Bergman, Deborah Kerr, Simone Signoret and her then-husband Yves Montand, Louis Jourdan and his wife, plus Pia Lindstrom, Ingrid's older daughter. I had worshipped these people growing up, and here I was at dinner with them. I don't remember one word that was spoken or one word that I said. I was that much in awe.

What was I doing there? Maybe I was invited because Ingrid's daughter Pia was also there, and Jennifer wanted someone else

Pia's age on hand. Who knows? But Jennifer was such a lovely hostess, and good hosting is a lost art to be sure. After that she became my biggest supporter, my mentor, like a second mother. Every young actress could use a fairy godmother, and Jennifer was mine.

My biological family was growing as well. Around the time *Slattery's People* aired, Diana and her husband welcomed a baby girl named Claire into the world. I was now an aunt. I remember going to see my little niece when she was just starting to crawl around.

"Look, Claire, it's your Aunt Sally," my sister said. Claire turned around and crawled in the opposite direction. She was adorable, independent, and spunky even then.

Slattery's People earned me some good attention. Not long after it aired I got a call from Shirlee, a stewardess who had at one time bought the entire contents of my apartment for $100. At first I was worried she was calling because she thought I'd overcharged her for the two twin beds, Morgan's grandmother's couch (the one I covered in orange burlap), and two chairs that Susie Pleshette had left me after our one hour of trying to be roommates. (That's all it took for us to realize that, with our strong personalities, we'd never survive living together with our friendship intact.)

"Hi kid, it's Shirlee," she said. "Listen, my boyfriend saw you on *Slattery's People* the other night, and he'd like to meet with you 'cause he's doing a play in New York. He thinks you'd be perfect for it."

Yeah, whatever, I was thinking. It's LA. Who isn't dating an actor?

"Do you know who my boyfriend is, kid?"

"No."

"Well, it's Henry Fonda," she timidly replied.

"Ohhhh!" I said brightly. Sure glad it wasn't about the furniture.

So I met with Henry Fonda in a deli on Santa Monica Boulevard, and Shirlee flew a reel of *Slattery's People* out to New York for the producers on one of her flights. In the end I didn't get the part. But shortly thereafter, while I was making what I consider to be my first "real" movie, *The Third Day* with George Peppard and Elizabeth Ashley, Henry got director Arthur Penn to come out and watch me shoot a scene. Arthur was overheard saying that I had so much presence just walking across the room. Sadly, that wasn't quite enough. Little did I know that Arthur was about to start production on a movie called *The Chase* starring Marlon Brando, my lifetime heartthrob. And who got the part of the girl? Jane Fonda! Oh well. Easy come, easy go. Marlon Brando . . .

Shirlee and Henry had a long, happy marriage. She took with her into that marriage Morgan Ames's grandmother's couch, though she got rid of my orange burlap. I remember Henry saying to me, when he was much older, "I'll never work again."

He sounded just like all us struggling actors. But all I could think was, *Doesn't he realize he's Henry Fonda?* Shortly thereafter he won the Oscar for Best Actor in a Leading Role working opposite Katharine Hepburn and his wonderful daughter Jane under the direction of Mark Rydell in *On Golden Pond.* It was one of his greatest performances—and at the age of seventy-six. There's hope for all of us yet.

• • •

STUART CONTINUED TO WORK PASSIONATELY FOR ME AND MY career. He probably believed in me more than I believed in myself. When I heard that David Mer rick, the famous Broadway producer, was going to do a musical of *Breakfast at Tiffany's,* I wanted it badly. I knew it would give me the opportunity to sing. It felt like a good fit; it felt like something I could do. I wanted to start to bring more singing into my career, and this felt like a good way to do that. Stuart went over to my agency, William Morris, to get me a meeting with Merrick and was told that David only wanted to see "stars." Stuart exploded and said, "If you don't think she's a star, she's out of here today!"

I got a meeting.

David already had around twenty Tony nominations under his belt, with several wins for musicals like *Hello, Dolly!* and *Oliver!* At the time I was shooting an episode of *That Girl* starring Marlo Thomas. And as embarrassing as this is, I always brought my dog and cat to work with me. So there I was in my jeans, scarf around my head, animals in tow, coming from the set for my appointment with Merrick. When he opened the door of his suite at the Beverly Hills Hotel, my yellow cat, J. R., leapt out of my arms and my black cocker spaniel, Holly, chased him around the suite.

It was a good meeting.

As he walked me to the door, he said, "If Mary Tyler Moore doesn't want it, I'll let you audition. And by the way, what is the real name of your dog?" David asked, thinking I'd lied about the dog's name to get the part of Holly Golightly. I ended up as Mary's standby with a guarantee that I'd get to play Holly three months in the second year of production. I also had two numbers of my own as the character "Mag Wildwood."

Doing the show was an incredible experience. Mary, an amazing performer, worked harder than anybody I've ever seen. My pal Larry Kert was cast, as was Dick Chamberlain from class. Both were wonderful. I treasured friendships I made with Bob Merrill, the lyricist (also the lyricist of *Funny Girl*) and the choreographer Michael Kidd, whom I will never forget saying to me, "It's not that you can't dance. It's that you won't."

David was a character. Still one to weep at the drop of a hat, I cried at my first wardrobe fitting. David's response? "Kellerman," he said, "you don't need to cry. Don't you think we can see that the dress is ugly?"

When the show was on the road, David would often take me out for tea. Our names got linked romantically, which was unfortunate, because he was married and there was no truth to it.

We spent a month in Philadelphia followed by a month in Boston before returning to Broadway. We were sold out in both places, a year in advance on Broadway. But despite the buzz, the play had its troubles. Abe Burrows, the director, had adapted the book himself from Truman Capote's novella. But David decided he wanted the play to have more grit, so he replaced Abe with playwright Edward Albee, and Abe promptly quit as the director. David then hired Joe Anthony to replace Abe while Edward Albee rewrote the play from start to finish.

In the end *Breakfast at Tiffany's* was memorable but unfortunately a flop: it closed after four nights of previews, despite an amazing performance from Mary Tyler Moore.

I was not happy in New York, and what I wanted more than anything was to get into films.

Instead, I returned to Los Angeles for more television. *Hawaii Five-O*—shot in Hawaii, gotta love that—and *The Rogues* with the lovely David Niven, whom I adored, as well as Charles Boyer and Gig Young, who became my friend. I guest starred in the pilot for a new show called *Star Trek*. When I arrived on set, I saw Leonard Nimoy. Oh boy, I was crazy about him, after knowing him for years. Bill Shatner was a delight—so casually funny. I didn't know what the heck was going on on that set, though. It seemed to be just a lot of standing around in awful outfits, waiting for machines to blink. My episode was actually the *second* pilot for the show, which true Trekkies are quick to point out. It was the first that featured Bill and Leonard, and I am still constantly recognized as Dr. Elizabeth Dehner. (If you sneeze on *Star Trek,* Trekkies know who you are.) To this day I happily attend conventions. *Star Trek:* the gift that keeps on giving.

These roles were all nice but not what I wanted. I hoped Stuart was telling the truth. I hoped he really could get me in the movies.

• • •

I ALSO HOPED THAT, NOW THAT I WAS HOME IN LA, MY LOVE life would take off.

Friends set me up with writer David Rayfiel, who had recently split from Maureen Stapleton, an actress who would go on to be nominated for four academy awards, winning for her supporting role in Warren Beatty's *Reds*. Right away, I thought, that would be wrong, dating someone who had just gotten out of a relationship. My friends warned me that he liked to get up at five and be in bed by nine. I, however, liked to stay up until five and get up at nine. So when he called, I said, "Listen, why don't you come by around four? That way you can get to bed on time."

The next day I returned from taking the dog to the vet—running late, as usual—and standing on my porch was this tall, handsome man with a gift in one hand and a jacket slung over his arm. I was dumbstruck. Later, as we talked, he showed me a photo of his home in the Adirondacks, and I felt myself falling fast. It was beautiful, it all seemed so romantic, so picture perfect—but then again, I was only looking at his pictures. When he asked me where I'd like to go to dinner one night, I heard myself mumble, "I'd go anywhere with you." After he left, I stood in the doorway of my latest apartment, a fourplex. My neighbor walked up and said, "What's the matter with you? You look like you're in love." And indeed I was.

My first proper date with David was breakfast on the beach in Malibu, which back then was a quick half-hour, traffic-free drive from West Hollywood. It was one of those dates that lasted all day: breakfast turned into a walk, then a visit to a market, followed by a picnic lunch on a massive rock high above the ocean, which was fenced off by a chain-link fence. After sneaking past the fencing, David and I climbed up on the rock and laid out our lunch. I looked down over the jagged edge and said, "Boy, I sure wouldn't want to fall in there."

Then, as we say in the movies, "cut to" David opening a bottle of wine as a huge wave knocks me over and halfway down the rock. David grabbed my arm with one hand as he held a broken wine bottle in the other. The surf tore off my bathing suit top, and I had blood shooting out of my arm.

David managed to drag me up, and we sat huddled together, trying to stop the bleeding. We went to a drugstore to get a bandage, which David assured me would help close up the wound.

The last thing I remember him saying to me was, "And don't get it wet." Two months later I had to go to the doctor to remove the keloid that had formed. I guess I must have gotten it wet.

When David left town, I moved on to other guys, but no one took his place in my mind. I was obsessed. He sent me letters, gifts, and candy—just enough to keep me hoping, to keep me hooked. When he came back to LA, I told him I was seeing someone else, which made him want to see me again.

And so it continued: LA, Adirondacks, absence, gifts. Around and around we went. Dribs and drabs of a relationship, mere breadcrumbs.

One day I decided I'd had enough. We were in love, weren't we? I spoke to David's closest friend, actor Walter Matthau. I told him I was crazy about David, but he was always either coming from or going to the Adirondacks, always just out of reach. Walter told me in no uncertain terms: "If you want David, you'll have to go up and get him."

So I called David and announced, "I'm coming to see you! Uh, remind me. How do I get there?"

David didn't take me seriously. "Well, telling you how to get here would be like sending bombs to Vietnam when you don't believe in the war."

"Well, I'm coming, anyway," I said. "I'll find it myself."

"Sally," David said, suddenly serious. "I've got someone else here."

I laughed. "Good, she can make us dinner when I arrive."

Another woman? Impossible. Our own relationship had been fairly chaste.

I flew to New York. I got on a bus that twisted and turned along rainy country roads and finally ended up at a muddy bus stop. Luckily for me, there was a taxi stand there, and I gave the cabbie David's address.

When the cab reached the house, I looked down through its streaky taxi window. Sure enough, I saw a woman sitting in David's living room knitting. Knitting. It was all too much for me.

As I got out of the car, David appeared.

"Kellerman, you are extravagant," he said, impressed by my grand gesture.

By the way, the woman did cook dinner for us. That night, we all slept in separate beds, and the next morning David drove me back to the bus stop. As he put me on a bus back to New York, he told me that I was part of a very small group of people who he cared about. *Oh boy,* I thought. I'd dragged myself across country on a plane, a bus, and a muddy taxi to be in his "small group"?

David later told me that the knitter, the woman who cooked dinner for us, had taught him how to love. By then I was truly happy for him. I don't think that, at that time, either one of us knew how. Not really.

I went back to LA with my tail between my legs, longing. I longed to break out of television and into films. I longed for David. I wondered if I'd ever achieve either: success in life or love. All around me people were moving on with their lives. Jack had married Sandra. I would occasionally hang out at their place or we'd go see Luana in a play.

My sister had taken a big step as well. Diana had left her husband, Ian, and was now living with a woman named Gloria. I knew that Diana was struggling with her sexuality, but learned Ian had had affairs as well, with other women. Gloria, a very talented clarinetist and conductor, had met Diana when she began teaching her recorder. My mother had rung me up to fill me in on the situation. I don't know how much of a shock it was for her and my father. We didn't really discuss it—that wasn't my family's style. But it certainly wasn't a shock for me.

Diana soon brought Gloria out to my apartment to meet me. Diana seemed so free, so much herself. I couldn't imagine what it had been like for her to live a lie for so long. That didn't mean her new life was easy. Quite the contrary.

Sometimes Diana would come over sobbing. What were they going to do about her daughter, Claire? Diana didn't want Claire shuttling back and forth between Ian's place in Santa Monica and

Diana and Gloria's place in Topanga Canyon. Diana thought that would be too confusing for Claire. Besides, it was hard enough for Diana and Gloria to deal with intolerance. Diana certainly didn't want her daughter to have to grow up with it. She thought it would be best for Claire if only one of them—either Diana or Ian—kept Claire. The other parent would not see her until she turned eighteen. It was soon decided that that person would be Ian.

I didn't fully understand that decision at the time, but I also recognized that I had never had to deal with the situation of being judged so harshly by society for who you were. It was their choice, and they had made it. I began to feel a much stronger pull toward my niece, though I didn't know what to do about it beyond visit with her whenever I could and help Ian out in any way possible. I had no idea yet the amazing impact Claire would have on the rest of my life. But that's how change usually is: it doesn't announce itself; it doesn't let you know when you're witnessing a moment that's going to affect you forever. You just have to pay attention. Things are changing all around you all the time.

Even my city was changing. I remember being on the Universal set of *The Alfred Hitchcock Hour*. The assistant director yelled, "Quiet on the set!" which means not a breath. Not a sound. I waited for action. But that's not what I heard next. Instead it was: *And on your right, you can see . . .*

"CUT CUT!!!"

We all looked up. It was a bus. A Universal Studios tour bus. One of the first. But I didn't think anything of it at the time, never imagined that the tour bus would be joined by an entire city, an outdoor mall, and amusement park rides.

Just beyond Universal lot was my Valley, my orange groves. Everything was changing. Everyone was moving on.

So why did I feel so stuck?

CHAPTER 6

Hit the Deck

OVER MY YEARS AS AN ACTRESS, EVEN A STRUGGLING ONE, I have gotten to experience a lot of things that I would otherwise have never had the chance to try. Robert Altman gave me the opportunity to do something I had never dreamed possible: be a cheerleader.

Unfortunately, before that could happen, I had to do something I had never wanted to do: get completely naked on film.

I was desperate to be in the movies. I had done small parts in a few films, but nothing of any real note. I had thought my big break was coming in 1965, when I did *The Third Day* with Roddy McDowell and George Peppard. In it I played a young mistress and wrote George Peppard dirty letters and got killed in a car accident. I danced around in front of a fireplace in a midriff top, thinking, for the first time ever, that I actually looked good. I really believed *The Third Day* was going to be my rocketship to stardom.

It wasn't.

I was finally thin, and nobody cared.

Back to TV I went. I had a promising turn in a pilot, *Higher and Higher*, playing the title character Liz Higher with a supporting cast that included Robert Forster, Alan Alda, and Dustin Hoffman. The show wasn't picked up as a series, but Robert became a lifelong friend. Then, a few years after *Third Day*, I landed a small part in the film *The Boston Strangler* with Tony Curtis. I like to think of myself as the romantic lead in that film, as I played the only one of the women who actually survived the strangler's attack. But again, a rocketship to stardom it was not.

More TV. And voice-overs. From the 1960s on, voice-over work was a mainstay of my life. I still remember my very first commercial, for a feminine deodorant spray that used to be all the rage:

I've grown up . . .
I'm a woman . . .
And now that I am, I'm glad there's FDS.
(Pause)
He's home!

Oh, how clean we women have to be. Where, I wonder, are the ads saying, "Hey fellas, let's get down there and really give your boys a good scrub."

No matter how long you've done voice-overs, you have to audition for every job. It's as if the producers of these things are thinking, "Well, sure, you may be able to say 'Sears,' but can you say 'Maytag'? You might be able to say, 'Revlon,' but are you sure you can say 'Clairol?'" Still, it's a great gig.

Finally I got another film role, in *The April Fools*. Again, the part was small, but the film featured Jack Lemmon and Catherine Deneuve, both of whom I admired. I even had one scene with Jack Lemmon. I was excited just to rehearse it with him. Then I found out it was his wife's birthday. Would I mind terribly running the scene with the script supervisor? "Of course not," I replied. What was there to say?

When I turned around, standing there in front of me was

Boomy, my next-door neighbor on Sweetzer Avenue. So that's who I shot my first "Jack Lemmon" scene with: Boomy the script supervisor.

Soon after *April Fools* my agent called me about an audition. I didn't know anything about the director or who, if anyone, had already been cast. The only thing my agent said was that I was reading for the part of "Lt. Dish," so I thought that I had better put on some red lipstick to look more "dish-y."

The audition room was full of men, scattered about, none of whom I recognized. I didn't even know which one was the director. I guess I did well because, all of a sudden, one of the men—he had the longest fingers I've ever seen, like birds about to take flight—said, "I'll give you the best role in the picture: Hot Lips."

The first thing that popped into my mind was Diana saying to me, when I sang as a kid, "Shut up, big lips, with your stupid voice!" I'd burst into tears every time. But the guy said he was giving me the best role in the picture.

"Really?" I said. I was so excited. Finally! The best role in something. I thanked the long-fingered man, took the script, and rushed outside.

The man was director Robert Altman, who later loved to tell anyone who would listen that I was down on the floor, chewing on his pant leg, when I got the part.

Not true.

I didn't even wait to get home before I cracked open the script to get a better look at this "best" role in the picture. Leaning against the building, I began thumbing through the pages looking for my part. And looking. And still looking. Nothing. On page forty, maybe I found a single line. Later I found a few more.

Fourteen years in Hollywood and my "best role" is the nine-line part of a soldier named Hot Lips? I staggered home, angry and bitter, and I called my agent, indignant.

"There's nothing to this part!" I told him.

"This guy is supposed to be really talented," he said, trying to calm me down. "I really think you should do it." I later learned that fifteen directors had said no to this film before Altman had said yes.

So I read the script again and then agreed to take another meeting with Altman. It was just the two of us this time, and I arrived in a huff. I didn't know him from Adam, but I hated him for thinking he could fool me. Hot Lips was a memory before the script was even halfway over. But as long as I had come this far, I was going to tell him what I thought.

"Why does she have to leave in the middle of the film?" I began.

I had spent years playing roles on TV. I was already thirty-one years old. I didn't want a career playing hard-bitten drunks in Chanel suits who get slapped by their husbands. This movie was supposed to be a comedy. Hell, I'd done two episodes of *Bonanza* just to prove I could be funny. I was capable of so much more than a few lines. I was capable of a "best" role—and so was my character.

"I'm not just some WAC—I'm a woman!" I shouted at Altman. "So why can't she do this? And why can't she do that?"

I was ranting. When I finally came up for air, Bob just casually leaned back in his chair. He said, simply, "Why couldn't she? You could end up with something or nothing. Why not take a chance?"

The minute he said that, something in me shifted. Here I was having a tantrum in his office, and there he was leaning back in his chair, smiling. Everything about him was so comfortable and relaxed. So sure.

Oh my God, I thought. *I love this man.*

So it was settled. The role of Hot Lips Houlihan was mine. The movie was *M*A*S*H.*

• • •

THE SHOOT BEGAN IN APRIL 1969. *M*A*S*H* WAS A MOVIE about an Army medical outpost during the Korean War—a thinly veiled commentary on Vietnam—and the doctors and nurses who lived and worked there. The storyline was unconventional, not the kind of predictable plot that audiences were accustomed to. Cinema was changing.

I hadn't known Bob at all before I threw my tantrum in his office, but evidently he quickly got my number. On that first day of shooting I stood nervously in front of the mirror, looking at my bright red lips. Bob strolled by and said, "Sally, if you're worrying about what you look like, you're fired."

Son of a bitch, he really did understand me.

So I had to get over the way I looked. Jo Ann Pflug, who was playing Lt. Dish, the part I had auditioned for, got to wear makeup and a scarf and get laid. I got to be uptight and buttoned up to my neck. On the set nobody looked at me twice.

Until the shower scene, when I was hoping they wouldn't.

I spent half my life backing out of rooms. I always went to the beach with a towel wrapped around my legs. For someone like me, who had ridden the roller-coaster of pregnant women's urine, dexamyl capsules, apple diets, and fruit fasts to always run back to cookies, brownies, and candy—the mainstays of my diet—getting naked was not at the top of any "to-do" list.

Now I was about to be stark naked on the big screen.

"Can I at least look pretty?" I asked Bob.

"Here's what we can do," he said. "Sure, we can have the entire crew of a hundred and twenty men light you for an hour, or as fast as you hit the deck, that's what we'll see."

I took the second choice.

There wasn't going to be anything sexual about it—that wasn't the issue. Nudity in films was becoming more common, if not the norm. These were the early days of the Motion Picture Association of America's rating system (Rated G, PG, R, etc.), which had been in effect for not quite a year when we began shooting. Frankly, I wonder if it's still in effect. Back then we had some nude scenes. Today we have munching on breasts, vaginas, making love, masturbation . . . Acting has certainly changed since I was a kid. I like to say I was lucky that all my nude scenes were done essentially alone—no munching.

Still, I was terrified. So I did what any woman in her right mind, who was anxious about her appearance, would do: I went to my shrink and dropped my pants.

This was shrink number two in my short line of therapists. (No one can ever accuse me of not trying to better myself.) This particular psychiatrist encouraged attending orgies as a means of overcoming virtually any kind of repression. It was the 1960s, after all. I ignored that suggestion, but I was pretty sure that nothing I did in his office would catch him off guard.

He had already been harping on me to stop dieting. "Get to the deeper problem," he had told me, and I had agreed to give it a shot. But now I had to do this scene. I had to know what kind of shape I was really in. I stood up, turned my back, and dropped my pants.

Silence.

"So?" he finally said. "That's it?"

As long as he didn't recoil in horror, that was good enough for me.

In that famous scene in the film, the Army doctors Hawkeye, Duke, and Trapper have placed bets on whether or not my carpet matched my drapes, so to speak. So they have invited a crowd to watch as they raise the flaps of the women's shower tent to expose me—and settle their bet.

On the first take I hit the deck so fast that Altman said I was on the ground before the tent flap was even raised.

I lay there, soaking and naked, on the ground, too embarrassed to stand. When I looked up, I saw Gary Burghoff, who played Corporal Radar in both the film and the TV series, standing directly in my sight line without a stitch on. Stark naked.

Take two.

I hit the deck again, this time making sure the tent hit the ground before I did. When I looked once more, I saw Tamara Wilcox-Smith (then Tamara Horrocks) who was playing one of the nurses, Captain "Knocko." Tamara was a comedienne, one of several from a comedy troupe in San Francisco who were cast in the film. Tamara is, shall we say, amply endowed. And there she was, standing in my sight line, bare breasts in the sun. But I still had Gary's anatomy burned on my brain, and so when I got a look at Tamara's boobs, I thought for a split second that I was looking at some sort of hermaphrodite.

Take three.

I hit the deck once more and again looked up, wondering what new vision was in store for me. This time, Tamara had her clothes back on but was being dry-humped by actor Kenny Prymus.

That third take was the charm. Thanks to my castmates, who bravely stripped and humped to spur me on, I'd done it! Bob had probably put them up to it to relax me because he knew how scared I was. Who knows—he was such a rascal. No matter how those antics came about, to this day I attribute my Academy Award nomination to my reaction to seeing my colleagues off-camera during the shower scene.

However, it still wasn't clear that I would have anything at all to do in the remainder of the movie. All I knew was that I had one more scene. After the shower incident I was supposed to storm into the tent of Colonel Henry Blake, played by Roger Bowen. How I got from the shower to the Colonel's tent was up to me.

Years earlier Joe Stefano, the guardian angel who had changed my life by promoting my career during my first appearance on *The Outer Limits*, had given me a piece of advice I had never forgotten: *Don't run on film*. Now, on the set of *M*A*S*H*, I hesitated for one second before saying to myself, *Sorry, Joe, here I go*.

Other words flowed through my mind. Gig Young had once said to me when I worked with him on an episode of *The Rogues*: *In comedy, you have to play for something*.

That inspired me to take really huge, hideous strides. With soapsuds running down my face, arms flailing—all five-foot-ten of me—I strode and stomped my way to Colonel Blake's tent. I'd worked myself into a rage until it hit me: Hot Lips was losing everything she cared about. So because Bob hadn't said "cut," I started whimpering, "My commission . . .my commission."

All of a sudden, Bob ran around the tent and grabbed me. "I had no idea you were going to do it like that!" he said. "Now you're vulnerable! Now you can stay in the movie."

After that, Bob kept making up scenes to keep me in the movie. There were no big intellectual discussions about the part. Every now and then Bob would just throw out an idea or a thought that would convey the whole sense of the character. Hot Lips wasn't in the script anymore, but she was still on screen. She was, for example, sneaking into the swamp to be with Tom Skerritt's character, Duke Forrest. She was playing cards. She appeared at a football game, as something I had always dreamed of being but had never had the chance in high school: a cheerleader.

Cheerleading was maybe the most fun I have ever had in my life. I got to be goofy and silly: doing cartwheels, making up cheers, getting hit in the face by my whistle as I spastically jumped up and down. Bob was in his element, hovering over the football field in a crane and barking directions through his megaphone.

"Sally! When the gun goes off at the end of the first half, say, 'My God, they've shot him!'"

"Hot Lips! You're a blithering idiot," Colonel Blake yelled, and I was. It was exhilarating.

Working on that set was like going to summer camp. The 4077th M*A*S*H was set up on 20th Century Fox's Century Ranch in Malibu. For someone like me, it was heaven: I was out in the open air, working with a director I now knew to be brilliant.

One day Bob walked up to me and asked, "Sally, where are you from?"

"San Fernando," I answered proudly.

"Whatever," Altman said. "Listen, when Don [Sutherland] asks you where you're from, say, 'I like to think of the Army as my home.'"

That, for me, was genius. That one line tells you that Hot Lips wasn't offended by the obnoxious doctors because she was a nasty, cold-hearted wench; she was appalled because they were not only disrespecting the rules, but they were also disrespecting her home, ridiculing everything she held sacred. Bob got that across to me in just a few words, with no book learning required. Speaking of books, I didn't learn to read until I was twelve.

Leon Erickson was a brilliant art director. I loved the way he worked my own personality into Hot Lips. When he was set dressing for my tent, he asked me, "Do you smoke?" I told him I didn't. "Well, what would you have in your tent?" My answer was, of course, "Candy." So he made sure to have a candy dish in there. It was also Leon who decided that I needed to wear garters. Bob loved the garters the moment he'd heard Leon mention them.

"Oh, garters!" he said. "Come with me . . ."

So we shot a scene of Hot Lips arriving at camp, exiting a helicopter, bending over and saluting—Hot Lips was always saluting. Chopper blades were whirring above my head as the updraft from the chopper blew up my skirt and showed off Leon's precious garters.

Robert Duvall was a joy, so talented and a delight to work with—just an easy, breezy absolute doll. I had the privilege of making love to his hilariously pious Frank Burns, while screaming at him, "Kiss my hot lips!"—the inspiration for my character's nickname. Tom Skerritt was a love and as enamored of Bob as I was. He was a dear—and another handsome fellow I got to romance on screen.

But my favorite castmate was the guy I spotted one day while waiting on the chow line. He was so darling, so androgynous looking that I had no idea what to make of him. The man was Bud Cort, who most people know from the cult classic *Harold and Maude*, had a small role in *M*A*S*H* as Private Boone. The first thing that popped into my head, looking at this fascinating creature in the mess tent, was, "Oh boy, we're going to be best friends." And we were. We still are.

For me the whole experience of making *M*A*S*H* was thrilling. But just as at real summer camp, there were mean kids. For me, the mean kids were the two male leads, as much as there are leads in Bob's films: Donald Sutherland and Elliott Gould. They loved to pick on me.

Prior to filming, I didn't know either one of them. Don had gotten some notice for his role in the *Dirty Dozen,* but at the time that was about it. Elliot had a little more buzz, having just appeared in *Bob & Carol & Ted & Alice.* I too had been offered a role in *Bob & Carol & Ted & Alice,* but in one of my less-than-stellar career moves, I decided to pass. Why? Because I was an idiot.

The movie, exploring the very 1960s issue of spouse swapping, was a major hit. Boy, oh boy, did I have a crush on Elliott. Both Don and Elliott knew it. Throughout the shoot they kept themselves apart from the rest of the cast, which was perfect for their characters and the tight camaraderie they had in the film. But they were absolutely horrible to me.

Their favorite gag was to invite me out and then pretend that we'd never made plans. Don usually started it. He'd say, "Hey Sally, we were thinking of going to the movies tonight. Wanna come?"

"Sure!" I'd reply.

The end of the day would roll around, and I would see the two of them getting ready to leave the set. "Hey, Don, are we going to the movies?" I'd ask.

Don and Elliott would look at each other, confused. "No, I'm going to the game!" Don would say, and off they'd go, leaving me behind.

I fell for this more than once, I'm sorry to say.

We were almost two months into shooting when my thirty-second birthday rolled around. I was walking off set when the two of them drove up alongside me.

"Sally, it's your birthday! Meet us at the Brown Derby," they said.

"Just go away!" I told them. I'd learned my lesson by now.

"Oh, come on . . . It's your birthday!"

So I gave in. I drove over to Beverly Hills, to the original Brown Derby restaurant at Beverly and Wilshire. The building itself was shaped just like an actual men's brown derby hat. So sad they tore it down. Sometimes I think Los Angeles has no sense of its history. I took a seat in one of the booths and waited for what seemed like an hour. Alone in the dim light, I kept sitting there. I'd look at my watch. I'd look up at the door. I'd look at my watch again. Nothing. No one. I felt like a total idiot. They did it to me again, I thought. When would I ever learn?

Gathering the little self-respect I had left, I began to head for the door when I heard, "SURPRISE!"

Don and Elliott jumped out of the shadows. There they were, the two devils, chocolates in hand. Unbelievable. Even when they were doing something nice, they still had to torment me. Six months after the picture wrapped, we had a reunion lunch. We all kissed and made up, joking about how mean they were to me. I think I laughed. Maybe.

Because I didn't mingle with the two of them, I didn't know how disaffected they felt. Although I was an instant fan of Bob's, Don and Elliott were not happy with the production. They even met with their agents to complain about Altman and discuss having him replaced; the two were concerned that Bob would not only ruin the movie but also their careers.

At the time Fox had two other war pictures in production—*Tora Tora Tora* starring Martin Balsam and Joseph Cotten among others, and *Patton*, starring George C. Scott. In a way this helped *M*A*S*H*, a third war picture, with its $3.5 million budget and unorthodox director, fly under the radar. The others were World War II movies. Although *M*A*S*H* was set in Korea, Bob worked hard to avoid references to the Korean War so that the film could just as readily evoke the current conflict in Vietnam.

But word was getting around—and it was obvious to anyone who saw the dailies—that the script was not being followed very closely. For some people, especially those of us coming from television, taking such liberties was amazing. In TV especially you didn't change one word. When I had worked with Rod Steiger a few years before on an episode of *Bob Hope Presents the Chrysler Theatre,* we used to joke that we were worried we'd get canned for changing "a" to "the."

The screenwriter Ring Lardner and lots of folks at Fox were increasingly bothered that people were improvising and, worse, constantly talking over each other. You just didn't do that in movies then. Bob liked to have cameras and mics all over the place, always hot to pick up whatever we did or said. But Ingo Preminger, one of the producers, loved what he was seeing in the dailies. If Bob hinted that something hadn't come out the way he wanted, Ingo would say, "So reshoot! I'm a happy man."

If Bob knew about all the behind-the-scenes grumbling, he didn't let on. He was so relaxed on the set. Few of us understood the kind of movie he was making, but he exuded confidence, no matter what. After shooting, we'd smoke a little grass, and some would have a drink. We'd all go to the dailies together. There was always a big crowd sitting there in the dark: actors, crew, agents, managers, and the occasional studio reps. The place was packed. If people hated what they saw, Bob didn't seem to care, and if anyone had a good suggestion, he had no problem using it.

The first time I had ever seen dailies, for *The Outer Limits,* I'd been ready to hang myself. If I ever doubted that Bob understood me, he kept reminding me of it during the dailies for *M*A*S*H.* I would appear onscreen, and his voice would come out of the darkness.

"Oh, I bet you hate yourself there, Sally . . . I bet you think you're looking ugly there . . ."

Then, one night, after the dailies were done and the drinks and the smokes were gone, Bob came up to me and said, "You know, you're going to get nominated for an Academy Award for this."

What do you say to something like that? I had no idea. I loved hearing that, especially from Bob, someone I loved and admired.

· · ·

ON JUNE 11, 1969, SHOOTING WAS COMPLETE. ROBERT ALTMAN
brought *M*A*S*H* in three days ahead of schedule and nearly a
half-a-million under budget. For directing the picture, he was
paid a mere $75,000. Bob's son Mike, who wrote the lyrics to
M*A*S*H's theme song, "Suicide Is Painless," ended up making
more money than Bob did on the picture.

But the war that had started on the set continued into the editing room. Bringing all of this footage together was going to be
challenge; the studio didn't even want to release the film at first
because they didn't know what to make of it.

In many ways *M*A*S*H* changed filmmaking. Bob brought
a new fearlessness to the screen, a new juxtaposition of blood
and gore with comedy and pathos. Horror movies always showed
some carnage, which we have certainly taken to the max now,
whether in slasher films or on cop shows. We show blood, livers,
hearts pounding. But Bob was the first to depict gore in a realistic
light, showing us the bloody hands of doctors working over an
operating table while blithely talking about the game. Back then
those scenes were scarier than a horror film's because they were
just too darn real.

· · ·

M*A*S*H WENT ON TO BECOME A MEGAHIT, EVEN A CLASSIC.
All the fears about its controversial nature had gone out the window. Two hours before a preview screening in San Francisco
there were lines around the block to get in. Elliott and Don, who
had wanted Bob fired, were just as thrilled as the rest of us. Elliott
later worked with Bob in *The Long Goodbye* and, to this day, raves
about him, as I do. But not everyone was happy with the movie's
outcome. The screenwriter, Ring Lardner, was furious the first
time he saw the completed film.

"What have you done to my script?!" he supposedly demanded
of Bob. "Not a word of what I wrote is in there!"

But in the end the $3.5 million production brought in more

than $80 million at the box office and garnered countless award nominations, including five Oscar nods. One of them, as Bob had predicted, was for me.

. . .

M*A*S*H WAS THE GREATEST EXPERIENCE OF MY ENTIRE CAreer, and I've had a lot of great ones. Still, I'd be lying if I said it doesn't push a button or two every time someone calls me Hot Lips. I've been working for more than fifty years and made at least fifty movies, but for better or worse, I'm most notably remembered as Hot Lips Houlihan. Recently, as I walked through New York City, a truck driver leaned out the window and yelled, "Hey, Hot Lips!" That put a big crooked smile on my face. Anything that keeps me connected to Bob Altman makes me happy.

Bob's was a world most of us hadn't seen—not in the movies, and certainly not on TV. But so much was to about to change—in Hollywood, in our culture, and in my own life.

CHAPTER 7

Never the Same Again

I WAS NOW WORKING ENOUGH TO BE COMFORTABLE FINAN-
cially and got my own place. No roommates—that was progress. I
loved my new apartment on Shoreham Drive in West Hollywood,
just above Sunset and Doheny. At the intersection of Sunset and
Doheny was Turner's Liquor Store, which was convenient when
I wanted cookies and candy. The neighborhood was so peaceful,
so beautiful, so sunny, and traffic-free.

But then the hippies arrived.

My beautiful white sidewalks were suddenly covered in gum.
Kids, thousands it seemed, were all over Sunset Boulevard, with
long hair and raggedy clothes, smoking joints on the street or
wiped out on harder drugs.

Now my neighbors and I had to put up with the occasional
ruckus in the parking lot below our building when it emptied
after business hours. One night, when things got too loud, I
strode out in my nightgown, having been awakened by crashing
bottles and somebody threatening to cut somebody else. I'd had
it. I stood up at the top of the wall that overlooked the lot, yelling,
"Excuse me! But you're on somebody else's property and you're
breaking bottles. You roared in here on your motorcycles, looking
like Hell's Angels—and maybe you are! Now you're screaming

your heads off threatening to cut somebody? I mean, who do you think you are? Some of us need to sleep!"

All of a sudden, the tough guys got quiet. "I'm so sorry, ma'am," someone said. "We'll pick it up right away." They immediately started cleaning up.

I had already called the cops, but when they arrived, I told them I'd solved the problem. Then I went back to bed.

It was a far cry from a dangerous neighborhood. Still, it was growing unfamiliar—more impersonal and less neighborly than the West Hollywood small town I had inhabited for a decade or so. Our enclave was coming to resemble a strange new America that we barely recognized. Early that summer of 1969 I had sprawled out on the bed of my friend Mark Rydell, who had directed me in *Slattery's People*. I joined him and his former wife Joanne Linville to watch in awe as Neil Armstrong walked on the moon. Talk about brave new worlds!

The times were turbulent. We'd lost JFK in 1963 and Martin Luther King Jr. in 1968. Bobby Kennedy was assassinated just a few months after King, at our own Ambassador Hotel in Los Angeles. Vietnam was always in our thoughts. The war and the assassinations affected us greatly, and I think we all struggled to make sense of those horrors, feeling a loss of innocence and a troubling certainty that our world would never be the same.

But nothing could have prepared me for August 9, 1969, when horror struck closer to home.

• • •

I GOT THE CALL EARLY THAT SATURDAY MORNING. I WAS already awake when the phone rang. The voice on the line—a friend, I can't remember who it was—sounded panicked, asking, "Is it true? Is it true?"

"Is what true?" I said.

"Is it true that Sharon Tate and Jay Sebring and everybody up at Rudi's were stabbed and hung?"

"Of course not!" I yelled. "What's wrong with you? Why would you even say something like that?!"

I hung up, feeling sick, and immediately called my friend Anjanette Comer. She confirmed the ghastly news: five people—Sharon Tate, Jay Sebring, Wojciech Frykowski, Abigail Folger, and Steve Parent—had been murdered at the home of Stuart Cohen's partner, my friend Rudi Altobelli. The housekeeper had found the bodies that morning. Anjanette came over to be with me, and we spent what seemed like the entire day huddled together, shivering and shaking and trying to grasp what had happened.

Rudi Altobelli and Stuart Cohen made a great management team. I was lucky to have them in my life. Stuart had the business head, and Rudi had the aesthetic sense, not to mention that he was endlessly fun and hospitable. He loved his dogs, loved having people over, and was a fantastic cook. Jack Nicholson always called him "Rudi the Rank" because of Rudi's on-the-nose sarcasm.

Back in the early 1960s Stuart and Rudi had bought an expansive property in Benedict Canyon, overlooking all of Beverly Hills. Rudi lived in and ran the house. The place was somewhat secluded, shrouded by trees and shrubs. For years we'd all spent time hanging out there—me, Stuart, sometimes Luana, and occasionally Jack, who would come up to play cards along with Rudi's many friends. The property included a main house and a detached guesthouse; it was beautiful but not overly fussy. Homey. It was the kind of place where you could put your bare feet up and relax.

The guesthouse was where we spent most of our time. It had a high, beamed ceiling and a large open living room, with a ladder that led up to a small loft. A large stone fireplace and a big dining room table anchored the living room. That was where Rudi would serve up his big pots of spaghetti to whoever had come around.

Walkways connected the separate areas of the property, bordered by split-rail fences and blooming plants. The property's smallish pool sat between the main house and guesthouse. It had smooth curves and was hugged on all sides by rock and stone landscaping, softened with greenery. So inviting, so mellow.

We would go over and just sit around by the pool, maybe smoke some grass, then eat some spaghetti when the munchies kicked in. That made Stuart crazy—he hated when we smoked pot. He would get in a huff and storm off like he was leaving. We'd chase after him, pretending that we believed he was really stomping out, and we would beg him to stay, though we knew he always would.

Sun, food, friends, good times—that's what the haven at 10050 Cielo Drive had meant to us. Rudi would routinely rent out one or the other of the buildings on the property. Henry Fonda had lived in the guesthouse. Record producer Terry Melcher and his then-girlfriend Candice Bergen had lived in the main house. A strange musician named Charles Manson, who had been in touch with Terry about some recordings, had once come up to the house looking for him. But Terry and Candy weren't staying there at the moment. Actress Sharon Tate and her friends were, while Sharon's husband, the director Roman Polanski, was in London making a movie.

I didn't know Roman and Sharon well, but I had gone to their wedding reception. Sharon was lovely, both in her look and her demeanor—very warm and sweet, approachable and kind. She was only twenty-six years old, due to deliver a baby two weeks from the night that Charles Manson's followers invaded Rudi's home.

Rudi, meanwhile, was working in Italy and hadn't yet been informed of the tragedy. Stuart was also overseas, in Ireland with Chris Jones, an actor I'd introduced to him who had starred in the TV series *The Legend of Jesse James*. Someone had to break the news to Rudy. The task fell to me.

I reached Rudi at the Hassler Hotel in Rome and delivered the terrible blow. He immediately flew home, and I met him at the airport. From there we went straight to the Beverly Wilshire Hotel, where we spent the night together in a suite, scared to death, sick and brokenhearted.

Nothing so monstrous and violent had ever happened in our lives and certainly not in our community. The Tate murders and the LaBianca murders, committed a night later by Manson's family members, were hideous, altering my consciousness and the consciousness of everyone I knew. Our world had come unhinged.

I thought about the way I'd lived at my old apartment on Sweetzer, not far from my current place on Shoreham. Every night I'd leave my door open a crack so that the cat could go in and out. Not just unlocked—open. I still slept like a log every night, without a care in the world. That was a Hollywood that didn't exist anymore.

The Manson murders not only changed Hollywood but the rest of America as well. The press coverage was horrific. You couldn't escape those images of bloody footprints and the word "PIG" scrawled in blood on a door. None of us had ever seen such gruesome scenes on the nightly news or in the newspaper. The coverage, bordering on sick fascination, was the beginning of a new level of gore and sensationalism that has become the norm in our modern-day media. Suddenly, we were no longer watching the news but rather a new and twisted form of entertainment, focused almost exclusively on the grisly and the macabre.

I'd argue that it has only gotten worse over the years. Since then Americans have heard about every atrocity, and this does nothing but make us live in constant fear. Some would say we're immune now to the police tape and the blood and the voyeurism. But we definitely weren't then. It unnerved us. It made us sick. I think something as heinous as those murders is supposed to make you sick. I never want to be numb to that. Ever.

For those of us in Stuart and Rudi's circle, there was a sad, aching irony to the tragedy. How could such a senseless act of violence take place in a home that was so beautiful, where we had all felt such happiness and peace?

• • •

AT THIS STAGE I WAS STILL PANICKED ABOUT WHERE MY CA-
reer was going. I thought I'd given one of my better performances
in M*A*S*H, but at the time I had no idea how the film would
do and what that success could mean for me. So I couldn't shake
the fear that I would never work in the movies again. I flat-out
didn't feel good about myself, and that self-doubt, coupled with
my desperate fear, led me to make bad choices.

I had met Larry Hauben at the Actor's Studio. He was an actor
and painter who would later write the screenplay for *One Flew
Over the Cuckoo's Nest*. The first night I met Larry I was sobbing
to him about my career, and he said that he'd like to shoot a little
film of me. I was so desperate that I said okay without asking
questions. My friendship with Larry quickly became an affair,
though I was still obsessed with David Rayfiel. I guess I needed
somewhere to put my energies, so to speak.

So Larry came over to my Shoreham Drive apartment and
walked into the narrow little bathroom. The tub was on left, the
toilet on the right, and on the far wall was a sink and mirror.
Larry put up a piece of tinfoil in the corner of the bathroom above
the tub to catch the light, then sat down on the toilet seat. Never
one for too much silence, I started talking.

"Save that for when I'm rolling," he said, cutting me off. "Now
roll your hair and then take it down again."

Well, I tell you, when I saw what he had shot that day, I said to
myself, "Tinfoil, baby, cool!" I'd never looked so beautiful in my
life. Tinfoil.

At times we'd get together at Larry's house, which was never
my preference because it was far too filthy for me; I'd bring my
own sheets just to sit down on his bed. Sometimes we'd smoke
some grass first, which helped me relax a little. Occasionally
there was also a cameraman present for this film Larry wanted
to make. One night we got in such a huge argument that the
cameraman fled, clearly afraid for his life. Furious, Larry yelled
after him, "Finally something real happens and you run out!"

On one particular evening Larry said, "Let's take psilocy-

bin"—'shrooms were a favorite of Timothy Leary. Once we'd gotten high, Larry made a new suggestion for the film. "We're going
to make love, but you'll only see our legs . . ."

Though I was terrified, I went along with it. Larry assured me
that I'd know what we were doing—really doing, not faking—but
the audience wouldn't see it. I had no idea what the film, which
would be called *Venus,* was going to be like until I saw it—along
with everyone else—when it premiered at a local theater.

In the meantime, thank God I got a real role in *Brewster
McCloud,* a new film with Bob Altman that was set in Houston. At that point it felt good to get out of town for a while. The
movie starred me and Bud Cort, the slight, unusual fellow I fell
in love with the moment I saw him standing in the chow line for
M*A*S*H. Bob had asked me if I thought Bud would be good in
the role of Brewster, an oddball loner living in a fallout shelter
in the Houston Astrodome who wants to build wings that will
allow him to fly.

A bizarre recluse who wants to fly in the Astrodome? Who else
could Bob possibly cast? Bud was perfect.

Bud and I had become fast friends, just as I'd predicted. Luckily
for me, he was a good listener, because all I talked about in those
days were my affairs and work. Bud was a nice Catholic boy from
New York, and I hope he found my stories riveting, for his sake. I
taught him to drive, and we loved tooling around town together.
Driving down Sunset, I would window shop from the front seat
of my car. Because there was no traffic, we could slow to a crawl
as I leaned out the window to see what my favorite boutiques had
on display. I can still do that today while I'm stalled in traffic. You
can always look on the bright side.

Bud bought me a pair of lovebirds once. They were a nice
symbolic gesture, but in reality they would never shut up. I
couldn't make a move without them squawking. If an overnight
visitor got up to use the bathroom, I would hiss at him, "No!
No! Don't move!! Don't turn on the water!" But I always said it
too late—the squawking would begin. The lovebirds did not last,

perhaps a not-so-subtle metaphor for my own romantic life at the time. But that was Bud: darling and generous, with a great eye for art, if not pets. I was happy to be working with him again as well as Bob.

I still hadn't seen the finished version of *M*A*S*H*, but Bob had believed in me then and now had cast me in *Brewster* without an audition. At the time I had no idea how rare that was—what a gift, what a vote of confidence. I should have been grateful, but instead, believing it was normal, I began to expect to land roles without competing for them.

For the most part Bob just made up my role in *Brewster*, as the title character's fairy godmother of sorts. After my recent experience as Hot Lips, making it up as we went along was fine by me. However, Bob knew very well that I wanted to portray real-life women in films, not a wacko. So what part did he give me? He chose me for the role of a very unconventional angel who walks around calm and lovely and ethereal, murdering people with bird shit, all the while dressed in a trench coat.

In one scene Bob told me to sit in a fountain, topless, like a giant bird. "No, Bob!" I protested. I'd had enough with taking my clothes off.

"It's five in the morning, and it's a long shot. We'll hardly see you," he argued.

Yeah, right. We'll see about that, I thought. But I did it, because it was Bob.

There is another scene in which my character gives Bud a bath. Again, I was to go topless. The day we shot that, I thought we were on a closed set. Only my naked back was supposed to be visible to the camera, so the audience could see the beautiful scars my wings left behind. Apparently, however, security on the set wasn't exactly airtight. Someone snuck in and snapped a picture of me from the front, and I soon ended up in *Playboy* as one of the new "Sex Stars of the Seventies." I suppose I could have sued—nowadays you would without thinking twice—but back then we just rolled with the punches.

And, hey, I got to sing in that bath scene! I sang "Rock-a-Bye, Baby." For me that was a big highlight of *Brewster McCloud,* right up there with working with Bob and being part of a fabulous cast, including Bud, of course, Shelley Duvall, Michael Murphy, and others.

I also loved our producer, Lou Adler. I developed such a crush on him, but nothing ever came of it. At the time he was dating actress and singer Peggy Lipton, a darling girl and so talented, who sang a song for the soundtrack, called, "Brewster, Don't Blow Your Mind."

Lou would go on to produce the cult classic *The Rocky Horror Picture Show,* among other movies. But he was also a legend in the music business, having produced the work of such famous artists as Sam Cooke, Jan and Dean, the Mamas and Papas, and so many more, including one of my favorite albums of the time, Carole King's *Tapestry.* He knew everyone in the business, and everyone loved to be around him—especially me.

All the movie people lived in the same apartment building in Houston, and on days we finished work early Lou would get his big old Rolls Royce with the tinted windows and take us to Neiman Marcus, which at the time was not a store any of us had ever heard of in LA. He gave all the actors peppermint oil, which I put it in my bath after work to give me the energy to go out. One night Lou took me to a ballgame. Because I found him so attractive, I was uncomfortable being alone with him and spent the entire game on the phone. Lou even threw a birthday party for me with twin pigs, ducks, and two astronauts. (Houston, we have landed.) Still, my favorite nights were when Lou, Bob, and I would go to a club called Patty's. There was a wonderful piano player there, and I'd get up every night and sing the same two songs: Bobby Hart's "Hurt So Bad" and "Lazy Afternoon."

Oh, how I wanted to sing professionally. Lou knew of that desperate longing. After singing at Patty's, I'd always turn to him and say, "Lou, I can do it! I know I can!"

I wanted Lou to produce a demo for me, a rock-and-roll song

that someone had given me. One night he finally agreed. I was all set to record it the next day.

But when I woke up, I was mute with laryngitis. Ladies and gentlemen, does fear have any power? My vocal cords that morning would have said, "Yes."

Brewster McCloud was quirky and goofy and magical—far ahead of its time, as far as I was concerned—cementing Bob's reputation as a maverick. I was lucky to be a part of it. But my life was not all movies, piano bars, and trips to Neiman's. Another huge change engulfed me: I was about to be married.

· · ·

THE MEDIA AND THE PUBLIC LIKE TO MAKE CRACKS ABOUT THE shelf life of Hollywood marriages. Marriage is work—period. I don't know if being married in my business is any more difficult than it is otherwise. However, I can confidently say that having your boyfriend show up on set and start picking arguments with you—as my soon-to-be husband Rick did on the *Brewster* set—does not bode well for your relationship or your career. Of course, I played my own part in those arguments. What they were about I have no idea.

I had met Rick Edelstein shortly after my relationship with David Rayfiel had dissolved. I was sitting, moping and heartbroken, in the bathtub of my friend Liz Hubbard—my "cousin" David Bennett's one-time wife—at her apartment in New York City, where she starred as Lucinda Walsh on *As the World Turns*.

"I know this guy who writes and directs some of our shows," Liz called from the other room. "He seems nice and intelligent, and I know he just got divorced. Would you like to meet him?"

"Does he smoke grass?" I yelled from the tub. "If so, tell him to come over!"

Sally gets back in the saddle. The Cowgirl Club rides again. Love, take two.

Rick was a writer and director not just of soap operas but also of other TV classics, such as *Starsky and Hutch* and *Sanford and*

Son. I used to joke that I liked him because he knew Barbra Streisand—not that I'm that shallow, but his knowing her certainly didn't hurt. Streisand had been one of my heroes since I first saw her in the mid-1960s in *Funny Girl* on Broadway. She was a revelation, proving that you could be funny and break hearts all in one song, that you could sing songs and star in plays and movies, all in one career. I loved her.

I was rebounding hard, still longing for David. I wanted someone to fill that void in my life without needing me too much. Rick was perfect, but what he had to offer was hardly the storybook romance I had imagined.

The truth was that Rick had a temper. He was tough, difficult, and even mean—just my kind of guy at that time. I once watched him put his fist through a parking lot attendant's glass booth because I had said something that ticked him off. But even rushing him to the emergency room wasn't enough to turn me off Rick.

We had planned to have a garden wedding in the backyard of the house we were renting in the Hollywood Hills. I loved that house. It had a yard—I had grass beneath my feet again!—a badminton court, and a little pool. In 1970 a working actress could still afford to rent a house with a pool in the Hollywood Hills. I had made a few movies—two already with Bob—but I was hardly rolling in the bucks at that point. And money management was never my strong suit, a personality glitch that would come back to haunt me.

But for now I was going to have the big wedding I'd always dreamed of as a little girl. All my friends from the beginning of time. A beautiful dress. My parents were coming, and a renowned photographer named Alfred Eisenstaedt from *Life* magazine was to shoot the event. Then Rick and I had a fight over one of the guests, his friend. Rick wanted him. I didn't. Rick's famous temper flared up, and he announced that the wedding was canceled. That was it—no discussion, no two ways about it. All the invitations had gone out and the arrangements had already been made. My mom, who had planned a beautiful party in Palos Verde with all my family and friends, said, "Darling, we'll just have the party anyway." And we did—at their club. It was lovely, but it was no fairy tale wedding.

At the time I didn't see the wedding debacle as an opportunity to leave, to simply learn from my relationship with Rick and get out, sparing both of us more upheaval and damage. Apparently I had three rules for love: keep people at arm's length if I think they might be capable of loving me too much, ache for the ones who never would, and—the most important rule of all—marry the one you fight with constantly. Anger and arguing felt safer than longing and needing and loving a little too much. "Mean" made sense to me. So I waited for the dust to settle.

It settled by the time *Brewster* had its New York premiere. There was some buzz building around me at this point. *M*A*S*H* had been released, and it was a blockbuster, surprising everyone—probably even Bob himself. The film that had worried the studios, the one they had even considered not releasing, was—along with *Airport* and *Love Story*—one of the highest-grossing films of the year. Now everyone was looking to see what that *M*A*S*H* director was doing next. And more people now knew my name, too, and were curious about my follow-up to such a successful movie, one with the same director.

I was booked to shoot a layout for *Harper's Bazaar* and for interviews with Dick Cavett and David Frost. Suddenly I was being touted as a sex symbol. The problem was that I never felt sexy. No matter my size or whether I was playing a cheerleader or sitting in fountains with my top off, I still felt like the chubby girl. This "I'm not good enough" attitude seeped into my personal life and explains, to a very sad and great extent, my first marriage.

Rick and I decided to squeeze in a wedding ceremony between the film premiere, the *Harper's* shoot, and my television interviews. We were staying at the Sherry-Netherland, a stunning hotel on Fifth Avenue at the bottom of Central Park. But the glamorous surroundings were not nearly enough to keep me from sobbing uncontrollably the night before our quickie wedding.

As we prepared for the not-so-big event, I looked around the suite and saw nothing of the kind of wedding I had envisioned for myself, nothing that had anything to do with "me." The closest thing I had to an item of some sentimental value was a plaid wool scarf that belonged to my sister Diana that I had brought along with me. That would have to count as both "old" and "borrowed." In an effort to have something in the ceremony that reflected who I was, I hung Diana's scarf over the curtains in our suite's windows. The "blue"-est thing around was my mood.

Someone else might have taken bursting into tears as some sort of—I don't know—"sign" that getting married things wasn't a good idea. But not me.

There were only a handful of people at the ceremony. My family couldn't attend because it was all too last minute and my father wasn't well. No one was sure what was going on with his health. Among the few guests was, of course, Rick's friend, the very man I did not want to have at our wedding in Los Angeles. That will teach me. He had sparked the fight that had resulted in the cancellation of my beautifully arranged garden wedding, which had now led to this sad excuse for a wedding ceremony in a hotel suite with a scarf draped over the window for decor. To add insult to injury, after Rick had kissed the bride, that friend announced, in one of the cheesiest lines ever uttered at a wedding ceremony: "That's a wrap."

Boy, was it ever.

I felt ill. After the ceremony Rick and I walked down Fifth Avenue together, with New York City's skyline closing in on us from every direction. Tourists shuffled by, wide eyed and bundled up against the cold. I was numb. It was the loneliest walk I've ever taken. We weren't right for each other and I knew it. The marriage wasn't fair to Rick or me. But good or bad, I got what I said I wanted.

CHAPTER 8

The Wheel of Fortune

ON THE BIGGEST NIGHT OF MY PROFESSIONAL LIFE SO FAR, I was saddled with some inescapable truths: neither my dress nor my marriage was a good fit. One of these problems I thought I could fix in a jiffy—at least I hoped I could. I had about two hours before it was time to walk down the red carpet.

My Oscar night story starts with a drug-fueled trip to Mexico, as I'm sure many ill-advised adventures do.

It was April 1971, and the Academy Awards were fast approaching. I hadn't for one minute taken Bob Altman seriously when he predicted that I would be nominated for an Academy Award for my performance as Hot Lips. When he turned out to be right, I was over the moon.

About two weeks before the big night a writer friend invited Rick and me to join him in Puerta Vallarta for a minivacation. His wife wasn't free to join him, and he wanted some company. Before leaving for Mexico I went in to get fitted for my dress for the Oscars.

Studio costume designer Donald Lee Feld, aka "Donfeld," who had worked with me on the film *April Fools*, had kindly offered to design my Oscar-night dress for me. That's how we did it in those days: costume designers from the studios usually made award ceremony dresses, if they weren't simply bought off the rack at a boutique. It was not a time when nominees attended shows in Paris and New York, eyeing outfits by Versace, Marchesa, Dior, and Armani hoping to spot something for the big night. The great costume designer Edith Head was good enough for Grace Kelly, after all. And almost nobody borrowed $2 million worth of jewels for the ceremony and had to be shadowed by a security detail the entire evening. You wore what you had, or if there was any borrowing to be done, it was from a friend who had better bling than you did.

My old friend Donfeld, who himself had already been nominated twice for an Academy Award, for *Days of Wine and Roses* and *They Shoot Horses, Don't They?* (he would go on to be nominated twice more) and who was sought after by the likes of Bette Davis and Ingrid Bergman, was certainly more than good enough for me. I was lucky he offered. The dress he created for me was beautiful: a sumptuous, champagne-colored velvet-and-chiffon gown, with long sleeves and a softly plunging laced neckline, bounded by bronze and gold bugle beading. My fitting went just fine, and Rick and I were off to Mexico.

On the agenda for our jaunt was a different kind of side trip: we were all going to take peyote, because my husband had taken it before and claimed to have seen God. Well, that sounded like a plan. As soon as we arrived in Puerto Vallarta, I went into town and bought a long, flowing diaphanous white gown. If I was going to see God, I wanted to make sure I was appropriately dressed.

The house where we were staying was lovely. Rick and I were given the guest room—and waterbed—on the lower level. Every room in the house, it seemed, opened to the outdoors. There were verandas in every direction, some of them looking out onto lush flowers and greenery whereas others opened out onto a view of the Pacific Ocean. Perfect. Serene. God, here we come.

Not so fast.

When I finally got a look at the peyote, I thought it looked like a wooden button. Rick, our host, and I all dropped it together. I have no idea exactly when it began to kick in, but I do remember one thing very clearly: I *hated* it. I wasn't tripping or relaxing; I was wildly speeding, and there appeared to be no stopping anytime soon. Maybe all the diet drugs I'd taken over the years had burnt out my nervous system by this point, but for whatever reason I felt like I was going to jump out of my skin. Not only did I not see God; I was ready to take myself to the emergency room.

Finally the three of us began to come down—me, only a little. "Please, let's go downstairs," I said to Rick. "I can't stand the way I feel."

Rick agreed. I had no idea what time of day or night it was, but we told our host that we were turning in. He didn't argue. I think it was obvious I needed to lie down. As we talked, I stared at the man's nostrils. They were huge, like caverns—he had been shoveling in coke. Just before we made our way downstairs, our friend handed us a comic book and a portable tape recorder.

"Play this," he said.

When Rick and I got to our room, I took a closer look at what he'd given us. It was an S&M comic book. I didn't even know they made those. The two of us got into the waterbed, and I prayed to the God I never saw that I would be able to get some sleep. (Note to self: in the future, avoid waterbeds when tripping on peyote.) As we lay awake, Rick decided to turn on the tape recorder. There was no music, just sounds. Percussion? Maybe. But there was something . . . different.

"Oh," Rick finally said. "Snare drums . . ."

We listened some more.

"Honey, those aren't snare drums," I said.

They weren't. The rat-tat-tat we were hearing was actually the sound of someone beating someone else with a whip. Our host had provided us with a soundtrack to go along with our comic book.

Snare drums . . . it still makes me laugh.

That was one of those moments when I loved Rick, even though we were often at each other's throats.

I did manage to sleep. The next day when we awoke, we said nothing to our friend of what we'd heard the night before. We all piled into an open-topped Jeep and drove through the bush until we arrived at the most pristine, untouched, breathtaking beach. We got out on the beach and just walked.

In the distance we saw a dark shape on the sand. As we got closer, we saw that it was a dead horse, lying there on its side, its clouded eyes staring at nothing. There were no flies, and I wondered if the poor animal had just died. I was fascinated, but I couldn't bear to look too closely.

Moving on, we soon found a good spot for a dip. Tearing off our clothes, we ran into the clear greenish-blue water. That was by far the best part of my short trip. But by then the peyote, the S&M mood music, and the dead horse had gotten to me. I couldn't wait to get back to Los Angeles.

I went to see Don for my final fitting. Whipping out his measuring tape, he quickly discovered that I had lost weight while I was away. I actually couldn't remember if I'd eaten anything the whole time I was in Mexico.

"I'm taking it in," Don said, marking the gown. "If you have any problems the night of the Oscars, a seamstress friend of mine is on the second floor. Go see her."

The night of the Academy Awards I was to get dressed onsite at the Dorothy Chandler Pavilion of the Los Angeles County Music Center, which was only about two years old at the time. I was not only nominated, a thrill in itself, but I was also presenting an award. Even better—making the night near perfect—I was going to get to sing. Sing!

Rick was the one who pushed me to tell the Academy that I sing. I didn't think they'd believe me. But, lo and behold, Quincy Jones was the musical director for the Academy Awards that year, and he knew me.

I had worked with Quincy about a year before on *The Music of Antonio Carlos Jobim: Music from the Adventurers*. My friend

Morgan Ames, by then established in the music business, had helped me land the job. Quincy had done the arrangement for the album, featuring the Ray Brown Orchestra.

Harold Robbins, the author of the best-selling book, *The Adventurers*, had adapted it to film. Harold was working with Quincy on the movie's soundtrack and asked to direct my track personally. What Harold wanted me to do was moan.

Harold's directions from the booth were hilarious, in that he was so serious.

"Okay, Sally, let's try a vaginal orgasm . . . No, no, no! . . . That's more clitoral. We have a clitoral orgasm already. All right, let's go again . . ."

Although I didn't really know there were two kinds of orgasms, I took direction quite well. Harold and Quincy were pleased. On the *Adventurers* soundtrack my credit reads: "Coming and Going (Vocal Inspiration: Sally Kellerman)."

And hey—that hilarious gig led to my singing spot on the Oscars. I was to perform "Thank You Very Much" from *Scrooge,* along with Petula Clark, Burt Lancaster, and Ricardo Montalban. Nothing could have made me happier.

The big day came. As show time approached, I went to get dressed so that I could walk out one door of the Dorothy Chandler Pavilion, drive around the block, and walk in another. I slipped on the gown. I looked down. The "V" was no longer plunging softly. It skirted my breasts. On the outside.

I was totally bare chested.

Rick walked in to find me in a panic.

"Rick, look at my dress!"

"Great!"

Something must have gone wrong. Either Donfeld overcompensated when he took in the dress, or I had gained back some of the weight I'd lost—or a bit of both.

I had only two hours until red-carpet time. Then I remembered: the seamstress! Racing around the building, I finally found her.

She pulled and tugged and stretched what she could of the fabric. Thanks to a needle, some thread, double-sided tape, and sheer dumb luck, she finally got the dress up over my nipples. Barely.

Rick and I made the drive around the block and stopped in front of the Pavilion. Now it was time to make my red-carpet entrance. The media lay in wait, with flashbulbs erupting outside the tinted glass of the limousine. I was a nervous wreck, not because of all the attention—I liked that part—but because of the dress.

"I can't get out of the car!" I said to Rick.

"Well, you have to," he told me.

I sat for a few minutes, paralyzed. One false move, and I knew I would lose what little fabric was clinging for dear life to my boobs. At last, I braved it. I took a deep breath, froze every muscle in my body, and stepped out into the throng. When you're in the middle of such frenzy, all you can see is who's next to you and what's straight in front of you. You recognize some people, but most appear as a blur. Cameras flash, and people call your name. It's disorienting. So it wasn't until later, when I saw an aerial shot of Rick and me standing in a sea of photographers and reporters, that I got an idea of just how insane and exciting the entire scene really was. And how low cut that gown was.

My first wardrobe test of the evening was my stint as a presenter. NFL-great-turned-actor Jim Brown and I were presenting the Oscar for what was then referred to as "Short Subjects." Onstage I moved like I was in a full body cast, terrified I would lift right out of the dress. When I turned to hand over the Oscar, I moved like someone spun me a quarter-turn on a pedestal—but nary a nipple slip.

My musical number, "Thank You Very Much," was a blast. To my huge relief I sang in a backless black halter that made no threat of leaving my body. What a thrill to be onstage, doing what I loved with such amazing performers. I was so happy I forgot for a minute I was nominated. Then someone ran back and said, "Sally, get in your seat. Your category is up." I raced back into the audience, sat down, and waited.

It may sound like a cliché when someone who's up for an Academy Award says, "It's an honor just to be nominated," but it really is an incredible honor. Yes, it's true that the coolest thing is doing the work, being on the set, having a part you can sink your teeth into, and having 5 A.M. burritos and doughnuts at craft services or hanging out in the makeup trailer. But being nominated is amazing because it's your peers' acknowledgment of your work. That's humbling!

It was fun that people I had started out with in the business were nominated that year too. Jack Nicholson and Carole Eastman were nominated for *Five Easy Pieces*—Jack for his lead role and Carole for writing the screenplay. Jeff Corey had launched all three of our careers in his garage fifteen years earlier.

Bob Altman had already won best director at Cannes, and *M*A*S*H* had gotten the Golden Globe for best motion picture (musical or comedy). People today talk about how the Golden Globes are so much more fun than the Oscars—looser and more easygoing. Alcohol is served, so people get relaxed. But believe me: today's Globes seem uptight and formal in comparison to the ceremonies back then. Why? Because back then they weren't televised. Without the unforgiving eye of the camera, people really cut loose. I had also been nominated for a Golden Globe, along with Elliott Gould and Donald Sutherland. For that show I didn't bother having a gown specially made; I just dug into my closet for something I'd probably bought on Sunset.

*M*A*S*H* was nominated for five Academy Awards: best editing, best picture, best director, best adapted screenplay, and best supporting actress—me. Back then you didn't "campaign" for a film or an actor as you do today. The most campaigning you'd ever see was one ad in *Variety* and an appearance on Merv Griffin. Today you can't get away with less than a full military assault. For an Oscar voter—which I am—the blitz can have the opposite of its intended effect. I can start to doubt my love for a film by the time I've had a hundred ads for it shoved down my throat. (But, of course, not if it was *my* film.)

My friend Gig Young from *The Rogues* was presenting the Oscar for my category. That was fitting, as he'd inspired me with the advice, "In comedy, you have to play for something." I sat up straight and listened as the nominees were announced, all too aware that a camera would broadcast my every expression.

Helen Hayes, for *Airport* . . .
Karen Black, for *Five Easy Pieces* . . .
Lee Grant for *The Landlord* . . .
Sally Kellerman, for *M*A*S*H** . . .
Maureen Stapleton for *Airport* . . .

People ask if you prepare your speech ahead of time. I had had an Academy Award speech nailed and ready to go since I was seven years old. Of course, my speech has changed over the years. But was I ready? Yes.

I would have loved to have accepted an award from my friend Gig. But from the stage I heard: *And the Oscar goes to* . . . *Helen Hayes.*

Helen Hayes. The First Lady of American Theater. Never mind all the fine work she'd done over the years—she won best supporting actress for *Airport.*

Bob was sitting behind me. I could feel him lean forward.

"They're voting for a different war this year," he said.

That took away the sting—not that I ever expected to win. Hoped, sure, but never expected. And Helen Hayes had long since earned any award she was nominated for.

Still, I appreciated Bob's words, which proved true. *Patton* took home best picture, best director, best actor. A different war.

The only Oscar *M*A*S*H* took home that night went to screenwriter Ring Lardner Jr., who had also won best adapted screenplay at the Golden Globes and an award from the Writers Guild of America—all for the screenplay that Bob had supposedly ruined.

No matter who won, it was fun to be with Bob and his wife, Kathryn. Rick and I spent the evening with them at the Gover-.

nor's Ball, which, at the time, was the only party in town. Today you can't even keep track of all the "official" Oscar parties. I frankly think that's rather divisive, turning one of the few nights our industry celebrates together into high school. Where are the cool kids? Where's the best party?

One year I watched the awards at the Bistro on Cannon Drive in Beverly Hills. That was the domain of Oscar party legend Swifty Lazar; he threw a party there after the Oscars for almost thirty years. Then there are the countless "viewing" parties, one of which is the Night of 100 Stars. I've attended that a couple times just to see my friend Norby Walters, the event's producer. But my favorite place to watch the Oscars is at home in my pajamas.

Unless, of course, I'm nominated.

The day after the Oscars, reporters from all over the world were commenting on my dress, my accidentally risqué, daring, fabulous dress, with the neckline virtually at my navel. My look was a huge hit, and the dress got so famous that, years later, it was auctioned off at Christie's for charity. Today that dress would hardly warrant a whimper, as everybody's dress is practically falling off. I guess I was just ahead of my time. And it's funny to think that the mistake that caused all the uproar and attention—making me the precursor of J Lo in Versace—resulted from my peyote-enhanced Mexican getaway.

• • •

SHORTLY AFTER THE OSCARS I HAD AN ENTIRELY DIFFERENT kind of premiere: the film Larry Hauben and I shot finally hit a few theaters. I went to see it, not sure what to expect. Although I was relieved to see that Larry had told the truth about the sex scene we filmed—only our legs were visible—I was shocked to see some other moments that Larry had included, moments when I hadn't known that the camera was rolling.

There were scenes of us talking to friends on the phone and other scenes of Larry just goofing off. But what really got me was the footage of Larry breaking up with me over the phone. He had captured the entire conversation, including my end. I sounded so needy that it was utterly humiliating.

It was obvious even to the reviewer from the *Los Angeles Times* that I hadn't known Larry was recording us. Discussing the scene that took place in bed, the reviewer wrote, "While one does not mean to be insulting, we nonetheless can only hope that Miss Kellerman knew she was being photographed."

The rest of the review was not exactly glowing, either, saying it was "impossible to tell where reality leaves off and fiction begins and, more importantly, whether the film is saying such a distinction is even possible . . . In intermingling two favorite forms of underground filmmakers, the potpourri of fragmented, super-imposed images and the cinema-verite interview, *Venus* demonstrates the limitations of both." It went on:

> [Venus] has the look of a scrapbook record of a broken romance, and is finally too personal to mean much to anyone but Hauben and his friends. . . . In short, we never really learn much about Hauben or his motives. As for Sally Kellerman, sexy, beautiful, talented and funny—a modern-day Venus, to be sure—we do know that she thought enough of Lawrence Hauben to trust him completely.

Evidently I did. Maybe I thought enough of Larry but didn't think enough of myself. I know that my parents saw that review, but my father never said a word. Thank God they never saw the film. Note to self: there is a difference between feeling desperate for work and taking work out of desperation.

• • •

THE FOLLOWING YEAR I WOULD RETURN TO THE OSCARS AS A presenter. Alongside Richard Harris, I gave the award for the best supporting actor to Ben Johnson for his work in *The Last Picture Show*. But that time, instead of getting Donfeld to make a gown for me, I just went down to my old favorite boutique, Holly

LEFT: My dad, Jack Kellerman, looking very smart in his fedora.

BELOW: Me at 18, ready to take on the world!

RIGHT: Posing with a "co-star" on the set of *The Outer Limits.*

BELOW: "Hitting the deck" on the set of *M*A*S*H. (Photo by Twentieth Century Fox/ Getty Images)*

LEFT: Enjoying time with my favorite scoundrel, Robert Altman, and actress Nina van Pallandt.

BELOW: Enjoying an Oscar after-party with my friends Jack Nicholson and Michelle Phillips. *(Photo by Max Miller/ Fotos International/Getty Images)*

In Scotland with the other love of my life, my long-time manager Stuart Cohen.

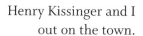

Henry Kissinger and I out on the town.

My "other mother," Jennifer Jones Simon, and I catching up with Cary Grant.

LEFT: Feeling
exhilarated and at
home doing what
I love: performing.

BELOW: I fulfilled a
lifelong dream when
I went out on tour
with my band in 1974.

ABOVE: My mom, Edith, and I loved visiting our budding equestrian Claire at camp.

RIGHT: Relaxing with the man who "named" my daughter: the great Groucho Marx.

ABOVE: Jonathan and I on our wedding day. It was nice to get married in front of friends instead of extras!

BELOW: Hitting the trail with Tony Curtis.

ABOVE: My two mid-life angels: Jack and Hanna.

BELOW: Jonathan and me with Claire, Jack, and Hanna. Bliss.

Harp's. I attended the awards with Jack, who at the time was dating Michelle Phillips of the Mamas and Papas. I have no idea where we went before or after, but from the pictures I've seen, it looks like we had an awful lot of fun.

It's telling that I didn't attend that Oscar show with Rick. Our marriage, never peaceful, had hit the rocks. I don't blame Rick for that—it takes two to tango. We fought over ridiculous things. But our conflicts didn't stop me from turning down work that I probably should have taken and from listening to Rick when I should have known better.

Little things got blown up into big ones, as they often do in relationships. There were warning signs, all of which I ignored. Some of them had to do with work, others with our personal life, family, and friends.

My family life had been painful. My father had died. His feeling of being run down never did go away. It turned out that he had cancer, which took him fairly quickly. The weaker he got, the more he worried that my mother would just up and leave him. He couldn't imagine anyone staying with him as his condition worsened. Vitality, strength, never wavering in every way—Dad valued these attributes and wanted to instill them in his daughters. My mother was different—caring, comfort, spoiling, understanding, hot cocoa with cinnamon toast and sugar. That was why she would never have left my father, ever, during his illness.

Everything we need is within us, Sally, she always said to me.

I knew that I had left so much unspoken and unresolved with my father. "I can't die," my dad had said during one of my last hospital visits with him. "I have to see you kids grow up." After his death I found those two beautiful letters, full of love and support, reminding me that I had talent. At the same time I couldn't forget his anger and disapproval and how stern and critical he could be of everything from my language to my wardrobe. Every transgression of mine—or my mother's—was worthy of the same level of anger. Neither of us had reached a point in our lives when we could talk about any of that.

Mom insisted that she stayed in the relationship because she loved my dad—a lot. As for me, I could never find a way to reconcile his good side with his bad side, his encouragement with his reprimands. But I had noticed some changes. "I've even learned to like Gloria," he had written me the year before his death, referring to Diana's partner. "I must be becoming modern."

My dad was growing, just like the rest of us. He had worked very hard to accept Diana's coming out and also to see the good in Rick.

. . .

I MYSELF WAS HAVING TROUBLE SEEING THE GOOD IN RICK. Things flared up in 1971 while I was in New York City, rehearsing for the film *Last of the Red Hot Lovers* with Alan Arkin. I was living at the Plaza Hotel, where we also rehearsed. I was loving the work. I had a fantastic part playing one of the women that a frustrated—and married—Alan Arkin gets involved with. Great parts are all about the writing, whether it's a film or a voice-over gig, and this was a work by Neil Simon. You don't get better writing than that. *Last of the Red Hot Lovers* remains one of my proudest accomplishments.

Unfortunately for me, every time Alan Arkin would do something during rehearsal, Neil Simon would start to laugh. But whenever I did anything, all I heard were crickets. At first it was just a little annoying, but then it really started to get distracting and was making me paranoid. Instead of becoming my character, I felt like I was trying to please Neil. So I had the director, Gene Saks, ask Neil if he would mind not sitting in on our rehearsals. Neil never said anything to me about it, but he did stop showing up when I was filming.

As our director, Gene was tenacious about getting what he wanted from his actors and crew. He always wanted me to play harder and tougher, displaying no vulnerability whatsoever. Gene was brilliant—and he was right. But when the film came out, reviewers tuned in to—you guessed it—my vulnerability. The harder I played it, the more you could see how vulnerable the character was. My character and I were similar in a lot of ways. The more I tried to show everyone how confident and together I was, the clearer it was to those close to me that I wasn't. Not by a long shot.

What made the time in New York even more special was that my mother came to stay with me. After my father's death she needed to get away, and she'd never been to New York. I was busy all day, but in her typical self-starter style, my mom got all the brochures and maps, familiarized herself with public transportation, and went out into the city every day, taking tours and visiting museums. At night, when she returned from her adventures and I was done with rehearsal, we would sit in our beautiful two-bedroom suite at the Plaza, eating clams on the half shell and sipping glasses of white wine. I loved having the chance to spoil her as she had spoiled me all my life.

Edith Kellerman was such an example of how to live and love. She always took care of herself, plump or thin, tired or raring to go, hassled by my dad or standing tall on the pedestal he had for her in his mind. I'd always thought of my parents as Victorian and repressed, the source of all my neuroses. But during our time in New York my mom confided in me that she and my father were having sex until they fell off the bed because the cancer had made him too weak. So what the hell did I know?

Having Mom around was both a comfort and a reality check. Here I was with a woman who never looked to a man to make her happy, who did not stop living her life because he was gone. And here I was in a marriage with an expiration date that I felt was fast approaching, wondering how—and if—I could make it on my own.

• • •

WHILE I WAS IN NEW YORK GRACE MIRABELLA, EDITOR-IN-chief of *Vogue*, contacted me. Grace offered me a ten-page spread in her magazine, one that would include modeling some furs for my "cousin" David Bennett, who now had his own shop. It would have been wonderful exposure for me, great publicity for David, and a lot of fun. I loved being around Grace who, despite her prestigious job, was a warm, real, down-to-earth girl. She was one of fashion's triumvirate of divas, succeeding Diana Vreeland at the magazine and preceding Anna Wintour. I sometimes thought that, if the acting went south, maybe I could work for her. Whenever I was in the *Vogue* office, there was someone buzzing around with belts for shoots, belts for advertisements. Someone always seemed to be looking for the right belt. *Maybe I could be the belt person,* I thought.

I called Rick to let him know that I wanted to extend my stay a few days in New York so I could do the *Vogue* shoot. He was furious.

"What about me?" he said. "You've been out there nineteen days. You need to come back."

I was terrified of losing Rick. I didn't want to upset him. But when I told my agent, the legendary—and notoriously somewhat prickly—Sue Mengers, that I was going to pass on Grace's offer, she was beside herself. She was as furious with me about passing up the *Vogue* shoot as Rick was about me taking it. She knew very well that, after your Oscar exposure, a window of opportunity opens wide for you, but it doesn't remain open long. What did I think, that *Vogue* was going to ring up and offer me another ten pages the following week or month . . . or ever, for that matter? They never have again, or at least not so far.

It was a horrendous choice, but ignoring everyone's better judgment—including my own—I finally told Grace no. I'm sure I lost her respect and cost David a great opportunity to expand his business. But at that point I just couldn't stand up to Rick.

Before leaving New York I did some interviews about *Last of the Red Hot Lovers,* a few other films I had in the works, and my budding music career. My first album would be out soon, and I was so excited. But was I insightful? Not very. I saw a quote of mine recently that was published in December 1971, a year after Rick and I got married:

"I am finally all put together," I told a reporter. "I couldn't be happier."

Yep. I was an Academy Award nominated actress, all right. Happy? If they bought that, they would buy anything I was selling.

The problem was, I bought it too.

• • •

IT'S HARD TO POINT TO JUST ONE THING THAT FINALLY UNDOES a marriage. Although I was annoyed at Rick for helping sabotage my career—intentionally or not, but certainly with my acquiescence—probably the straw that finally broke my back was the issue of Claire, my sister Diana's seven-year-old daughter. I wanted to play a bigger part in Claire's life.

Claire was still living with Ian in Santa Monica. Diana was far away now. She and Gloria had decided to leave not only Los Angeles but the United States. They were living in the south of France, where Diana had lived before and where she and Gloria felt more comfortable. Furthermore, it would be some time before Claire reached eighteen, the age when, according to Ian and Diana's agreement, she would be able to see her mother.

I knew that Ian was struggling—physically, emotionally—to take care of Claire. What had initially appeared to be some sort of depression—Ian was sleeping all the time, not working—was becoming much worse. What we did not know then was that he had Parkinson's. Very little was understood about that disease at the time. I would run over to Ian's place whenever I could to cook or take Claire out, but now that Rick and I were settled in a lovely rented house with a yard in the Hollywood Hills, I found myself longing to be with her more permanently. So I had Claire over often, but I must confess that those visits sometimes took a tragicomic turn.

I still hadn't shaken the horror of the Manson murders. Every time I heard a car making its way down our sleepy little street in the Hills when Claire and I were outside, I'd fly into a panic.

"DOWN CLAIRE!!!" I'd shout. For some reason I felt compelled to make sure that the approaching driver could not see that a child was playing behind our white picket fence. It didn't matter to me what kind of neighborhood we lived in or how much money we had; there was still that residual fear that maybe there were some people from the Manson gang that they hadn't yet found.

Then, not long after we began renting our house, a group of men moved next door. *What's going on over there?* I wondered. *What kind of group living situation is this?* There weren't any women around, and none of the men seemed to have jobs. They brought in very little furniture. The men just stayed indoors all day, and occasionally I heard loud music. I was convinced they were some sort of cult, part of the Manson gang. Whenever I was in the yard and I saw one of the men leave the house—to go to his car or take a walk—I'd grab Claire and shuttle her inside as fast as I could.

"Down, Claire! Get in the house, Claire!"

Poor girl. She was only seven or eight years old. I know I must have scared her to death. But I just wanted to keep her safe. Luckily, she had great spirit.

One day I was gardening with Claire. The weather was lovely, and I was enjoying the sun and the breeze and the flowers in our small yard. Suddenly I looked up. It was one of them! I whipped around and scanned the yard. Oh my God! Where was Claire?! I finally spotted her. I ran over, but the Dangerous Man was already on the move. He wasn't going to his car. Oh God, Oh God, he was walking toward my house, toward us. *Oh no, oh no . . .* I was thinking. I tried, but I couldn't grab Claire and make it back in the house in time.

"Excuse me . . ." the man said.

I turned around. He was still walking toward us.

"Excuse me . . ."

I froze.

"I just wanted to say hi," he called out to me. "We're going to be living next door for a while. We're in a band called Bread."

Ah yes. The murderous cult/soft-rock band that sang love songs like the number-one hit, "Make It with You."

I introduced myself and blurted out my entire insane story. Thank God the man laughed. I'm surprised he didn't start running into his house to hide from me.

Okay, so maybe my maternal instincts were a little off at times. But I loved Claire. I didn't know how I could live without her.

More and more I hated her situation with her ailing father. She would call sometimes and say something like, "Aunt Sally, I have gum in my hair . . ."

"Sorry, Rick, I have to go see Claire," I'd say. I'd hop in the car, drive over to the apartment she shared with Ian in Santa Monica, and by time I got there, she would have already lopped off a huge chunk of her lovely chestnut hair with a pair of scissors.

After the gum incident, while I was taking a walk in the neighborhood with Rick, I told him that I wanted to spend more than few days here and there with Claire.

"She needs me," I said, biting my nails and fearing his reaction.

"If you want her, fight me for her," Rick said.

"Okay, then I want her here on weekends."

I started having Claire spend weekends with us, but the battle wasn't over. Everything had to be a fight in our house. One fight I almost lost related to having Claire come for Christmas, which was two months off. Rick agreed to let Claire come, but her father, Ian, who was suffering from Parkinson's, was not welcome. I would never have Claire spend Christmas apart from her father.

We then learned that we could no longer stay in the house. The lease was up, and the landlord didn't want to renew. I hated the thought of losing that house. It was so lovely, so quiet, and having a yard meant everything to me. I was still a country girl from the orange groves of the Valley. I needed my grass. I needed my trees.

We had friends in the neighborhood who offered to put us up until we found a place that really suited us. But Rick wouldn't have it; he was intent on finding a house that was big enough not only for us but also for his four daughters from his first marriage. They still lived back east in the Bronx. The house he found was enormous. I hated it—all house, no yard. No land whatsoever. But again, I didn't stand up to him the way I should have. I didn't say no.

Instead, I took it out on him. In my mind we lived precisely four days in that house before we split up. Maybe it was longer. Maybe not. We were already going in such different directions. I know that, even though Rick was the one who physically walked out of that house, I was making it as unpleasant as possible for him to stay—even if he had still wanted to.

Looking back, when Rick and I met, he was recovering from a marriage that had produced four children. I was on the rebound from a relationship that only existed in my mind. I don't think either of us loved ourselves enough to have a relationship. When I was younger, I blamed Rick for everything. Today, I see clearly my part in it.

My marriage was over. It was for the best. And Claire and Ian came to Christmas and all was right in the world.

CHAPTER 9

Flirting with Politics

My first date after splitting from Rick? Henry Kissinger.

It was all Jennifer Jones's doing.

At that point I was all over the map, so out of touch with myself. I was in the midst of my divorce, wondering why I had ever married Rick and why we'd bought this huge Spanish-style house with six bedrooms, six baths, and a living room the size of Dodger Stadium when we had no furniture to fill it. The house had been on the market for two years before we moved in. Now I was trying to turn around and sell it again. I was determined.

I did what I could to make it look attractive to anyone who might stop by. I hung scarves from the windows. I would come home from work and get the fireplace going, turn up the music, and sip a split of champagne. I did my best to make it feel homey, but I had never wanted to live there in the first place.

I was there alone, except for weekends, when I had Claire. Claire loved the house. With no furniture to get in the way, she could do all the cartwheels, headstands, and backbends she could dream of. But I couldn't wait to get that white elephant of a house, with no yard and all those empty rooms full of unhappy memories, off my hands.

Meanwhile, I was keeping busy. I was working on the film *Lost Horizon* and had just finished shooting two other movies, *Reflection of Fear* with Robert Shaw and *Slither* with James Caan. Both men were rascals, each in his own distinct way. I loved them both dearly.

William Fraker, who had been the camera operator on *Outer Limits* and another love of mine, was the director on *Reflection*. On the first day of shooting I had to take a long walk across the lawn. It was my first shot.

The assistant director called, "Roll it!"

"Relax, Sally! It all depends on you!" Robert Shaw yelled out in the middle of the scene. "Everything is pointing right at you!"

Thanks, Robert. I thought. *Now I don't feel self-conscious at all.*

Another day Robert came into the makeup trailer and said, "God! You look gorgeous!" In his enthusiasm he walked over, picked me up, threw me over his shoulder, and tromped me off to the set, with my hair blowing in the wind. I'd just spent forty-five minutes fixing my hair because I'm neurotic. But still, his caveman act was utterly endearing,

I'd have to say Robert Shaw was an alcoholic. He said, "I only drink when I'm acting. It's so boring." But he was also very funny and sweet. One night on the set he kept telling me, "You should have a glass of wine, Sally, to help you relax." I kept saying no, and he kept insisting, "Don't be silly." So I had a glass of red wine. I guess I felt guilty. I ended up getting as drunk as he was, and Bill could have killed us. I have since only had a glass of wine on set one other time, with Harry Dean Stanton.

Slither was James Caan's first film after *The Godfather*. I almost didn't get the part. "You don't have to hire me," I had said to the director, Howard Zieff. "How about we take ten minutes and have a meeting, just talk about things?"

I had initially been offered the film by MGM, turned it down, and soon after had a change of heart. Then one weekend I'd found myself on a picnic with friends. Howard Zieff was with us. I was wearing big, checkered pants and four-inch Candie's high heels, looking like the Jolly Green Giant. Howard and I got to talking, and he told me about his brother, a land developer, who built much of the tract housing in the San Fernando Valley. I was not a fan of tract housing in my Valley and let him know. The next day I got a call from my agent.

"Sally, Howard is not sure if you're right for the part . . ."

Can't say I didn't see that one coming. So I decided maybe I should call.

"Howard," I said, "don't be like your brother and ruin the Valley. How about we have a meeting first?"

He agreed. I wore tight jeans, a T-shirt, and flats. As we talked, I learned that James Caan was worried I was too tall to star with him. So I said, "Well, you want somebody good or somebody short?"

I finally went in to do the reading. When it was over, everyone in the room, including Jimmy, stood up as I was leaving. I looked around and said, "I don't think Jimmy's too short."

I got the job. And in every production office, at all of our locations, my picture hung next to Jimmy's on the wall—six inches higher.

Slither was a road movie, and my character, Kitty Kopetzky, was on the run with Jimmy. He had great charm and was so much fun; I loved him from the first day. Jimmy taught me to box; he practiced lassoing on me. He was irreverent and adorable.

For a while we were shooting near some cliffs that overlooked the Pacific Ocean. The location was invigorating. Jimmy was all brawn and machismo. I was free, unattached, as Rick and I were split up by that point. Maybe a little affair would be just the ticket, I thought.

One night when we were on location in northern California, we were all wandering around a small town. There was some sort of festival going on, and I arrived just in time to see a young woman being crowned "Little Miss Rodeo" or something. I went back to my room at the motel and was lying on my bed, thinking about Jimmy. At a certain moment I happened to look up.

Strolling past my window, on the way to his room next door, was Jimmy—arm in arm with Little Miss Rodeo.

Well, I thought. *I guess that won't be happening.*

There would be other nights, other girls, other locations, other towns—and Jimmy made the most of them. One night I got locked out of my hotel room. Jimmy's room was next to mine, as always, so I went next door for help. It was a huge property, and it was late, and the office seemed too far away. Jimmy gave me a choice: he would be happy to help me break into my room, or I was welcome to stay in his. Believe me, I was torn, but having seen the steady parade of women past my window; I just couldn't do it. Sweetheart that he was, he did help me get into my room.

Jimmy was one of only two men—the other was Bob Duvall in *M*A*S*H*—who I ever slept with on film. Jimmy had the decency to take the gum out of his mouth before we kissed. At the end of the shoot he presented me with a photo—of my ass. You see, before all of my takes, I used to bend over and flip my hair in front of me to fluff it up. Jimmy was a devil. He must have gotten the set photographer to snap the photo when I wasn't looking. As a parting gift, he wrote notes all over the picture like, "I can't believe I ate the whole thing," and other lovely remarks. One of the reasons I love him.

I still really hadn't had a date since Rick and I broke up. Jimmy wasn't going to break my dating ice, so it had to be someone else. That's when Jennifer Jones stepped in.

After David Selznick's death, Jennifer had married philanthropist and art collector Norton Simon. She was having one of her fabulous dinner parties and phoned me in my big empty house to say, "Sally, Henry Kissinger would like you come as his date to my party."

"Ewww, Jennifer!" I said. "I'd be embarrassed to be seen with him! Besides, I'm working for McGovern." It was election time, 1972, and George McGovern was running against Richard Nixon, who had made Kissinger his national security adviser.

I was not a Nixon fan or a supporter of the war in Vietnam.

Jennifer laughed and said, "Well, would you at least sit next to him?"

I loved Jennifer so much; I couldn't tell her no.

"All right," I said, "if I have to."

I told my mom, who at that time was a good Republican. She was over the moon and mailed me a newspaper article about Kissinger and Nixon's historic trip to China.

When Jennifer married Norton, she bought a modern beach house from director John Frankenheimer. Norton was a passionate art collector; in fact, his collection is now housed in the museum named for him in Pasadena, California. Jennifer and Norton had hired Frank Gehry, the famed architect behind the Guggenheim Museum in Bilbao, Spain, the Walt Disney Concert Hall in Downtown Los Angeles, and countless other stunning structures, to construct a second house next door. A beautiful garden, with mirrors hidden in the landscaping to reflect the greenery, connected the two houses.

The night of the party, as I entered Jennifer's house, the first thing I saw was Vincent Van Gogh's *Mulberry Tree* hanging in the foyer. The second thing I saw was Henry Kissinger, sitting across the room in a low chair. I walked over. After being introduced, I asked him, "So, how was China?"

"Why?" he asked. "Did your mother send you an article?"

"Yes," I said. "How did you know?"

Damn, that made me like him right away.

We adjourned to our table, sitting with Rita Hayworth, Dorothy McGuire, Joseph Cotten and his wife, and Paul Ziffren, a successful Hollywood lawyer, with his wife, Mickey. The food was great, and somehow the conversation got around to *M*A*S*H* and why Henry hadn't seen it. He said that Nixon wouldn't allow it in the White House. Henry had a wonderful sense of humor and an easygoing manner.

It was a very enjoyable evening. At the end of the dinner we all stood up from the table, then Henry asked—in front of everyone there—if I'd like to accompany him to a dinner honoring the

Soviet ambassador coming on his first trip to the States, another historic moment in Cold War relations. My politics reared up again. A public dinner with Henry Kissinger, Nixon's key adviser? I was a lifelong Democrat, picketing the Vietnam War alongside Jane Fonda. But all eyes were on me. I couldn't say no.

The week before the event Henry called to make sure I was still going. I finally came clean. "Henry, I feel ambivalent about going with you because you guys are murderers, and I'm working for McGovern."

He responded, in his low distinctive voice, "Sally, I'm sure you don't mean 'murderers.'"

"Well, maybe not 'murderers,'" I mumbled.

On the night of the dinner Henry picked me up at the white elephant. There was nowhere for him to sit, but he seemed to be a good sport. I got in the car and began grilling him about why we were in Vietnam and why the Nixon administration was keeping us there. Henry started to reply, "The president—" when I interrupted him, saying, "I don't care about the president. What are you doing there?"

He seemed to take it all in stride. I guess that's what being a diplomat is all about.

We arrived at the Bistro, an elegant Beverly Hills restaurant that the Who's Who of Hollywood used to patronize. The maître d' escorted us upstairs to a private room. He opened the door, and instead of seeing fifty people, which is what I was hoping for—easier to get lost in the hubbub—there were only about fifteen people, among them Cary Grant, John Wayne, and the Soviet ambassador and his wife. Just my usual crowd.

While mingling before dinner, I heard John Wayne talking about Vietnam.

"We should have gone in there and wiped them off the face of the Earth," he said. In spite of our significant differences on that issue, I liked John and always found him warm and respectful.

During dinner Henry asked me to stand up and welcome the Soviet ambassador. It was the last thing I wanted to do, and I don't remember one word of what I said. After a nice meal and many toasts, Henry and his two bodyguards—who barely fit in the car—drove me home. We were an odd pair, especially politically, but I had fun.

. . .

IT WASN'T AS THOUGH I WAS SPENDING HOURS ON END WORK-ing the phones for George McGovern, but I did my best to spread the word. I did my share for different causes, but the bottom line was that I was a follower. McGovern was about getting out of Vietnam, cutting back on defense, and getting the Equal Rights Amendment ratified. I was on board with all that. I wanted Mc-Govern to be president instead of Nixon. End of story.

I worked as an usher at a huge benefit concert held in his honor called, "Four for McGovern." Warren Beatty was the driving force behind the event, which was held at the Los Angeles Forum. My friend Lou Adler was producing. No matter what the media says today about the growing ties between Hollywood and Washing-ton, DC, that relationship is hardly new. Warren even convinced Barbra Streisand to perform, along with Carole King and James Taylor, all backed by Quincy Jones and his orchestra. It wasn't just a single performer stepping out to support a candidate, Warren pointed out to the press, remembering Frank Sinatra's concerts for Hubert Humphrey in 1968. Rather, it was the group effort and solidarity that he felt made an event like this different and more influential, giving it the power to unite a larger section of the population.

Someone called and asked me to usher for the benefit, and I said, "Sure." Because I was going to be ushering, I pulled together what I thought would be appropriate usher attire: I showed up that night wearing a straight black skirt, a plain white blouse, and carrying a flashlight.

When I arrived at the Forum, it was positively swarming with media. I was shuffled into a room full of television cameras and reporters. I looked up: Standing across the room was Warren

Beatty, never looking more handsome, and Julie Christie, never looking more beautiful. Both of them were dressed to the nines. Even Jack Nicholson was wearing a three-piece suit. And there I was, in a dowdy black wool skirt, wearing hardly any makeup.

Just my luck, one of the cameras turned on me, and a reporter thrust his mic into my face.

"Why is it, Miss Kellerman, that all of you people are rushing out to vote for someone with so little charisma?" he asked.

"This is not about charisma," I huffed and puffed in response. "This is about content!"

Thank God they didn't ask me anything about McGovern's platform. I would have been in pretty deep water. Luckily, I got to play Miss Indignant.

Ushering along with me were Jack Nicholson, Julie Christie, Peggy Lipton, Michelle Phillips, James Earl Jones, Jacqueline Bisset, Mike Nichols, Shirley MacLaine, Goldie Hawn, Gene Hackman, Elliott Gould, Marlo Thomas, Burt Lancaster, Jon Voight, Raquel Welch, Michael Sarrazin, Britt Eklund, and more. (But I was the only one in proper attire.) Gregory Peck and Joni Mitchell were in the audience. Some tickets were $4 and $10, but Golden Circle tickets were going for $100. And those were 1972 dollars. Warren was right about the crowd—more than eighteen thousand people showed up.

Streisand killed. The screaming crowd, wearing "I rocked with McGovern" buttons, throbbed and got revved up to vote by Barbra, Quincy, Carole, and Sweet Baby James. There was a choir, and Quincy strolled onto stage in a long velvet robe. Too far out.

Barbra's performance led right into McGovern's appearance on stage. Finally. The man. The moment. The crowd surged forward. We all waited. He stepped forward and said, "Let . . . the sun . . . shine . . . in . . ."

My God, I thought as I watched McGovern address the crowd, *why are we voting for someone with so little charisma?*

McGovern made $320,000 that night. The campaign may have failed, but Barbra's resulting album, *Live Concert at the Forum*, was fantastic. I met McGovern years later, when he was signing his book, and found him one on one to be warm, charming, and charismatic after all.

The war in Vietnam mobilized a lot of people, actors and civilians alike. Like a lot of my friends, I was very much against the Vietnam War but not against the men and women who fought in it. In my mind we were *for* the troops: We wanted them to come home from the war alive. I know that was Jane Fonda's motivation too.

I've always greatly admired Jane's curiosity and her ability to throw herself into her interests, learning everything there is to know about her passions. She has done so much good for so many people. I also took part in a poetry reading, along with Jane, Donald Sutherland, Jon Voight, and others, in support of Daniel Ellsberg, a former military analyst who released what became known as the Pentagon Papers. At a rehearsal one afternoon, we were standing on stage at the Coliseum when Henry Fonda strolled up with Ellsberg himself. After the handshakes were done and Henry and Daniel were on their way out, Ellsberg turned back and called out, "Sally, I know your sister!"

Ellsberg had been working at the RAND Corporation when he made his now-infamous copies of documents related to US policy in Vietnam. My sister had worked at the RAND Corporation as a secretary during his time there. I dined out on that all afternoon. What a strange small world: Me, Diana, Ellsberg, Kissinger. . . .

Not long after that rally, a postcard arrived in the mail from Russia. It had a picture of Red Square and the Lenin Mausoleum. It read:

From Russia with love, Henry (Kissinger). Hope I see you soon.

Thank God he put "Kissinger" in parentheses. I was always getting postcards from the Soviet Union in those days.

• • •

Several months later Mickey and Paul Ziffren hosted a dinner for Henry, and he invited me to come as his date. Paul Ziffren was an entertainment lawyer for people like Charlton Heston and Danny Thomas. Paul and his wife, Mickey, often hosted get-togethers that brought candidates together with people from the entertainment and corporate worlds. Paul was very tight with Henry. By this time, fall of 1972, I had finally sold the big house and moved into a tiny little rental in Malibu, right down the beach from the Ziffrens'. I'd unloaded the gargantuan house in less than a year.

My entire new home could have fit in the living room of the house I'd just sold.

I had decided to save money for the first time in my life. So I borrowed a friend's camper and packed up what was left for the trip across town, thinking I would move everything with the help of some friends. When it was time to unload, Jerry Brown—the future governor of California—was the only one who showed up to help. You can see why I have to campaign for Jerry for the rest of my life, no matter what office he's seeking. I even did a promotional video for him when he ran for president, which may be why he wasn't elected. My "cousin" David Bennett had a fantasy I'd marry Jerry and that one day I would be standing in the White House Rose Garden in my notorious pink nightgown. David, however, would be standing on the balcony chatting with President Jerry. David's fantasy, not mine.

So I had gone from a huge house with no furniture to a tee-ny-tiny house crammed to the rafters. It was adorable, though: a little Spanish-style house right on the beach. Wendy Stark—now Wendy Stark Morrissey—the Los Angeles editor of *Vanity Fair* and daughter of the movie producer Ray Stark, lived next door. Robert Redford shot a scene in that house for *The Way We Were.* I could never look at Wendy's house without thinking of Robert and my idol, Barbra, in that film, so achingly in love.

I wasn't ready when Henry arrived to pick me up for the party.

I stuck my wet head out of the shower and yelled, "I'll be out in a minute!"

I emerged one hour later.

In the meantime Henry had little to do. No crackers or cheese or drinks. All he could do was sit and wait while my trusty Cocker spaniel, Holly, barked incessantly at his Secret Service men outside.

Henry assumed we'd drive to the Ziffrens, which I thought was ridiculous.

"Come on, Henry," I told him. "It's only a few houses down the beach. Let's walk. We can carry our shoes."

"Sally," Henry chuckled, shaking his head. "You're trying to ruin me."

On the walk over he turned to me and said, joking, "I know you're working for McGovern, but when we win, we'll still give you a passport."

It was a nice party, a nice night. At the end of it Henry gave me a kiss on the cheek and off he went.

About a month later I got the following letter, dated October 29, 1972:

> Dear Sally:
>   Sorry to be so remiss in writing, but I've been busy stopping a war.
>   What have you been up to lately?
>   Best,
>   Henry

Henry Kissinger never intimidated me. I loved his humor, which made mine better.

One day Henry called from the White House and as we were talking on the phone, he said, "Sally, the red light is on—it's the president."

"So?" I'd reply. "Who's more important?"

"Sally, you're trying to ruin me," he said with a laugh.

Directors made me nervous; other industry people could make me feel competitive, insecure, or desperate for validation. But someone like Henry Kissinger, easily one of the world's most powerful men? I wasn't worried about what he thought of me. He couldn't get me a role. He couldn't do anything for me except maybe get me a passport.

And just a few weeks after his letter arrived, Richard Nixon won reelection as president of the United States by a landslide. I sent a telegram to Henry at the White House:

All right, I give up. You win. Will you still get me a passport?

The following year, when Watergate broke, I was at home lying in bed with actor, singer, and songwriter Clifton Davis, with whom I was having a nice romance at the time. He was the only man I was ever with who wasn't angry. Claire adored him.

The phone rang. It was Henry. He had called, in essence, to let me know that he had not been involved in the scandal. It was the last time we ever spoke. I liked Henry a lot, but geography and travel and schedules and international crises can be real obstacles. We drifted apart.

My time in Malibu was short, but it capped off a hectic couple of years. I was ready for a change, personally and professionally. And this time I wouldn't need Rick or anyone else to help sabotage my career—I was going to do it fine all by myself.

CHAPTER 10

Advice Given and Ignored

"Where the hell are any answers . . . Inside me, I guess."
—Sally Hughes, my character in *Lost Horizon*

"Everything we need is within us . . ."
—Edith Kellerman, my mother

I HAVE BEEN GETTING THIS MESSAGE IN VARIOUS FORMS FOR years—from my mother, my characters, and my psychotherapists. Sometimes it sinks in; other times I misinterpret it as justification for ignoring the well-meaning and better-informed advice of others. It's all in the interpretation. The devil is in the details.

Hollywood may have changed a lot since I played my first big role in *Reform School Girls* in 1957, but one thing has remained the same: it has a very short memory. You blow some good will, and Hollywood moves on to the next flavor of the month. And why shouldn't it? Every time I land a part, I know there are thousands of other women lined up around the block who could do just as good a job as I would if they were only given the chance.

So why blow the chances you're given? Well, if you're me, you do because you're convinced that you should follow your bliss. This was the 1970s, man—come on.

My bliss was singing. As much as I loved acting, I never wanted one career instead of the other.

Unfortunately, I wasn't the sharpest tool in the shed. I had no idea how to build a career as an actor or as a singer. I didn't understand that when opportunities come to you, like being in a hit film and being nominated for an Oscar, you have to go with them. Instead, my inner monologue was, *Good. I'm all set as an actress. Now I've got to work on my music.*

. . .

I DID SOME SINGING IN THE FILM *Lost Horizon*. AT THAT TIME Burt Bacharach and Hal David were on top of the world. Burt is so talented, so brilliant and handsome; and Hal was a genius lyricist. I knew Burt slightly before the movie, and though it was my first time meeting Hal, he would grow to be one of my dearest friends. The only reason I did *Lost Horizon* was because I wanted to sing with Burt and Hal.

I didn't have much of a character in *Lost Horizon*; it was one of those films with twenty-five stars, each of whom got seven lines a piece. I wasn't crazy about the script. There was a scene in which I committed suicide, but for the life of me—pun intended—I had no idea why my character would do such a thing. But, hey, that's why I'm an actress—to figure things out. I was willing to look past a lot of my concerns because of the people involved. Along with Burt and Hal, my friend Morgan was working on the music, and the cast included Sir John Gielgud, Michael York, Charles Boyer, Olivia Hussey, Liv Ullmann, and Peter Finch.

People had loved James Hilton's book about a group of people whose plane crashes in the Himalayas, where they come upon a lost Utopian world. The legendary Frank Capra had directed the book's first film adaptation. But that was back in 1937. This time around Shangri-La was going to be in color.

In many ways it was such a joyous time. I got to work with Hermes Pan, the choreographic genius behind Fred Astaire's moves. We had exercise classes in which Hermes—gorgeous

Hermes, who actually looked a little like Fred Astaire—had me (and I am no dancer) sailing over library tables and dashing up ladders with Olivia Hussey. She was five-foot-two (and slightly pregnant, rumor had it), whereas I was five-ten and so thin you could hardly see me sideways. (That's what divorce will do to you, no dexamyl spansules needed.) I thought Olivia and I made a darling couple.

In one of my more confident—more like cocky—moments, I had actually said to my agent that I wouldn't do the film unless Burt Bacharach wrote a song for me personally. In my mind I was going to get something smoky and sultry that stuck in people's heads, like Dusty Springfield's "The Look of Love," which Burt and Hal had composed for *Casino Royale*. The camera would come in on a close-up, and there I would be: an instant singing phenomena.

Burt had said the actress Ursula Andress inspired him to write "The Look of Love." Ursula and I were friends; we'd met through my close friend, actress Lizabeth Hush. I remember watching Ursula emerge from the surf one day out at the beach. I turned to Liz and said, "I don't think she has such a great figure."

Cut to: Ursula Andress, legendary Bond Girl in a bikini and overnight sensation.

In the end I did get to sing my own song: "Your Reflection Reflects in Everything You Do." Smoky and sultry it wasn't. It was a rather jaunty tune that I sang while jumping over garden stones with Olivia.

The other actors were lovely. Michael York was a sweetheart, and I was in awe of Sir John Gielgud. Then there was Liv Ullmann. She had already been director Ingmar Bergman's leading lady of choice—professionally and personally—and was just as sweet, funny, and unassuming as you could ever want anyone to be. We became very good friends over the five-month shoot. One day Liv asked Morgan if she thought I would come to her house some afternoon, even if there weren't any men there. Morgan replied, "Sure, as long as you talk about men."

Men or no men, I enjoyed visiting Liv at her rented house in Beverly Hills. We'd sit out by the pool and watch her little darling daughter Linn play-vacuum and talk to herself in Norwegian. Or was it Swedish? Liv speaks both languages, plus a few more, and I could never tell the difference. One time we decided to have a party and invite only men—Liv's idea, as she was newly single—except for herself, Morgan, and me of course. Jerry Brown came. Then Peggy Lipton showed up with Quincy Jones. They walked in, sat down in the middle of the party, and started necking. Gotta love those two. We didn't mind. Our odds of flirting with the invited men were still pretty good.

But though I loved my castmates, *Shangri-La* itself was not exactly a utopia for me.

I locked swords more than a few times with the producer, Ross Hunter. I'd get furious with him if I was given an A.M. call time and then didn't actually go to work until 5 P.M. So I started showing up at noon—bad form. I still didn't start working until 6 P.M., but Ross got wind of my defiance. When I complained, Ross retaliated in a way that he knew would silence me. Shortly after one angry episode, he sent a note over to my trailer: I was no longer allowed to bring Claire on the set. As for excuses for my behavior—besides me just being a jerk and unprofessional—I was still reeling from my divorce. It had forced me to really look at myself. I wasn't ready for that, and it showed.

We worked on the film for five months—plenty of time for Ross and me to get under each other's skin. When I had finished—or thought I had finished—shooting my suicide scene, I was informed the following day that we were reshooting it because the mountains in the background looked too fake.

Well, you would have thought the world was coming to an end by the way I reacted. Like I wasn't getting paid. "We have to do that again?!"

Then someone quietly said to me, "What's the problem? Is that the best you can do?"

Wow. That shut me up.

After we wrapped, Ross and I made up and exchanged some nice letters; I really grew to appreciate who he was. Ross was a real showman, for starters. He knew how to produce a film and promote it. He was like an early Harvey Weinstein in that he was great at getting the press excited about a project. And in Old Hollywood style, he didn't scrimp on glamour either.

Lost Horizon had its world premiere in Los Angeles at a massive theater in Westwood that, sadly, no longer exists. Ross got Liv out of a play in Sweden for two days and flew her to the premiere. I was so happy she was going to be there. I invited Jerry Belson, a comedy writer and friend I was crazy about, to be my date. Jerry had worked with Garry Marshall on such comedies as *The Lucy Show, Gomer Pyle, Dick Van Dyke,* and together they developed *The Odd Couple* for television. I thought he might offer some comic relief if I hated what I saw onscreen.

Seeing a movie I'm in for the first time is never my favorite thing. For me, it's hard to be objective about the film, my performance, and the way I look. We all know that looks are not the most important thing, but boy, it's hard to see yourself up there, thirty feet high and seventy feet wide. It didn't ease my anxiety when Jerry and I took our seats to find Rona Barrett, then the biggest gossip columnist in the country, sitting directly behind us.

So we watched the movie, frozen, not daring to move a muscle for fear that we'd telegraph our reactions, good or bad, to Rona. I loved the music, loved Hal's lyrics, loved all the actors—I just wasn't so sure about the script. I remember there was a lot of gardening going on.

The minute the lights began to come up, it was as though Jerry had read my mind. We both made a beeline for the exit. We were the first ones out. The minute we got outside we had to run the gauntlet of fans and press and people calling out to me, including my friend Liz Hush, who was waving and yelling, "Sally!" Jerry and I just blew past them as fast as we could without breaking into a full-on sprint.

We got to the car. I dove in and closed the door.

"Drive, Jerry. Drive," was all I could say. Jerry and I both started in with the jokes. (I was beginning to think that bringing my own comedian was a stroke of pure genius.) As we pulled away from the crowd, Jerry asked where we were going.

"Drive, just drive."

There was a premiere party, and I knew there was no way I could miss it. But until I felt ready to face it, Jerry just kept circling around, driving up and down Santa Monica Boulevard.

Finally we had to attend the party. I scanned the room—people talking, congratulating each other, eating and drinking, a lot of drinking. When I saw Liv across the room, I thought of her onscreen, wearing that powder-blue eye shadow. She was so ethereal and gorgeous—why mess with near perfection? I walked up behind her and tapped her on shoulder. She turned and looked up at me. We stayed like that for a moment, just looking at each other. Not a word was spoken. I guess neither of us knew what to say, how to react in such a public setting.

After the premiere there was a world tour, which meant London, Edinburgh, Manchester, and Leeds. Not quite the whole world, but it was so much fun. Stuart Cohen—my beloved manager, my best friend, and an indispensable part of my emotional life—accompanied me. On our way overseas we stopped in New York for a premiere party. The event was held at the Rainbow Room, high atop Rockefeller Center. The entrance was decorated with giant, cardboard Himalayan arches so everyone knew we were in Shangri-La. More than five hundred guests were invited.

I asked David Rayfiel to be my guest, but he said no—that instead we could meet up after the movie. Still a little stuck on him, I jumped at the chance. So I rushed into the party, gave somebody a high five, and dashed out the back to meet David. Sadly, I think David had the same feeling about having dinner with me. Rushed in, rushed out. In no time I was back at the party. Oh well...

As for the rest of the tour, I will say this: no expense was spared. Ross Hunter was definitely Old Hollywood in that respect. I don't remember any promotional experience then or since that could compare. Bottomless supplies of the best wine and champagne. All the caviar you could eat—and I can put away some caviar. Bring some friends over to visit? Sure, absolutely. The sky was the limit for any kind of comfort you desired. And plane travel . . . oh, how I miss old first-class European airline travel. This was the tail end of the era when you dressed to fly. Stewardesses—they were still called stewardesses then—strolled down the aisle of the cabin with an entire roast, carving off steaming slices for passengers, as much as you'd want.

On the flight over I was sitting next to some very nice men—strangers—and as we were nearing London, I overheard them talking about clearing customs, and it hit me: *Oh my God . . . I don't have my passport! I'm going to meet the Queen and I don't have my passport.* I wondered, *How on earth did I even get on the plane?*

Once the plane landed I stuck with the rest of the cast, hoping I could slip through customs unnoticed.

No such luck.

"Passport, please," the customs official said, in his plummy little accent.

I smiled. I stuttered a bit.

"You don't have your passport?" he asked.

"Well, no," I said. "But I am here to meet the Queen!"

He looked at me, and then he waved me through. Talk about a different time.

After Manchester and Leeds, the tour put Stuart and me, along with the publicist, in a Daimler, complete with fur rugs, for the drive from Glasgow to Edinburgh. The Scottish countryside was beautiful. Moody skies hung low in every direction; emerald green sod and thistle dotted the landscape. It was late afternoon, and we were alone on the road, reveling in our luxurious isolation.

And then the car conked out.

The poor driver felt absolutely terrible and started trying to summon help on the CB radio. Stuart saw headlights approaching. Draped in his fur coat, with his trademark diamond ring glinting, he leaped out into the middle of the road and stuck out his thumb. A huge truck, almost two blocks long, with a little cab in front, screeched to a stop. The driver opened up the door of the cab—no worry about stopping any traffic—and we started to explain our situation.

"Mumble mumble Edinburgh mumble mumble," the driver said in his heavy Scottish accent.

Edinburgh? We were sure we heard the word "Edinburgh." Stuart and I hopped in the truck's cab, along with the publicist, all squashed and lying on top of each other, leaving our luxurious car and driver behind. We pulled into Edinburgh in grand style in our gigantic truck.

Next stop: London, where the highlight of the tour would be meeting Her Royal Highness, Queen Elizabeth II. After the screening we were shuttled through security, then lined up with others to be presented that day.

Stuart Cohen was standing behind me in his fur coat. Sir John Gielgud was standing next to me, and on my other side was Peter Finch (who would later gain fame in *Network*). Peter was a great English actor, and told me he'd met the Queen many times. So in my mind they were going to have a nice chat. Leslie Caron was ahead of us in line, and I watched as she performed a curtsy so magnificent that it took my breath away. With her graceful arms extending out from her sides, she looked as though she was about to take flight.

You're briefed on etiquette before you meet the Queen. "Be sure to bow your head," I was told over and over. "No one ever does it right," my English friends had told me. I was as prepared as I could be, standing there in a painfully dull white dress, jazzed up with one of David Bennett's furs. We'd been instructed not to initiate conversation with the Queen, but she asked all of us the same thing: "And are you also in the film?" I looked up and blurted out, "Sure nice to meet you!"

Leslie Caron, I was not. The Queen chuckled at my rebellion, then moved along and said the same thing to Peter.

Before arriving in London I had received a letter from Sir John Gielgud about *Lost Horizon*:

> *Dear Sally,*
> *I shall look forward to seeing you again tomorrow night . . . It seems you have made the only acting success in the picture. I knew you would. Congratulations.*

He may have been full of malarkey. But hey, I'll take it where I can get it. What do you do when someone of Sir John Gielgud's character and reputation takes the time to write you such a thoughtful note? I just tucked it in my boot and got on about my business, and I never said a word to him about it. What a jerk I was.

Despite Sir John Gielgud's estimation of the film and its poor early reviews, *Lost Horizon* has become a cult favorite today. I'm tickled to death when people come up to me and ask about it. I even met a man who attended one of my shows at the Roxy who told me that he and his family watch it every Christmas without fail. I guess everyone needs a little Shangri-La in their lives.

• • •

I WAS ABOUT TO STRIKE OUT FOR WHAT I HOPED WOULD BE MY own Shangri-La—my singing career.

While I was finishing up *Lost Horizon*, I had run into Neil Diamond on the beach in Malibu. He wasn't an idol of mine in the way that Harry Nilsson or Rod Stewart were, but I respected him and his incredible success. So I asked his advice about singing. What he told me was simple: "If you want to be taken seriously as a singer, you have to get a band and go on the road."

I decided to heed what he said, even though my friend, the legendary record producer Richard Perry, told me, "Stay in the studio, Sally. Keep recording." Stuart tried to talk me out of it initially too.

But I soon found myself back up at 10050 Cielo Drive, the site of the tragedy in August of 1969. When I needed a place to rehearse—in this case, for my upcoming music tour—there was only one choice in my mind: Rudi Altobelli's. All of us who had history with Rudi's home refused to let what had happened color our memories there forever. We chose to focus on the good times we had had there in the past and to make new memories as well. For me, rehearsing at Rudi's was a clear and easy choice.

I have Lou Adler to thank for my first record deal. After we got back from filming *Brewster McCloud* in Houston, Lou was producing Carol King's album *Tapestry*. He slipped me into the studio, and I got to record my first demo with Carol King's rhythm's section. *Life* magazine's Alfred Eisenstaedt was there too, and he took some wonderful photographs of the session. My album, *Roll with the Feelin'*, produced by Gene Page and his brother Billy, had been released in 1972. It was rock oriented, a departure from the standards I used to sing when I was younger. The track titles speak to me even now: "Roll with the Feelin'," "Sweet Journey's End," "Take a Chance," "Child of Mine," "It All Works Out." *Billboard* magazine gave the album four stars—a huge thumbs-up for me, or for anyone else for that matter.

But I had done little or nothing to capitalize on that good buzz because I had been on location shooting *Slither*. I was so excited just to have made the album that I never thought about promoting it. Through the thin walls of our motels I could hear Louise Lasser, my costar on *Slither,* along with James Caan, listen to my album almost every night while we were on the road. I was thrilled. I'd gone from singing in the grocery store to hearing a colleague grooving to my music on an album I had actually recorded. It was heaven.

I had announced in a newspaper article in 1973 that I was

going "all out" with my singing. It's not very helpful to your career as an actress to announce that you are focusing all of your efforts on a different profession. Now that I was planning a singing tour of three months straight, not everyone was happy, especially not my agent, Sue Mengers.

Sue passed away in 2011, but she remains legendary, one of the most powerful agents of the last half of the twentieth century. She had started out as a receptionist at MCA, the mammoth agency that grew into Universal Studios. (There's still a little white colonial building in Santa Monica, where MCA was once housed.) Sue's client list was like a Hollywood walk of fame, including Marlon Brando, George Burns, Michael Caine, Cher, Faye Dunaway, Gene Hackman, Barbra Streisand, Gore Vidal, Ali MacGraw, and Warren Beatty, to name just a few.

Sue's sense of humor was famously acerbic. Whenever I was with her in a group setting or at one of her parties, I was always afraid to go to the bathroom. I was sure that the minute I stood up to leave she would rip a hole in me big enough to drive a Mack truck through. People loved her evil humor, though; the truth always came out when she was around.

Sue's patience with me was wearing thin. She was furious that, just when my film career was thriving, I was turning down a movie and disappearing for three months to tour. I could easily have done a movie, then gone on the road for a bit, then continued to alternate acting and singing. But I wanted soul. I wanted to earn my stripes in the music world, just as I had as an actress. I wanted the Billie Holliday story but without the drugs—well, maybe a little grass every now and then.

I was getting to the point when no one could tell me anything, not even people who had my best interests at heart. Part of the problem was that I had begun to believe my own press. I went from feeling like a nobody to seeming arrogant. Arrogance is often just the flip side of low self-esteem. If you ever meet an arrogant asshole, chances are there's a big mess of unresolved, low self-esteem lurking beneath the surface.

Worse yet, I had no comprehension of how the film business worked. For example, after *M*A*S*H* came out, Fox wanted to make a picture deal with me. To my mind, that meant a seven-year deal, the kind they used to make at places like Universal, when you'd get $750 a week and they owned you. Please! I was too big for a seven-year deal. I would be trapped! Only when it was too late did I grasp that they were offering me a deal to make films, not a weekly retainer. Oops.

Then there were films I turned down:

The Poseidon Adventure: pass. Why? From the script, it didn't seem that I'd have enough to do in the picture. *Poseidon* apparently was good enough for Gene Hackman, one of my acting heroes, and for Shelley Winters, whom I adored, but it was not good enough for me. The studio kept offering me more and more—more money, back-end profits—and I just kept saying no. Don't get me wrong—it's okay to turn things down. But if you're going to build a career, you have to say yes sometimes. And I was becoming very stubborn.

I didn't realize what a hit the film would be—no one can predict that. You can have the greatest talent in the world and still not have a hit. But hits make you more viable, more bankable.

Perhaps one of the most painful mistakes I ever made was turning down the man who gave me a career: Robert Altman.

I had just finished filming *Last of the Red Hot Lovers* when Bob called me one day at home.

"Sally, do you want to be in my picture after next?" he asked.

"Only if it's a good part," I said.

He hung up on me.

Bob was as stubborn and arrogant as I was at the time, but the sad thing is that I cheated myself out of working with someone I loved so much, someone who made acting both fun and easy and who trusted his actors. Bob loved actors. Stars would line up to work for nothing for Bob Altman.

Life is all about choices. There isn't necessarily a right or wrong about choices, but there is living with the consequences. It is never bad to make unpopular decisions or to go against the grain, but what is important is that you make those decisions from the right place. Trust your judgment, trust the writing, listen. Look, there isn't an actor in town who hasn't turned down some fabulous thing. There was just too much of that in my case. My choices weren't made from a place of any real *confidence* but rather mostly from fear.

Oh, the Altman film I turned down? *Nashville*. In that part I would have been able to sing. Bad choice.

• • •

WHEN STUART SAW HOW STRONGLY I FELT ABOUT GOING ON tour, he got behind me all the way. In fact, Rudi Altobelli was going to come on the road with me. All the arrangements and preparations would be done by Bob Esty, a man I've been musically codependent on for about forty years now—and one of my dearest friends—who happened be living in Rudi's guest house at the time. An amazing arranger and producer, Bob has worked with people like Cher, Barbra Streisand, and Donna Summer, and I had him for musical director of my first-ever tour.

My dress designer and friend Donfeld stepped up once again, this time teaching me how to pack. A couple of black-and-white boas and I was good to go on a three-month tour.

I'd be touring with a band of five guys, plus a group of three backup singers, called Gotham. Stuart begged me to get rid of Gotham. The money was too much, he said. The band, three backup singers, me and Rudi, and our road manager—I'd be paying for all of them. Furthermore, Stuart pointed out, a big group onstage could look awkward if the clubs weren't packed. I didn't listen.

Sue made one final plea before I got the show on the road.

"You believe in magic?!" she yelled. "You think all of this will still be here when you get back?!"

Stuart and I looked at each other, smiled, and said, "Yeah, we do."

And that was that. I was off.

· · ·

I WAS SLATED TO DO THREE SHOWS A NIGHT. THAT PROVED more exhausting than I had imagined—and sometimes demoralizing to boot. There were often more people in the band than in the audience. (So Stuart was right: if I had traveled without a band, it might not have looked so damning.) In Denver that particular problem solved itself: Gotham wanted to sing more in the act, and one of its members threw a fit with the road manager about it. A few punches flew, and the next thing I knew, Gotham had quit, taking their sparkly costumes with them. The next night I went on faced with the challenge of covering as many different parts as I could while still appearing to be the lead singer. We needed emergency rearrangements for the music. And I needed to get to know that road manager better.

In Denver the sound engineer offered me a piece of advice: "Sing to the mic," he said. "Talk to the mic, not the audience." That suggestion made a big difference at the time. Every little bit helped. I was learning.

Every town had its tale. In El Paso we played the opening of some hotel. My hotel room was red, and there was a trapeze above the bed. I was tempted to use it, but I resisted. The hotel did not appear to be finished—there was a large, dirty plastic dome over the outdoor venue where they wanted me to sing. When I caught a glimpse of myself in the mirror that night, I looked like the Bride of Dracula. I had really overdone it on the makeup. The crowd didn't seem to care, although I thought if I heard, "Where's Hot Lips?!" one more time, I would call it a night and retire to my trapeze.

In Atlanta we had a run at the Playboy Club, which was in a dicey part of town. The management advised us that leaving the hotel after dark was not a great idea. Luckily, we could enter the venue through a rear entrance of our hotel, sidestepping the little piles of rat feces on the stairs. Our mecca was the coffee shop in the hotel lobby. We practically lived there—between shows, before shows, after shows. Bob Esty had joined us in Atlanta, and he and Rudi were practically stools at the counter in there. One night, after we'd finished the second show, we headed to the coffee shop to get a snack.

"Wait! Wait!" someone shouted. "Don't go in there! There's been a murder. The cook and one of the customers were just shot!"

For the rest of the stay I ordered pizza and smoked a joint in my room.

I was excited to play New Orleans, not just for my shows but also to soak up the scene, the food, and some of the other music in town. For our performances at the Blue Room in New Orleans Bob decided to use a full orchestra. I was blowing through money, using all my movie earnings, but I felt I had to. If I was going to crash and burn, I was going to crash and burn with a string section.

I never thought a hurricane would upstage me.

The warning came: batten down the hatches, seal the shutters, tape the windows, and fill the bathtub. I waited in my hotel room, hoping that the storm would pass us by. Then the booker came up to ask if I would please go down and sing for all the tourists, who were so nervous about the hurricane. So down I went to perform for a panicked audience, trying to think of what to say to ease their fears. The words, "Don't worry about the hurricane," actually came out of my mouth and, needless to say, were little comfort. *Hot Lips Sings!* the posters for my shows announced. No one cared. The wind howled outside, the rain began, shingles shook loose, and traffic lights swayed like they were made of papier-mâché. In the end we all came through fine, but I put on a terrible show.

When I was leaving on tour, my then-boyfriend, producer and director Chuck Shyer, had said to me, "Fool around, but don't fall in love." That wasn't the way I wanted a man to feel about me. It was a nice offer—very freeing, as I soon discovered—but didn't suggest the kind of committed relationship I would be interested in. However, because it was on the table, by the time I got to New Orleans I had taken Chuck up on his offer and was having a full-on affair with the gorgeous road manager.

New Orleans proved to be a lot of fun. We would wander around the French Quarter late at night after shows. One night we ended up at some house party full of spectacular drag queens. "Sally!" everyone yelled, racing up to me. I reveled in the attention until a guy nearly threw up on me.

Another night we wound up in the French Quarter, a wonderful maze of courtyards and alleys and little secret hidden nooks and crannies. Suddenly someone pulled out a ball of coke the size of my head. Never my thing, cocaine, thank God; I have enough trouble sitting still. But whether or not I was going to take it was beside the point. I was scared. I thought, *If anyone sees us with this bowling ball of drugs, we'll all go to jail for the rest of our lives.*

Music poured out of every doorway. So did drunks. One night we went to see a great horn band we'd heard about. Joe Cocker was lying on the floor of the club with a crowd of people standing over him saying, "Have another drink, Joe!" It was like a Tennessee Williams play. Happily, the last time I saw Joe perform, he was sober and brilliant.

My room in New Orleans was next to Rudi's. He was a devil and a lot of fun. I'd drop in on him while I was wearing my trusty pink nightgown, and Rudi would stop by my room draped in just a towel. Neither of us would think twice about giving press interviews dressed that way. Then there the nights I spent smoking grass and eating pizza in bed with the road manager. I was having the time of my life.

But I was getting exhausted. So one night Rudi and I called Stuart.

"Stuart," I said. "I can't do three shows a night anymore. It's too hard."

Stuart was brief and to the point.

"Sally, if you don't do a third show, you'll never work in this town again."

I did three shows.

New York City, mercifully, was a two-shows-a-night town. We were booked for two weeks at the Rainbow Grill above Rockefeller Center—a great gig. It was packed every night, mostly with foreign visitors who came to take in the fabulous city views, but I didn't care. I loved the place.

I opened with what I now consider an unsingable song called, "Dear Friend." It had no melody or rhythm. We had three new backup singers flown out from LA, as we'd lost Gotham. Because I knew so little about running a music tour, it hadn't occurred to me that I needed a show director and a lighting designer for a venue as sophisticated as the Rainbow Grill. Before I left LA, Chuck had me do a show in front of Garry Marshall, Jerry Belson, and Harvey Miller. They were all brilliant and gave me some funny things to say between songs. But that was now two and a half months ago, and not much of it had stuck with me. I still hadn't learned to take notes.

So there we were at the Rainbow Grill, me strutting around in pants, a white halter top from Holly's Harp on Sunset that was practically falling off me, and a feather boa, backed by three new singers, performing a show with no director, no lighting design, and no writing. However, my two-week run garnered me some wonderful reviews.

The tour had been bleeding money. After New York City Stuart called to say that if I was willing to go to a couple more towns, I could possibly break even. He emphasized the word "possibly." I banged my head against the wall, and off we went.

One of the last gigs I remember was in Pennsylvania at a place called Host Farms. The word "farms" made it sound like my kind of place: I pictured trees, meadows, horses. I called Chuck and asked my mom to bring Claire, telling them all it was a farm and we could have Thanksgiving together. No one could come.

The motel was one of the strangest I'd ever seen. It was practically underground. There was a little tiny patio and one window. There was a ping-pong table in the lobby. And we'd be there for a week, maybe two.

I was depressed and lonely. I had been on the road for three months—my own doing, of course. I called Stuart to whine; I called the shrink to sob. I begged anyone—everyone—to please come visit. Performances didn't do much to lift my mood because the audience sat stone faced as I sang.

I spent most of my downtime in my room, miserable. When I finally opened my door, there was the band, doing laundry, goofing around, and chatting out in the hall. I felt like I'd been hibernating. I was almost amazed to see everyone alive and well. Beyond the ping-pong table and a trip to Amish country, there wasn't much going on in that town. But today I would know better how to cope. I would make my own fun—some books, a ping-pong tournament organized by yours truly, or at least a good nap without tears.

When we got held over at Host Farms, I called Stuart to protest. "There is hardly anybody here!" I wailed. "This is so humiliating."

"Listen," Stuart said. "If you're not happy doing it just for yourself and the waiters, then it's all bullshit."

He was right. All I hoped to accomplish from this tour was to become a singer. If it was hard—and at times it was—then so be it. Hard knocks were good for the spirit. Let's face it: I wanted soul.

After the tour ended I went to record again, this time at Muscle Shoals, Alabama, the Hit Recording Capital of the World. Everyone recorded there, from local bluegrass legends to the Rolling Stones and Aretha Franklin. I was thrilled. In 1974 there wasn't much to see of Muscle Shoals except the recording studio, a motel, and a long stretch of empty highway leading to a coffee shop that served biscuits and gravy. But that was enough for me. It was a tremendously valuable experience to work with producers Terry Woodford and Clayton Ivy. We'd record until five in the morning, then play basketball. Their support helped keep my singing ambition alive. I think about them even today as I record, nearly forty years later.

The hard knocks kept on coming: For starters, I came back to Los Angeles $50,000 in the hole. That was a lot of money in 1974 and roughly equivalent to four times that or more today. Then, with perfect timing, the IRS called and said I owed $20,000 in back taxes. Now, my own debt I could deal with, but owing the IRS did not sound like a good idea. I did what I so often did in times of crisis: I called my mother. She loaned me the money. I paid her back.

Oh yes, and there was one more little hard knock: shortly after I returned from the tour I did a show at the Backlot in Los Angeles. I invited Neil Diamond, the man who had urged me to go on the road if I wanted to "be taken seriously" as a singer, to come see it.

Granted, it wasn't my best show, not by a long shot. But it was still me; it was still my voice. I sang. He listened. After the show Neil said he wanted to take me to lunch the next day.

At lunch Neil looked me dead in the eyes and said, in all sincerity, "You should never sing again. It's not your thing. You really can't do it."

I was again on the receiving end of more advice from someone who knew better than me. And guess what? I had ignored my business manager. I had ignored Sue when she told me not to leave town for months on end. I ignored everyone who told me repeatedly to take *The Poseidon Adventure*. I ignored Stuart when he said not to bring such a large band on the road. And here and now, I was going to ignore Neil Diamond and keep on chasing my dream to sing.

Only this time I was sure I was making the right choice.

CHAPTER 11

Reaching Down, Reaching Out

AROUND THE TIME OF MY MUSIC TOUR, MY HOME LIFE WAS going through serious changes—some wonderful, some trying, and some tragic.

As luck would have it, when I left the house in Malibu where I stayed during *Lost Horizon,* I got to move back into the Cape Cod house I loved, where I had lived with Rick. One phone call and $60,000 later and I was the owner of a house and yard, pool, and badminton court in the Hollywood Hills. Buying the house was one of the happiest days of my life. I still live there today.

With a place of my own now, I kept telling Ian I wanted to help him raise Claire. By now it was clear that Ian had Parkinson's disease. He slept all day, and he couldn't do much when he was awake.

"Let her stay with me," I would say.

"No," he'd insist. "She's all I've got."

I offered to help him find a place closer to me so I could cook breakfast for them in the mornings and help out after dinner. "No," he said. He had people in his building looking out for Claire, like the woman across the hall with agoraphobia.

I tried to help him locate a suitable nanny, placing ads with agencies and in the papers. Anyone we hired would work out for a bit. The first one, very loving and nurturing, wanted to be a nurse. She soon became a nurse. The second one, a darling young thing, seemed perfect: she played with Claire and was sweet with Ian, but she left after a few weeks to get married. Another girl was a health food cook. *Great,* I thought. Then Claire called: "Sally, Jan's in my bed naked." By the time I got there, Jan was gone.

I approached the neighbor across street to watch Claire. Rita was a very sweet woman and a real character. "I don't know if I can make it today, kid," she said. "But my boyfriend might be able to. He needs some work. He just got out of prison."

No, thanks.

I myself was trying to play a bigger role in Claire's life, but I had my share of screwups too. One day when I was having lunch with my agent at Ma Maison, the hottest restaurant in town, I suddenly realized that it was Claire's ninth birthday. I had forgotten. I dropped everything, jumped in the car with her presents, and raced right over. When I opened the door to Ian's place, I saw Claire sitting with two of her friends in the living room, at a tiny card table covered with a colorful paper birthday tablecloth. Some candy was laid out.

"Who did this?" I asked, bewildered.

"I did, Sally," Claire said. "I went down to Jerry's Liquor."

My boyfriend, Chuck, who had always been incredibly supportive of my relationship with Claire, told me that I couldn't leave Claire at Ian's. Either I had to take her, or we had to send her to boarding school. The night he suggested boarding school, I became so mad that I slept on the couch.

Claire would sometimes run away—who could blame her—and Ian, poor thing, couldn't keep up, being so ill. As soon as I heard she was missing, I would dash over, but sometimes the police would find her and bring her home, or Claire herself would call me in a panic.

So I did what many frightened adults do in situations like this: I began to threaten her.

"Claire, you can't keep running away! You have to listen to your dad. And if you don't, I'm going to have to send you to boarding school," I said to her one night on the phone.

"What's boarding school?" she asked, not sounding scolded at all but instead more curious. "Would I like it?"

"Well, I don't know. Would you like to go see? Shall we find out?" I was amazed by her reaction and so moved, because somehow she knew she needed a change in her life.

Through a friend I heard about a boarding school in Ojai, and the two of us drove up to check it out. As we drove past its split-rail white fences—there were horses—we immediately knew it would be perfect. The grounds and the buildings and the people felt real, not fancy. Claire would even have her own horse to ride and take care of. I knew I had to make this happen, to get her enrolled. I would even pay for it, though my business manager thought that would be a very bad idea. But I didn't care.

Claire was excited, and Ian agreed to let her go. That was his compromise.

With Claire settled in her new school, I had divided my time between rehearsing for the tour and nesting in the new house. I wanted some shelves added to the den, so I asked Chuck if he knew anyone who could do the job. He recommended a friend of his who did some fine woodworking, and brought him by to meet me.

The guy was in his early thirties, tall and fit, in that carpenter's sort of way, and very laid back. He lived nearby, drove an old beat-up truck, and had a couple of kids. With his brown hair and kind of cockeyed smile, he was so handsome—a real looker. *What a shame he's married and a friend of Chuck's*, I thought.

I told him I wanted a built-in couch in the den. I know: a built-in couch, but hey, it was the early seventies. There had to be enough room for two people to lie down side by side. I also wanted a couple of extra windows.

I would be in the living room, singing, preparing for my first

tour, while he was pounding away in the den. I would occasionally go in to check to see how things were going.

I thought the couch wasn't deep enough. Whining, I said, "I
wanted the couch wide enough for two people."

"That's the way it has to be," the carpenter answered.

Okay, then. I had told him I wanted some changes to the book-
case he built too, but—you guessed it—it was the way it had to be.
The carpenter was so damn sure of himself that it was impossible
to argue with him.

Of course, he was also an actor. He had been in *American Graffiti* and Coppola's *The Conversation*, but because his career hadn't
quite taken off, he was still working carpentry gigs here and
there. Over the two or three months he worked at my house, we
got into a little routine. He'd come in the morning, we'd have a
cup of coffee or maybe smoke a joint, then we'd both get about
our business.

My neighbor at the time was Phil Mandelker, a television
producer. I told him he should hire my carpenter on one of his
shows. During the time he was working on my house my young
handyman did two TV pilots, neither of which sold. I don't know
which, if any, Phil had a hand in. I was happy whenever the carpenter got a gig, but I was just as happy when he came back to
work on my projects. He would do a pilot, come back and ham-
mer, do a pilot, come back and do some more hammering.

Then one day he came in to take care of wiring the dimmer on
a lighting fixture in the den.

"Well," he said, in his deadpan cadence. "I was probably
their last choice, but I got some outer-space movie with Alec
Guinness."

"Oh, that's great!" I said, picturing him on a white wooden
ship, Alec Guinness standing at the helm in a long white gown,
holding a staff. "I really hope it works out."

The next time I saw Harrison Ford, he pulled up in front of my
house in a Mercedes.

"I hate to be Hollywood," he said when I answered the door, "but can I use your phone?" He came in and made his call. I joked with him that I didn't have a handyman anymore. "Neither do I," he said, "but I do know where you can get some tools cheap."

Star Wars, that "outer space movie with Alec Guinness," had indeed worked out quite well for him. And for everyone else involved, I imagine.

. . .

WHEN I CAME BACK FROM MY THREE-MONTH SINGING TOUR, I was exhausted. But there were real problems to deal with at home. Ian's condition was much worse. I didn't want Claire to be with me just part time when she was home from boarding school.

Chuck had heard enough. He had witnessed my frustration and scared phone calls, and he'd personally watched as Ian's health deteriorated.

"You asshole," Chuck said to me one day. "Why don't you adopt her?"

"What about my sister? What about Ian?" I said.

But he was right. Shouldn't I at least try to establish some official relationship with Claire?

Diana and Gloria were still living in France, and Diana's agreement with Ian was still in force: Claire was not to see Diana until she was eighteen. As Ian's condition deteriorated, my parents and I did our best to help out. I hadn't been in touch with Diana because I had felt, in a way, that it was unfair to Claire if everyone but her could be in contact.

But now I had to reach out.

I didn't want to call and put Diana on the spot. So I wrote to her in the south of France. How would she feel if I adopted her daughter? Diana wrote back almost immediately.

What are you waiting for?

I made the offer to Claire, who accepted. Then both Claire and I approached Ian, who had recently gone to Scotland. Rather than spend his remaining days in a home in LA, Ian's doctor knew of treatment he could seek near his family in Scotland. His final days would be much more comfortable there with so many relatives to take care of him. Claire's school was just an hour and a half from home, so if she needed me, I could drive up to see her. She'd come home for weekends.

Again, we made our proposal in writing. I let Claire compose the letter to her father, and what she wrote was remarkably clear, touching, and beautiful: *I would be in a nice loving home like I was with you the first ten years of my life,* she said. It is incredible to think that she was only ten years old when she wrote that letter. She had been through so much and had had to grow up alone in so many ways—abandonment, sickness, and care from a not-terribly-stable aunt. I wasn't ready; I was scared. But I knew what I wanted, and I wanted Claire in my life officially. Permanently.

Ian wrote back with his answer: *Yes.* I learned later he told his brother-in-law, "I can die now," knowing Claire would be okay. Not long afterward he passed away. It pained me to have to tell her about his death. We had a small memorial service for him. Claire soldiered through, like she always had, so much stronger than I was.

On the day the state adoption representative was coming to give me the once-over, I had been down the street visiting with my friend Jerry Belson and his wife, Joanne.

"You better go put on a bra before the adoption people arrive!" he said.

I rushed home to put on a bra. Claire, however, wanted to run around naked. "I think she should see the real me, all of me!" she giggled, referring to the adoption rep. So there I was, chasing naked Claire around, when I looked out the window to see a big black limo pulling up.

"Claire, she's here! Get your clothes on!"

I checked myself in the mirror and ran outside to meet the state representative. The limo door opened.

Groucho Marx stepped out of the car.

I knew Groucho only slightly. Bud Cort had been staying at Groucho's house, and Groucho would host salons. All kinds of people would stop by to sing or play or recite something. My friend Morgan Ames would play the piano. I would sing. But that was pretty much the extent of my and Groucho's relationship— thin, at best. A woman stepped out of the car after him: his companion, Erin Fleming. She had recently been accused of abusing Groucho who, at eighty-four, was getting visibly weaker but had recently starred in a tremendous one-man show at Carnegie Hall. Erin was not yet forty, and I didn't know her from Adam.

What could I do? I showed them both into the living room. Erin just stood there. Groucho immediately sat down at the piano and began tinkling. Claire—now dressed, thankfully—was loving every minute of it.

Now I heard another car's wheels hitting the gravel.

Shit.

I run out the door, flustered. Was I nervous? You bet your life.

Yep. This car had a state seal. I rushed over to the woman exiting the car, blurting each step of the way.

"Groucho Marx is in my living room! I don't really know him, but you have to believe me that I would do anything in the world to make Claire happy!"

The representative looked me up and down and then came right on in. I introduced her to Groucho and we got down to business. It went surprisingly well.

"You know, Claire," she said as we were finishing up the papers. "You can have any name you want now."

Claire had actually given this some thought. Her name was Claire Anderson Graham. She, however, wanted to be called "Malibu." Groucho, joining the discussion, yelled over from behind the piano, "Sam! Call yourself Sam!"

However, Claire thought he had yelled, "Sand."

So it was settled: Her new name was officially Claire Anderson Malibu Sand Graham Kellerman.

I didn't care how many names were in little Claire's lineup; the last one was all that mattered to me.

• • •

BETWEEN THE MONEY I'D LOST ON THE MUSIC TOUR AND MY debt to the IRS, I had to land some acting gigs. As if I needed another reminder, one day Sue Mengers called me in a panic. I don't think I had ever heard her in such a state.

"Sally! Have you seen *Cosmopolitan*?!" Sue asked when I picked up the phone.

"No, why? Who did I knock?" I asked, assuming I had said something mean about someone and it had come back to bite me in the ass.

I had unwittingly knocked a wonderful director a few months before in an interview with *After Dark* magazine. I had thought the interview was over, but I learned the hard way that anything you say in front of a reporter can end up in print.

"Nobody!" Sue said. "I knocked you.

Worried that I might have already heard about it, Sue was mortified.

Relieved that I hadn't put my foot in my mouth, I was delighted.

What had Sue said? She had told *Cosmo* that she thought I had lost my mind, passing up on so many opportunities and leaving town to follow my bliss.

"Who did she think she was?" the article read. "Last year's Sandy Dennis?"—the implication being that I wasn't even this year's Sandy Dennis. And for those of you who do not remember Sandy Dennis? Well, that's the point.

But I couldn't have cared less. Sue sent me a nice bouquet of flowers to apologize along with a note and vase that I kept for years.

As for my decision to go on the road when I was hot in the movies—well, what can I say? I followed my heart. I wouldn't recommend my career planning to anyone else, that's for sure. But I did what I felt I needed to do—and I lived to tell the tale. What I would recommend to anyone else is that that, no matter how good you are, you should value whatever opportunities come your way. I read somewhere that Clint Eastwood said that he has always felt lucky. That's wisdom for the ages. *Feel lucky.*

I was lucky to have people who were still willing to work with me, despite my ignoring most of their advice. Paul Ziffren, my old neighbor in Malibu, once said, "You don't build trust in this town. If they need you, whether you've robbed a bank or written a bad check, they'll hire you."

He was right. Hey, it's Hollywood.

My favorite Ziffren advice: "Make a call to someone every day, whether you're awake, drunk, lying down, whatever. You have to be proactive."

Boy, is that the truth. The buzz will never be "Oh, but how wonderful she was back in 1942 . . ." The question is always "What have you done for me lately?" Unless you're proactive and staying alive and working, then no one gives a shit about you. Hollywood has a short memory.

Before my music tour I had started saying no to everything, including the chance to work with Bob Altman again. Now I started saying yes to everything, but still not for the right reasons.

I was ambivalent about doing *Rafferty and the Gold Dust Twins.* I had already done a road picture with Jimmy Caan that I loved. But I did it anyway because I was going to get to sing. Also, it would be another chance to work with Alan Arkin, who had starred with me in *Last of the Red Hot Lovers.* On *Rafferty* Alan was very supportive of both me and my ideas, and I appreciated that. The director, Dick Richards, and I had completely different ideas about my character, Mac, a sympathetic yet droopy loser who longed to be a country singer. When I would make a suggestion about a scene or a way to play something, Dick would almost always say, "No, that's not possible."

But Dick would always listen to Alan's suggestions. After Dick shot me down, Alan would often chime in with a reiteration of my suggestion. "Why not?" Alan would say. "That's a great idea!" It was maddening, but thanks to Alan, at least I got heard.

Mackenzie Phillips, who was just a teenager then, was also a joy to work with on that movie. But I would love the chance to redo that character. Unfortunately, that's not how the movie business works.

· · ·

"A NEW BROOM SWEEPS CLEAN." THAT'S WHAT MY BELOVED manager Stuart used to tell me when we wanted to make some kind of change. Time to move on. Shake things up.

Get on with your life.

By now I had gotten to the point that I rang Stuart about ten times a day. He was so fabulous to me. I had come to rely on him for absolutely everything. People either loved him or hated him, but few would deny that Stuart was boundless in his energy for me.

He was my constant champion. When I was with the agent Jack Gilardi at ICM, Stuart would physically go into Jack's office and sit on his desk in the middle of the day, no matter who was in there. If the phone rang, Stuart would chime in, "Is that for Sally?" God knows how many jobs I got simply because someone was trying to get Stuart Cohen out of the office.

So one morning I rang Stuart up, full of energy and optimism. Ready for change, ready to reinvent myself in Hollywood.

"You know what I'm going to do?" I said. "I'm going to write a letter to everyone I've offended in this town."

Stuart laughed. "That'll be a long list."

I got off the phone, so pleased with myself. I was ready for change, ready to sweep everything clean. It wasn't long before the phone rang again. This time it was Rudi.

"Hello, am I speaking with the kinder, more benevolent Sally Kellerman?" Rudi asked. "The one who is going to write everyone in town and make amends?"

I laughed and said, "You got her!" Stuart had clearly passed along my ingenious plan.

"Well, that sounds great, but the only thing is that when you called, you forgot to wish Stuart a happy birthday."

Oh my God! I forgot Stuart's fiftieth birthday!!!!

I hung up in a panic. Stuart had been talking about his birthday for the longest time—how he was going to have a huge party and invite everyone he'd ever known, friends and enemies alike. Apparently he hadn't pulled that together. Now I had to add Stuart—my darling Stuart, my champion—to the long list of people I had offended.

David "my fake cousin" Bennett was visiting me from New York and had brought along some leftover furs from his shop. I raced upstairs to rouse him.

"David! David!" I yelled. "It's Stuart's birthday, and I totally forgot! What can I give him?"

"I have a brand new shaving mug!" David said, trying to help.

"Perfect!"

That was something. I threw a stodgy mink stole on over my famous pink nightgown and out the door we flew, me with a head of snarled, ratty hair and no makeup. We tore through town until we reached Stuart's high-rise.

Stuart opened the door and howled with delight at the sight of me. Bob Esty had come by with a bottle of champagne. None of us really drank that much, but we spent two or three hours just enjoying ourselves. It was perfect. David and I wished Stuart a happy birthday and said good-bye. Later that day, when I talked to him again on the phone, he said he had been invited to a party. I was very happy to hear that. I was so self-centered, worrying what *I* was doing, that it never entered my mind that I and all the other clients who loved Stuart could've thrown him a party. But Stuart didn't keep score. He didn't care. He was too busy enjoying life.

I, of course, was crying to him about something, possibly my love life. The more I fretted about my life, my work, my future, the more Stuart started to laugh.

"Are you laughing at me?!" I asked.

"No, no . . . I'm laughing with you," he said, chuckling.

I loved his laugh, so warm and sweet. When the phone rang the very next morning, I heard the voice of my darling Luana.

"Stuart's dead," she said.

At first I couldn't process what she had said. It was so blunt, so matter of fact. I didn't believe it, didn't know how to make sense of what I was hearing. I refused to believe what Luana, my closest friend, had told me.

When I got off the phone with Luana, I called over to Stuart's house, to the office—everywhere I could think of—to confirm what I had just heard. What I kept saying sounds so cliché: *But I was just talking to him . . . But I just saw him and he was fine. . . .*

When the truth finally sunk in, I went into my room, crawled into my narrow walk-in closet, and sat on the floor. I wanted to hide, to get away from light and sun and anything that would remind me of life and joy and the world outside that had now changed forever. I sat huddled in my closet for hours. The loss of Stuart was unbearably gut wrenching.

Our relationship wasn't just about business. We had traveled together, which was so much fun. He would tell me never to worry about Claire, that he would always be there for the two of us. I had confided in him about everything from my family to my love life as well as my career. *Stuart, what do I do? Stuart, what should I say? Stuart, what do you think?* Stuart was like my father in many ways, but with a manner that was capable of softening every blow, of taking the sting out of everything. I can still hear him saying, "You shouldn't worry, Sally. It'll all work out." And you know what? It does.

To think that life—especially such a precious life, one that touched so many others—could be over in two minutes. It was more than my mind could process.

"If only she knew she could have everything," Stuart had once said about me. He wanted me to have as much faith in myself as he did. He stuck by me, never giving up on me, even when I was difficult, scattered, calling yet again for a shoulder to cry on. Forgetting his last birthday.

Stuart is still with me in so many ways. I still think of him whenever I see a powder-blue Volkswagen convertible with a black top, his old car.

I cherish a letter he wrote me:

My darling Sally . . . I just wanted to put into words how proud I am of you. What a real delight you have become both in life and on the stage . . . Your love means so much to me. You constantly amaze me with both your personal and professional growth. You have inspired me as a friend.

My imagination is really going to be limitless and boundless in your behalf because of who you are as a talent and a person.

I love you,
Stuart
P.S: Remember your love for all will take you over the hurdles.

Well, Stuart, my love, this hurdle felt insurmountable.

CHAPTER 12

Chasing Garbo

In the aftermath of Stuart's death I began to look at my own life with fresh eyes. One thing I had to examine was my relationship with Chuck. I loved Chuck and had a wonderful time with him, and he had been so incredibly supportive of my relationship with Claire. But deep down I knew that something was not quite right. We split up.

But career-wise, I didn't exactly start things off with a bang. My first picture without Stuart was *The Big Bus,* a disaster-film parody about a nuclear-powered bus. I had said no to the real disaster film, *The Poseidon Adventure,* but jumped on board the nuke bus. Go figure.

Anyway, during *The Big Bus* shoot, I would be off someplace by myself crying, hoping no one would notice. One day Ruth Gordon walked by and heard my sobs. Now, Ruth was someone whom I not only admired professionally—five Oscar nominations with one win just a few years earlier for her role as the creepy yet kind upstairs neighbor and satanic cult matriarch in *Rosemary's Baby*—but I also admired her personally. She and Bud Cort had made the wonderful *Harold and Maude* together, and Bud had introduced me to her. I have never forgotten her Academy Award acceptance speech when she won the Oscar at the age of seventy-two, a good fifty years after her first film. "I can't tell you how encouraging a thing like this is," she told the Academy. Brilliant. I think of that line to this day. It still inspires me as I continue to rack up the years.

So when Ruth, who at the time was almost eighty, heard me crying, she stuck her head in the trailer.

"You know the difference between you and Garbo?" she asked.

"No." I answered.

"Confidence," she said, and kept right on walking.

Next up, I walked out on a film in which I was to star opposite Lee Marvin. I was getting a very nice six-figure salary (millions were not the norm for starring roles back then). Not the best career move for sure, but I was still feeling bereft without Stuart and needed to be with people I loved, whom I knew loved me.

So I flew to Canada to be with Bob and Kathryn Altman. Bob was working on a film there called *Quintet,* starring Paul Newman. As we talked, Bob asked me if I wanted a part in his then-protégé Alan Rudolph's upcoming film, *Welcome to LA.*

"I'm producing," he said. "There's a part for you. It pays fifteen thousand."

I immediately called Jack Gilardi at ICM, my agent at the time. I told him I wasn't doing the Lee Marvin picture. He pointed out not only that had I already agreed to do the film and was reneging on my contractual obligation but also the more obvious fact that I would be taking a huge cut in pay.

I didn't care. "I'm not doing the movie," I said flatly. It didn't matter how many people I hung up. I wanted what I wanted, but looking back at that behavior now sure doesn't feel good, even if I was in pain. I was determined to be with Bob and Kathryn, and that was that. Gilardi never mentioned the switch again, he is a great agent and a mensch, and even though it's 30 years later, I still owe him a deep apology.

Luckily, in those days lawsuits for breach of contract didn't go that far. In Hollywood today, well, it is a much different story. When Kim Basinger stepped away from *Boxing Helena*—violating what was called an informal commitment—she got slapped with about $9 million in damages, and she ended up losing her little town in Georgia. I guess my bad behavior got in just under the wire.

But then, of course, I've never had a town. I was lucky I still had my house.

Altman and Rudolph were shooting *Welcome to LA* in Los Angeles, and in it I played a real estate agent. I was excited about the character and had a great idea for my look, inspired by an outfit I'd seen on one of my neighbors: I would wear a bright red suit and put a big shock of white in the middle of my blond hair. But when I arrived on the set, wardrobe pulled out some nondescript suit and a pale pink blouse with a big, droopy bow. But I didn't want to be a prima donna. Because I didn't want Bob to think I was going to make trouble, I vowed not to complain about anything. "Just perfect!" I said. "That'll be great!"

Thus, my character turned out just like the blouse: droopy.

On the set of *Welcome to LA,* I had the joy of meeting the oh-so-lovely and adorable Sissy Spacek. Sissy played my topless housekeeper and was a sheer delight. Memories of her Texas drawl still bring a smile to my face.

"Hey kid," she'd say to me. "You should git some painter's pants jist like mine."

I absolutely *adored* her. Sissy has a unique talent. I always love seeing her in films like *The Help* and thinking back on all the interesting choices she's made throughout her career, from *Carrie* to *Coal Miner's Daughter.* And she's been married for decades to an incredibly talented art director, Jack Fisk.

The film turned out great and was praised by Jack Kroll of *Newsweek* as an "extraordinary debut" for Alan Rudolph, hailing the rest of us for our "sharp, distilled performances."

· · ·

SO LET'S RECAP MY BEHAVIOR SINCE ANNOUNCING TO STUART I was going to make amends in Hollywood: I appeared in some films but walked out on others. I'd left Chuck, who was available, only to fall for someone who was married. Maybe I needed a breather. A trip to Iran seemed to offer, if nothing else, a change of scenery and distance.

In April 1977 I was invited to the Tehran Film Festival. The idea was that afterward I would go visit my sister Diana and her partner, Gloria, who were still living in a small medieval village in the south of France. I hadn't seen Diana in years, not since she'd left Claire behind with Ian.

Tehran was full of half-finished cement buildings, bazaars, and enough traffic and smog to give LA a run for its money. The film commission had invited stars from all over the world in order to show off how Iran had stepped into the modern age and to celebrate its film history. Brenda Vaccaro (a wonderful actress and a good friend) and Kenny Solms, another friend, were on my flight. Kenny was a kick—a writer for the *Carol Burnett Show* and a producer of the *Smothers Brothers,* among a million other credits. All the invited actors, directors, and media people stayed in the same hotel.

Brenda, Kenny, and I spent a lot of time together looking for adventure, usually unsuccessfully. I saw the crown jewels in Tehran's museum, but the closest I got to the "real" Iran was the bazaar. We were warned not to drink the water or to eat raw fruits and vegetables. But on the upside, Iran's caviar is world class. One night Brenda, Kenny, and I went to a hookah bar. I don't know what we were smoking, but I didn't get high and ended up coughing up green gunk for the next three months. These were my adventures. Oh—and I bought a tiny rug.

The festival itself was held in the Roudaki Hall, Tehran's opera house. It was stunning. The local papers called me Sally Keller, which I thought was pretty funny. The afternoon of the event Brenda and I got our hair done, slipped into our evening gowns, and headed off to the bus, only to wind up standing in our high-heeled shoes and holding on to the strap for the two hour-long, half-mile trip to the Hall. I ended up squeezed in next to Paul

Mazursky. Years earlier I had turned Paul down when he offered me a part in *Bob & Carol & Ted & Alice*. Now I was mad at him because he didn't hire me for his upcoming movie *An Unmarried Woman*. So Paul was cold, and I was peevish. One of us was justified in behaving that way, and it wasn't Sally Keller. But boy, was that a long bus ride.

Shortly after the festival ended, my pals Brenda and Kenny joined the exodus of movie people leaving Tehran. But I was stuck. Somehow my schedule had gotten turned around, leaving four days before my sister was returning to her home in France. So I wandered down to the hotel lobby, looking for people I knew. There I saw Otto Preminger, a famous director who had made many well-known films.

I had met Otto in 1967. He was a notorious hothead, and my first interaction with him confirmed that. My agents at the time at William Morris had thought it would be a good idea to test with him for *Hurry Sundown,* even though Faye Dunaway had already been cast. Otto was still casting for one of the male roles, so he had me read with three men.

When the first guy stumbled over a line, Otto jumped on to his feet.

"You don't know your lines?! Bullshit! I go to my office!"

He stomped out and did not return.

The next day Otto let the poor guy try again, only this time he made him audition in front of the other two actors. Brutal.

I don't think I'd seen him since, and now here he was, exploding as only Otto could, this time at the restaurant management.

"What do you mean you're not open?!" he bellowed. "I am Otto Preminger! I take my shirt off!"

Dear God, he was just as arrogant and awful as before. And as luck would have it, he remembered me. So I could hardly avoid joining him at his table in the restaurant, which had now decided to stay open.

Next to enter was John Simon, a reviewer for the *New York Times,* whom I knew to be particularly cruel to any actress who didn't look like a Barbie doll. My friends had all left, and I was lonely. I had days to kill before my sister got back to her home in France, and I was sitting at dinner with two of the most miserable men on the planet, Otto Preminger and John Simon. Perfect.

I shared my lodging predicament with the two of them, and Otto, oddly enough, had a solution.

"You will come to my house in the south of France. You will stay there until you can go to your sister."

Maybe I misjudged him, I thought. I felt so desperate. As much as I loathed Otto, I did not want to stay alone in Tehran. So I made all my arrangements—called the airline, booked a flight to the airport closest to Otto's home, and reserved a car. When the day of our departure arrived, I found Otto in the lobby.

"Oh no, you can't come!" he said. "My wife would be too jealous."

In your dreams.

"Don't worry about it" was all I could say.

But I was worried about it. I went back to my room, called the front desk, and begged them to extend my stay. I had a good cry and then decided to make the best of it. The only person I knew for sure who was still in the hotel was John Simon. So I quickly signed up for a tour, feeling that would at least get me away from the city and the cranky critic.

Of course, the moment I boarded the tour bus, who was the first person I saw? John Simon. Then, like a mirage, I spotted Arthur Hiller, the director I had worked with back in the 1960s on the television show *I'm Dickens, He's Fenster*. I plopped down right next to Arthur, and John Simon never said a word to me again. Soon Dick Guttman, a publicist friend from LA, boarded the bus along with his daughter, who wound up being my roommate on the short trip. We visited Shiraz, Isfahan, and Persepolis, where we saw beautiful mosques, and Arthur and I ate more caviar together than we would ever see again for the rest of our lives. In the end it was a wonderful trip. Then it was off to France.

This was the first time I'd seen my sister since she had left

Claire for her new life. She looked older, kind of weatherworn, and I remember her hands being very rough. Still, she looked so happy, like she'd lived through a very hard time but come out the other side happier, more complete. As hard as it was for Claire, it wasn't easy for Diana, either, deciding to leave. But she was convinced that Claire's life would be easier, considering the times and the intolerance, if she herself were out of Claire's life. I didn't stay long, but man, I had some delicious meals. I love my sister, and it was so good, so important to have that time with her. And to get to know her partner Gloria.

When I got home, I decided that I wanted to take Claire on a trip somewhere. As luck would have it, I was offered a part in a film shooting on some island and thought that would be perfect. We packed, we got Claire a passport—I made sure not to forget mine this time—and we were both getting excited about the trip. Then, one afternoon, we came home from some pretrip errands to a ringing phone. The picture had been canceled. We were crushed.

Then, like an angel out of the blue, Sissy "my formerly bare-breasted housekeeper" Spacek called to ask if I would like to play her best friend, a 1940s B-picture ballad singer, in a PBS special titled *Verna: USO Girl*. It was part of PBS's *Great Performances* series.

Would I want to play a singer? Would I ever! There was only one drawback: I couldn't bring Claire. It was a low-budget film, and the money wasn't there. I would miss Claire badly, and I hoped I could make up for our canceled trip.

We shot in Idar-Oberstein, a tiny town in Germany known for its jewelry industry. I loved being with Sissy again and also enjoyed working with William Hurt. It was one of Bill's earliest jobs. Just a few years later he would be wowing us all in *Body Heat*. And I got the chance to sing, which of course always thrills me.

When you're working with a small budget, out of necessity things move quickly. As the clock ticks, the dollars fly. So almost as soon as we stepped off the plane we had to shoot a scene—

Sissy's death—though I didn't yet have a sense of our respective roles and had had no rehearsal with her. But Ron Maxwell, the director, was so easy to work with and so spontaneous that we worked it out. We shot on Hitler's training grounds, where US servicemen were living and drilling. Half the time we were so close to the firing range that we felt like we were dodging real bullets. Ron took full advantage of our military setting and the access to so many "extras."

At one point Ron came running over to our trailers, yelling, "There's a parachute drop!!" Piling into a Jeep, we raced over. Nothing in the script had anything to do with a parachute drop, but Ron figured that kind of drama was just too good to pass up. So he made up a scene on the way over. That's the beauty of a lower budget; it's freeing in so many ways. If you have the right kind of director—Ron was one, and Bob Altman, certainly, was another—the creativity that kicks in can make up for a lot of the bells and whistles that come with a bigger budget. I see that kind of creativity in many of the up-and-coming filmmakers of today, the ones working with limited funds. So here we are again, in Hollywood's new Wild West.

In *Verna* I got to sing songs like Billie Holliday's "I'll Be Seeing You" and work with Donald Smith, a fantastic Broadway choreographer. The costumes were all originals, refashioned from vintage 1940s outfits. Ron shot me performing my "USO act" in a variety of different venues—the action was taking place during the war, after all. On one amazing night, when the rain was really coming down, I sang in front of nearly a thousand actual servicemen— Sissy, the amateur tap-dancer, and me, the ballad singer. I prerecorded my vocals at a nearby Marine base, just me and a Marine and a pair of headphones—no director, no choreographer.

Because I was always dieting, when Sissy, Bill, and other members of the cast and crew would go to dinner, I would head off to the *hallenbad* and swim laps with a bunch of sweet German women. Then I'd go back to my room and eat a candy bar alone before bed. But I loved my fellow cast members as well as the project itself. I am forever grateful to Sissy for bringing me on board.

While in Germany I got news of another job: *Magee and the Lady*, a television movie, in which I'd star alongside *The French Connection's* Tony Lo Bianco. It was set to shoot for two months in Australia. And this time I'd get to bring along Claire and my mom as well.

We landed in Sydney and it was heaven, worth every minute of the sixteen-hour flight. We enrolled Claire in school, where she made great friends. My mom shifted into classic Edith Keller-man mode, quickly finding a bridge group and going on tours and joining a local lawn bowling league to keep herself occupied during the day. I worked six days a week and was in every shot. It was such a blessing to have Mom with me, both for moral support and to help with Claire.

The minute we landed in Australia I had raced to the nearest candy counter to see what kind of sweets they had that I had never tried before. That's when it hit me: I had a real sugar problem. So I decided I would use the time away from home to try to give up sugar. The cooks on the set made me whipped cream without sugar, scones without sugar, and jams without sugar. Oh, and my poor mother. My experiment with living life without sugar meant that the minute I returned home from shooting, I would storm into the apartment and start yelling, "Mother! Mother! Where's my diabetic chocolate bar? Where are the raisins?!"

On Sunday, my day off, I would treat myself to honey on my pancakes and take Claire on a ferry ride. Tony Lo Bianco and I didn't exactly turn out to be Hepburn and Tracy, but we had a lot of fun. I've never seen the finished film. Maybe it was better than I imagined. Maybe not.

* * *

WHEN WE GOT BACK TO LA THINGS ALMOST SEEMED TO BE finally starting to fall into place. Claire was happy at school, and I was working with people I liked. But Paul Mazursky's snub on that bus in Tehran reminded me that I had burned more than my share of bridges. The roles I was getting offered weren't what they used to be. I didn't have Stuart to rely on, and I was now a very unprepared single mother to my sister's child. However, I was concerned about the "single" as well as the "unprepared."

Jennifer Jones Simon, my fairy godmother, had recently told me, "If you ever have any trouble with men, call Milton Wexler."

Milton was her therapist. I was no stranger to psychotherapy, of course, and had recently stopped seeing my latest therapist. I wasn't quite ready to dive in again.

No, not me. First I needed one more misguided affair. This one was with Warren Hoge, an editor at the *New York Times* who had the reputation of being the East Coast Warren Beatty—maybe not as good looking, but close. You'll recall that I actually knew the original Warren Beatty in his single-man heyday. I can attest to the fact that "Warren II" had a similar love for the ladies. I would fly in to visit him in New York or see him if I was performing there. A month or two might pass between our encounters. But there were always pictures of his other girlfriends on prominent display in his apartment. Maybe this was a not-so-subtle hint that he never intended to get serious with anyone—or at least not with me.

But Warren was smart and charming, and our time together was fun, interesting, and passionate. During one of my trips to New York he threw a dinner party with people like the journalist Carl Bernstein, gossip columnist Liz Smith, and my friend Brooke Hayward, who was seeing the pianist and bandleader Peter Duchin. (Brooke and Peter later married.) Those were stimulating evenings.

But after about six months of seeing Warren, I arrived at his apartment for a visit with all my bags in tow. Normally, I couldn't get past the front hall of Warren's apartment before we were both in some state of undress. But this time was different.

"I'm not attracted to you anymore," he said.

I laughed. But that was it—the defining moment. I left, found the nearest phone, and called the number Jennifer had given me for Milton Wexler. Warren Hoge might have been the final straw, but life had been leading me to Milton for a long time.

"Come in and see me," Milton said over the phone. "I will tell you some things about yourself that people are afraid to tell you."

"Why would I want to do that?" I asked.

Maybe I was a masochist, but I couldn't wait. People telling me what I wanted to hear hadn't really been working out anyway.

CHAPTER 13

Love and Therapy

IN MY VERY FIRST SESSION WITH MILTON HE SAID, "GET RID of the self-pity. It is ruining your life."

That was just one of so many things he told me that smacked of truth. I'd always been a crier, which I assumed meant that I was emotional and sensitive. So the idea that I felt sorry for myself threw me. The first thing I had learned in Jeff Corey's class was that audiences don't want to watch self-pity.

Should I spend another thirty-nine years figuring out why I had the self-pity? Or should I just get rid of it?

"Get rid of it," Milton said.

Milton blew my mind, and he made me laugh. His observations were the complete opposite of what any other shrink had ever said to me, when Jeff Corey first sent me off to therapy so many years before.

I may have had a sense of spirituality, but I didn't have any real understanding of myself. I had gone to a therapist at UCLA because I didn't want to be fat. At one point in 1969 I was going to therapy five days a week. But Milton was different. He was a genius and also kind. He was very real.

"Get down to forty," he said, referring to my tendency to operate at around 100 to 110 on the spirit and fervor scale. "Enthusiasts are bores. No one likes a punster."

"But my mother always said, 'In Theo!' One with God!" I told him. "I thought God loved enthusiasm." Milton assured me he didn't mean I had to become lifeless; I just had to dial it down to forty. He then described seeing me at a couple parties before we had officially met.

"Sit down and let people come to you," he said.

That was a little embarrassing to hear. I would go strutting up to guys I liked or to important people I thought I should know, beaming a big ol' "Hi!" Here I was, working in the career I loved, nominated for an Academy Award, and I was still acting needy. Studio heads, directors, even other successful actors, intimidated me, so I overcompensated with enthusiasm. But when you don't like yourself, people can smell it. Milton saw through my act. And he let me know that, even if they didn't let on, other people could see through it too.

"When you pretend you feel good about yourself, people know it," he explained.

That first hour with him was mind blowing. I had work to do.

• • •

PARIS!

Before I could really get down to work with Milton, I had to focus on my day job—acting. As an actor, you do a lot of location shoots, usually in pretty unremarkable places. This was certainly true for me. But the great director George Roy Hill, who had given us movies like *The Sting* and *Butch Cassidy and the Sundance Kid,* was shooting his latest film, *A Little Romance,* in Paris. I was cast as the disapproving mother of Diane Lane, who was making her film debut as an American ingénue who falls for a French boy while in Paris. Sir Laurence Olivier played the gentleman who befriends the young couple. Diane was adorable, around fourteen years old and just learning to put on makeup. Having worked with her at that young age, I can say that I am not at all surprised that she has grown into such a tremendous—and stunning—actress.

I would be in Paris for two months, and Claire would join me for the second one. The hotel they booked for the cast was right off the Champs-Élysées. *This can't be Paris*, I thought. I wanted what felt like the "real" Paris, the more soulful, atmospheric Left Bank. Before Claire arrived I resolved to find a little out-of-the-way apartment or bed and breakfast there so she could have more of a true Parisian experience.

My trip started off with just that. My first night there, my co-star, David Dukes, and I went to a little hole-in-the-wall Left Bank café and drank two bottles of red wine. (I'm not even a drinker. But I've played one on TV.)

Working with George Roy Hill was a joy. He was the complete opposite of Bob Altman, whom I admired in an entirely different way. Bob was improvisational, whereas George's direction was more hands on, more specific. Still, I found him encouraging. We shot our first scene in a gorgeous historic building just outside the city. After the first rehearsal take I asked him if I was working in the right direction.

"A little less of this," he said to me, batting his eyes, "and I think we've got it."

My other favorite piece of direction came while I was shooting a scene sitting at a table with David Dukes.

"Sally," George said, "can you raise your voice?"

Take two.

"Sally," George said, "can you raise your voice *and* lower your arms?"

The tone of his voice made me giggle throughout the shooting of the entire film. George was another great artist with a very personal directing style. Even when he sounded stern, he never killed your spirit.

The first day I met Sir Laurence Olivier he was sitting at his desk in his trailer. Before he'd arrived he had sent a letter to the production to let the cast and crew know that they should please call him "Larry." Along with Marlon Brando, Sir Laurence Olivier was one of the biggest idols of my acting generation. It was hard to think of him as "Larry."

We had already been shooting for a month when he arrived to do his scenes. I had had a day off and had just returned from strolling Paris when my makeup artist came up to me.

"Larry is here, and he would love to meet you!"

I followed him to Olivier's trailer, where my makeup artist practically shoved me in the door.

"Who's there?" came Olivier's lovely voice.

"Oh, I'm so sorry, Larry. It's Sally Kellerman."

"Oh, my dear beauty!" he gushed. "Now I shall sleep like a dear boy having met you."

Talk about charm. I staggered, speechless, out of the trailer. The closest I came to having a scene with Larry was a shot in which I was standing across the road. I whined to Larry how disappointed I was not to get to actually act with him.

"Just being across the street from you is more than an actor of my character could hope for," he said.

He was so effusive and generous and humble, worrying George didn't like his accent.

I told "Larry" not to worry. He was irresistible.

Before Claire arrived I found the perfect hotel for us on the Left Bank. We had a little two-story flat, big as a postage stamp, looking out over the rooftops. There was no room service, just café au lait and croissants in the morning, and every night we went to a different bistro for dinner. We were really in Paris.

I always swim laps when I'm on location, and while at lunch with Peter Ustinov's wife, Helene, she suggested that I sneak into a health club she frequented on Fauborg St-Honoré, an exclusive street packed with high-end boutiques and embassies. I did sneak in, and it was *gorgeous*.

Then one day while waiting for a taxi, my ego got the better of me, and I started making conversation with one of the nicer-looking attendants. The next day, midstroke, I heard a voice as my head bobbed out of the water.

"Madame! Excusez-moi, MADAME!"

I came to the surface and grabbed onto the side of the pool, looking up at the club manager with all the innocence I could muster.

"I'm sorry, madame, but you will have to leave," he said curtly. *Dammit,* I thought.

"But, why?" I protested, in an effort to keep my favorite luxury Parisian swimming hole.

His answer was simple, to the point, and had nothing to do with the fact that I wasn't a member.

"We do not want any actresses in here."

So I took up walking.

. . .

ALL IN ALL THE TRIP WAS HEAVENLY FOR BOTH CLAIRE AND ME. But then you get back to Los Angeles, and guess what? Life is just how you left it. Not bad, but definitely not Paris.

I started seeing Milton in earnest. "Why are you people so devastated when you see there's something you need to work on in yourself?" he once said to me. "Why aren't you fascinated?" I never left Milton's office without learning something, and I always left feeling better than I did when I arrived. Of course, that didn't mean I didn't cry.

In many of our sessions together I talked about my relationship with marijuana. I began to connect a lot of my unhappiness to the fact that I smoked, even though I enjoyed it with friends in the moment and never smoked when I was working. Still, I always felt guilty. When I could next smoke a joint was always in the back of my mind. I'd think, "Okay, I'm working the next two weeks, but then I'm off for a week. So I can smoke that Sunday night." I know it's popular to say that marijuana is not addictive, but for me it was.

Milton never said much about my marijuana use. Then one day he turned to me in our session and said, "What if I told you, hypothetically, that if you lived a disciplined life for a year, you could have just about everything you wanted?"

I quit smoking marijuana that day.

Milton made another suggestion: Try group therapy.

Group was mind boggling for me. I was blown away by how much I could absorb just sitting there in Milton's office with a group of strangers. But it wasn't without some knocks.

Milton wanted new members to tell their story, get the group's impression, and give their own. Being an actress, I jumped right on this. *Boy, when they hear my story, they are really gonna love me,* I thought. So my first day in group I told the dozen or so group members that I had fallen hard for a married man and that it wasn't working out. I told everyone about Stuart, my guiding light and my rock, and how he had always promised to take care of Claire and me, no matter what. That now he was gone.

Sharing was never a problem for me. Neither was crying. I just put it all out there, adding a modicum of charm to the tears, laughing here and there as I told my story. After I finished pouring out my heart, I waited.

"Lady," one of the group members said, "I don't know you, but you're so full of self-pity, I could've hit you."

"I felt *exactly* the same way," someone else chimed in.

Ouch.

Then a third guy spoke up, saying, "I thought she was charming." Sadly, he never returned to the group. My only fan never came back for an encore performance. But that taught me, once and for all, that people really don't love you for your tragic tales. I also came to see that people's first days in the group were often the most revealing.

The members of our group were fascinating and included enough industry types that we could have seceded from Hollywood. Actors, painters, directors, landowners, and lawyers were drawn to Milton. Along with my darling Jennifer Jones, Milton's group welcomed Robert Loggia, Donna O'Neill (whose family owned half of Orange County), agent Ira Barmak, the spectacular architect Frank Gehry, Jean Coleman, and Joanne Linville along with a couple of civilians just to keep it real. Luana, Morgan, and my friend Anjanette Comer came for a little while. Director Blake Edwards offered Dudley Moore his famous role in *10* in the hall outside of one of our group sessions.

I began to see how much I got in my own way. For example, because I knew Blake had hired Dudley to be in *10*—and I was not yet the evolved woman I hoped to be—whenever Blake came into the room, I could feel myself sit up straight and fluff my hair, hoping I'd be the next group member chosen for a part in one of his films. I had originally met Blake in London years before. He had sent me the loveliest letter after I locked horns with Ross Hunter on the set of *Lost Horizon* and Ross expressed some not-so-nice opinions about me in the press. Blake wrote,

> The trouble with you, Sally, is that you are just not Doris Day for all the Ross Hunters in the world and there is no chance you ever will be. But cheer up. There will always be some grubby, second-rate, noncommercial director like Bob Altman, Stanley Kubrick, Bertolucci, Visconti, Bogdanovich, Lean, Zinnemann, Bergman, Kurasawa, Godard, or Fellini, for a grubby, second-rate, very special lady named Kellerman.

I had no idea I had ever met Blake before group! I didn't remember the letter! I only found it when I started working on the book. Think of it, I wouldn't have had to be nervous around him if I knew he liked me that much. But in group therapy I felt nervous around Blake, conscious of trying to impress him. But because he wore thick, dark glasses, I could never tell what he was thinking.

We were in group, after all, so I had to be honest with Blake and everyone else. I confessed my uneasiness to the whole room.

"Don't worry what I'm thinking of you," Blake said. "I'm too busy worrying about what people are thinking of me."

And Jennifer: Now the thing about my beautiful, adorable Jennifer was that she had her hair done every day of her life. The way that most of us would brush our teeth, Jennifer would have a set-and-style from her favorite hairdresser. One night Milton suggested to Jennifer that maybe, just maybe, if she were more relaxed about her appearance, she might have more opportunities for intimacy in her friendships. Well, Jennifer—the Jennifer of *Duel in the Sun*—did not like that idea one bit. Gesturing angrily to me, sitting on the floor in my ripped jeans with my legs spread and not a trace of makeup, she snapped, "Oh fine, then. I suppose you want me to look like Sally." "You don't have to look that bad," I said, laughing. Ah, Jennifer, my second mom. She tickled me so.

Everyone was drawn to Milton in part because he was more than a therapist; the way he lived his own life was an inspiration. He was legally blind, and his eyesight grew worse over time. This meant that he couldn't read or write, but that never stopped him from learning. When I would arrive at his office door for my appointment, I would hear audiotapes playing—literature, scientific studies, all sorts of stuff. He seemed to keep up with the latest developments in his field.

In 1974 Milton started the Hereditary Disease Foundation, which focuses on finding a cure for Huntington's chorea, the degenerative brain disease. Milton's ex-wife had three brothers with the disease, and when she herself developed it, Milton took care of her even though they were no longer married. Eventually his daughter Nancy would head up the foundation. Milton's remarkable talent at leading groups like ours to psychological breakthroughs carried over to his foundation work, as he encouraged scientists researching Huntington's to brainstorm together. Years later, when he died, the *Los Angeles Times* called Milton "a visionary who led the genetic revolution."

And through all this—his blindness, the sickness in his family—he sought to help others.

"It's all relative," he would say to me when I talked about looks or image. "After fifty years old, character is all that matters." Milton had character in spades.

We all overuse words like "genius" and "brilliant." But I remember how my friend Frank Gehry put it: "I would never have been able to achieve what I did without Milton."

The same was true for me. I always say that I'd met the Queen, but I didn't have any insides until I met Milton. Without Milton I would not be in a marriage that has now lasted more than thirty years. In fact, without Milton I would never have met my husband.

• • •

WHEN JONATHAN KRANE JOINED OUR GROUP IN AUGUST 1978, I had already been working with Milton for about a year. He was a handsome twenty-six-year-old in tight Italian pants, seething with sexuality. I was forty. I was instantly attracted to him but thought, "Oh God, I hope he's not too sick." According to Jonathan's memory, I was sitting on the floor—with my shirt open, braless—and I was crying but stopped the moment I saw him. His inner dialogue went "I got that chick."

Milton always asked newcomers to share their first impressions of everyone else in the group. Jonathan said that he'd "never be afraid" of me. Sometimes I think I should have headed for the hills right then.

In December I was leaving for a month to work on a film. The day I said good-bye to the group I turned to Jonathan and said, "And don't get married." We hadn't yet spent one minute alone together.

When I returned I was invited to a New Year's Day party at Susan Spivak's house. Jonathan was going to be there. I had since learned that he was an international tax lawyer who was instrumental in helping to develop the Wilshire Boulevard corridor. I wore my favorite high-heeled, wooden Candies and a green jumpsuit.

I brought Claire, then about fourteen years old, along as my date. When I saw Jonathan, I pointed him out to Claire. "That's the guy I've been telling you about. I think he's so cute."

Claire took one look at Jonathan and said, "Mom, you don't stand a chance."

Later I encountered Jonathan in Susan's cramped little kitchen, and that's where we spent the rest of the party. We weren't alone. The kitchen was crowded with people shuffling in and out for drinks and snacks. But there was something that kept us there. Maybe the proximity to the London broil on the cutting board—who knows? But I couldn't tear myself away, and neither could he.

The day after the party I had to have one of the many dental operations I have endured throughout my life, the result of so many years of indulging in sugary treats. Whenever I had these procedures, my entire face would swell up. One of my diet gurus, Judy Mazel (of *The Beverly Hills Diet*) told me that yams with cayenne and butter would help me heal more quickly. Susan rang from her office, and Jonathan was with her. They were checking in on me to see how I was feeling. And the next night, as I sat, swollen from head to toe and eating yams, the doorbell rang. It was Jonathan. He was drunk.

"I like you better like this," Jonathan said, looking at the bit of yam dangling from the corner of my swollen mouth. "Less threatening."

That night, after he left, we both broke things off with the people we had been seeing and started dating each other exclusively. For the first couple weeks we took it slow, keeping the romance to just a little kissing. But then the big night arrived.

Jonathan said, "Alright, is this something you really want to do?"

"Yes!" I said. "Yes!"

"Are you sure?" Jonathan kept asking.

"Yes!"

Getting together was not so simple because we were still in

group together. We would have to go back and tell everyone that our relationship—and, therefore, the group dynamic—had changed. Jonathan wanted to be sure the group knew that deciding to take our affection to the next step had been a "shared responsibility," as he put it. And it definitely was. Once we told the rest of the group, everyone was very supportive.

One of the more poignant things Milton said was that we should bring every little thing that bothered us into group and talk about it.

"You might not end up with a relationship," he explained, "but you'll learn a lot about yourself."

That advice sometimes led to some roof-raising arguments in the group. One night Milton calmly said, "You two don't want a relationship. You'd rather be right."

We both jumped in, saying, "No, we don't! We don't have to be right!"

Another problem was that, being an actress to the core, I was still overly eager to share. At one point Jonathan said, "If she shares one more word about her old boyfriends, I'm going to throw her out the window."

That first year Jonathan and I were together, we were absolutely crazy about each other. Still, the first time Jonathan said he loved me, all I could hear was Milton's voice in my head: *Don't tell anyone you love them until you're married for a while and then think about it. Let somebody else do the giving.*

And I had to admit that the more Jonathan liked and loved me, the more I wanted to bolt. That first year I tried to keep things as light as possible, working not to jump to love or marriage. If Jonathan ever said, "I love you," I would say, "Oh, that's great. Hey look! That Edith Piaf film is playing!"

He hated her, it was snowing, and we both had colds, but off we'd go to the show. Jonathan did everything I wanted. To this day Jonathan says that was the worst year of his life, and I say it was the best year of mine.

Jonathan is so different from anybody else I've known—so

smart, so supportive, so encouraging—not to mention drop-dead gorgeous. He has incredible confidence, and at the risk of sounding corny, he is the wind beneath my wings. He's always believed in me, encouraged me, and had faith in my music when no one else did.

For example, I've been blessed with the best voice-over career anyone could ever ask for. But at certain points I've felt overly entitled. I remember once having a radio voice-over gig when it was pouring down rain.

"Oh! I don't want to go," I told Jonathan. "It's only $500, and it's raining so hard."

He said, "Get your hat, get your coat, and get every dime, nickel, and penny you can until you've built yourself an annuity."

That was wise advice. I've had another twenty-five years of fantastic voice-overs.

My mom used to say about me, "Darling, don't you want someone in your corner? Your father was always in my corner."

Jonathan is and always has been in my corner.

Maybe Milton was right, and my newfound, non-pot-smoking, therapy-loving discipline was paying off. I had six films coming out in 1980. And I had Jonathan.

CHAPTER 14

God Laughs While We Make Plans

IN 1980 I SHOT TWO PICTURES AT THE SAME TIME. *FOXES*, directed by Adrian Lyne, which also starred Jodie Foster, Cherie Currie, Randy Quaid, and Scott Baio, and *It Rained All Night the Day I Left*, in which I worked alongside Tony Curtis and Louis Gossett. I went from playing Diane Lane's sophisticated mother in Paris to teenaged Jodie Foster's widowed one in *Foxes*, a coming-of-age story set in the San Fernando Valley. *Rained* was about ambushed weapons dealers (Tony and Lou) in Africa and the conniving woman—me—who hires them. It was definitely worth flying across time zones to work with that pair, and I was nominated for a Genie for Best Performance by a Foreign Actress.

We shot *Rained* in the desert above Eliat, Israel. There was nothing there—not scrub, not a bush, not a rock—just the changing colors of the sky and, occasionally, a Bedouin or two with camel in tow. Sometimes the Bedouins would venture up to where the film's horses were stabled where they would sit and make hash tea for themselves. Each day we shot till about four in the afternoon, when the light began to transform everything in sight. It was beautiful. I'd get back to the hotel by about 4:30, swim laps, take a bath, listen to the sole radio station, which only played classical music, read the *Herald Tribune*, go to dinner with a couple friends, and then head to bed. That was my routine. I loved it.

Because I was supposed to be a top-notch equestrian in the movie, I got a daily horseback-riding lesson from a darling Israeli. One day I looked at some of the Bedouins near the horses and thought about their hash tea. At that point I hadn't smoked grass for nine months. But it wouldn't be smoking if I drank some tea. So I asked my trainer to see if the Bedouins would let me try a cup—and to tell them to put lots of hash in it.

They gave me some. But as we made our way down the hill from the desert above town, I didn't feel a thing.

Dammit, I thought. *They didn't put in enough hash.*

After all, if I was going to cheat, I wanted to feel something. As I headed back to my hotel room, I looked at the ocean outside the bay window at the end of hall. It began to sway, then started surging up and down. The water seemed to rise like a tsunami. I ran into my room, slammed the door behind me, and stood in front the mirror for two hours, sobbing. Then I passed out on the bed until I got a call.

"We're ready for your costume fitting, Ms. Kellerman."

Mumble, mumble, mumble.

A second call came.

"Hi, are you ready for dinner?"

Blah, blah, blah . . .

And then I passed back out.

When I came to, I had to ask myself which was more fun: dinner and a swim or passing out after a good cry? The answer was obvious. So that was the end of my getting-high time.

The last time I had worked with Tony Curtis was on *The Boston Strangler* in 1968. That had been exciting because it was only my second big movie. I'd seen Tony socially every now and then and had really been looking forward to working with him again, until the first day of shooting, that is.

He was standing at the top of a staircase, and he suddenly began yelling, "I hate this piece of crap. I hate everyone on it!"

Thinking I could somehow help by talking to him, I said, "Well, you don't mean me, do you, Tony?"

"Especially you!" he shouted.

I stood behind a row of fake bushes to stay out of his line of sight until he calmed down.

The next time I saw Tony we were out in the desert, and he was yelling at the top of his lungs at the director. There was no place to hide in the desert. Then one day, when were out on location, I suddenly I felt an arm slip around me. It was Tony's.

"Ah, Sally," he said. "Life is really something, isn't it?"

This was the Tony I had first met years earlier—so sweet. And for the rest of the picture, there was no sign of Mr. Hyde. Tony remained as talented and easy to work with as ever. I guessed at the time that he had a substance abuse problem, and indeed, not long afterward I heard that he'd sought treatment. Boy, those addictions can be cunning.

Jonathan joined me on the press junket for *Foxes* in Chicago, his hometown. We were in the hotel with the journalist Irv Kupcinet, Jodie Foster, and her mother. After the interview with Irv we went to dinner and some jazz clubs with him and his wife. When we got back to our hotel room, I was fidgeting around while Jonathan was sitting on the floor watching David Janssen—TV's original Fugitive—on his new show, *Harry O.*

Suddenly Jonathan asked, "Do you want to get married?"

"No!" I screamed. "Not with *Harry O.* in the background!"

So romantic, eh? Just like in the movies. I got up, walked over to the TV, and turned it off.

"Ask me again!" I said.

He did—and I said yes.

The next day I called Irv to give him the news.

"You and your wife inspired us last night, and we're going to get married!" I said.

"I only hope that you'll be as happy as we might have been," Irv replied. To this day that still makes me chuckle.

• • •

WHEN JONATHAN AND I GOT BACK TO LA, WE TOLD THE GROUP our big news.

"We're getting married."

"At my house!" Jennifer Jones immediately said.

Sold. We had already secretly decided that if Jennifer didn't throw us a wedding, we would elope, because at the time we did not have a lot of money. Jonathan was a young lawyer, and I had not, shall we say, kept very good track of my finances. In fact, my new business manager announced that he would never tell me how much I had made over the previous ten years so that I wouldn't feel so bad about where it all went. (Note to young actors: pay very close attention to what you make and how you spend it.)

We decided on a date—May 11, 1980—and ran it by Jennifer to make sure it was okay. "Yes, that's perfect," she said. Only later did we realize that it was the anniversary of her daughter Mary Jennifer's death. Mary Jennifer had committed suicide five years before by jumping from a twenty-story building. But Jennifer didn't want to change the date.

"It will bring light and happiness," she said of our wedding. "And you're like my daughter."

I had the two greatest moms in the world.

My other mom, Edith, had loved Jonathan from the very first moment she had laid eyes on that handsome face. Then she found out he was a lawyer to boot. What more could a mother want? She was thrilled about our upcoming wedding.

"Wear whatever makes you feel pretty" was the only instruction we gave our guests. For my wedding gown I bought a white off-the-shoulder dress for $35 during a weekend trip with Jonathan to Mexico, which I paired with a $250 veil I found at Holly's Harp.

Jennifer planned the wedding perfectly. She and her husband, Norton, had two houses on the beach, connected by a patio lined with mirrors and greenery. One was a single-story contemporary that Jennifer had bought from the director John Frankenheimer. On the day of my wedding, guests arrived at the Frankenheimer house to mill around and drink champagne. The walls were graced with artwork: a Van Gogh in the entryway and, around the corner, a Cezanne and a Henry Moore sculpture of the family. What a difference from my first wedding, when the only festive note was Diana's scarf.

Next door was the Frank Gehry house, which had an entirely different feel: Indian art and stucco. That's where I was, getting dressed with my bridesmaids—my closest friends, Luana Anders, Morgan Ames, Anjanette Comer, Elizabeth Hush, Joanne Linville, as well as my housekeeper, Vivianne Carter—and my maid of honor, my daughter Claire.

My "cousin" David Bennett, who had come out from New York, took charge of upholding the wedding etiquette. David shooed all the bridesmaids out of my room because, according to tradition, I was supposed to be left alone to reflect on my new life. Up until that moment there were so many people around that I felt like I was getting married on TV, as I had so many times in various roles over the years.

The wedding wasn't huge, only about a hundred people. Mark and Joanne Rydell's children, Amy and Christopher, were, respectively, my flower girl and ring bearer. My very dear friend Bud Cort helped Jonathan pick out a tie and gave me huge bunch of calla lilies to carry, each about three feet long. Bobby Walker, Jennifer's son, and his wife, Dawn, were there. Darling Jennifer, who had done so much work to make my wedding day perfect, resisted posing for pictures. She hated being photographed. One day when Claire and I had stopped in to visit, we had found her cutting up these giant, gorgeous images of herself. Claire and I grabbed them and put them in the trunk of my car.

My mother read a lovely poem during the ceremony. Both my

fathers—my dad and my Stuart—were gone, so Milton gave me away. As he began walking me down the aisle, I realized, *Wow! I know these people! I love them! They're not extras!*

This wedding was real.

When David Bennett got ready to launch us on our honeymoon, we realized that he had already sent my mother off with our luggage in her trunk. So we would just have to go to Vegas dressed in our matching white suits—my idea—looking like twins. We were giddy, surrounded by people we cherished and so very happy and in love. We both wanted this. This time there was no crying the night before.

I was about to turn forty-three. Jonathan was twenty-eight. I used to kid him that if he were one day older, he'd be too old for me. But I wasn't entirely kidding when I said, "If you tell me when I'm fifty that you want kids, I'm going to kill you."

. . .

ONE OF THE FIRST TRIPS THAT JONATHAN AND I TOOK AS A married couple was to Monaco, to attend the film festival that had nominated me as Best Actress for my role in *The Big Blonde.* Part of PBS's *Great Performances* series, the film was based on Dorothy Parker's O. Henry Award–winning short story of the same name about a blonde who embarks on a desperate, alcohol-fueled search for popularity and love, faking her way through life and finally ending that life via suicide. Upbeat? Maybe not. But I loved the challenge of playing a character I could really sink my teeth into.

When my agent, Keith Adice, first mentioned the part, I said, "Keith—that's gotta be me." I then proceeded to call Jack Venza, who was producing the series, to tell him the same thing.

"Jack, I gotta do *The Big Blonde.*"

"They really want a star . . ." he began.

"Yeah? That's why I'm calling," I said.

"Well," Jack went on, "we really think of you as more of a Garbo type."

"Yeah, right, I know I'm too beautiful," I replied. "But listen: I haven't lived this long to be this big and this blond and not get this part. Don't hire me. Just let me meet with the director."

So I flew to Chicago on my own dime to meet with Kirk Browning in an airport lounge. We hit it off, I got the part, and I hopped right back on a plane to fly home.

My instinct proved correct. I found it a joy to work with Kirk, and my costar, John Lithgow, was a living doll. And I loved the part—most of the time. We had to learn the tango on set in twenty minutes worth of lessons. *Ouch . . . turn . . . crunch . . . swoon . . . My feet!* We laughed and laughed, despite our flattened toes.

But there were days when playing a wiped-out alcoholic wore on me. Once I called Jonathan, crying, "Jonathan, I have been playing drunk all day, and now they want me to shoot my wedding, and I'm supposed to be feeling good and happy. I can't do it. I'm too tired."

"But you love acting, darling," Jonathan said. "Acting is your life, remember?"

"Fuck you," I said and hung up. He may have been right, but it wasn't what I wanted to hear.

Kirk Browning knew how to handle me too. "You know, Sally," he said one day, "if you spend less time in makeup, you'll have more time on screen." Message received. I found that such a kind way to tell me to get it together and stay on schedule.

My experience on the set of *Serial* was altogether different. Much lighter fare, it was a parody of the 1960s, with a wonderful ensemble cast that included Tuesday Weld, Martin Mull, and Tommy Smothers. It was a lot of fun, except for one big drawback: Bill Persky, the director. He wanted me topless. "No," I said. "I'm not doing it. I'm not going to be topless on camera ever again." I gave at the office.

"We'll just shoot you from the back," he insisted. "You won't see anything. It will be a closed set."

Where had I heard that story before? Sure enough, when I arrived on the set, the camera was in the wrong position.

"Hey," I protested. "You said you were going to be behind me."

"We won't see anything," he said again. "We're just going to pan above you."

So I gave in. How could I have believed him? There I was, sitting topless in the lotus position with Tommy Smothers, and I really thought he was going to pan above me. So when I was finally sitting with the audience at a screening at Paramount, I was shocked to see this slow, almost clinical pan across my breasts. I could have decked Bill, and I wish I had.

Our trip to Monaco for *The Big Blonde* was so spectacular that it eclipsed such indignities. We had two first-class tickets to Europe with lodging in an exquisite hotel. The first night we were too excited to sleep, so we went to a late night bistro, drank red wine, and ate *croques-monsieurs*. We didn't get to bed until 5 A.M. and missed practically the entire next day. When we finally woke up, Jonathan said, "We have to go get a hot dog."

"Oy," I thought. Jonathan had been going on about eating hot dogs and crepes on the streets of Paris. He may have lived there as a student, but I thought myself the more sophisticated of the two of us. But down we raced to the water's edge for a hot dog, which came wrapped inside a hot baguette. It was the most incredible hot dog I ever had. When it came to food, I'd never doubt him again.

But the highlight of our trip was dining with Prince Rainier and Princess Grace. Cheryl Ladd, our fellow guest, was about to portray the princess in the television movie *Grace Kelly*. Cheryl was beautiful—perfectly cast. In the long, formal receiving line Grace greeted Cheryl and me just as one actress to another. She was so warm, embracing us both. At the dinner Cheryl sat next to Grace and I sat across from her, next to Prince Rainier. Unfortunately, Jonathan and Cheryl's husband, Brian Russell, were stuck at the far end of the table and forced to drown their sorrows in lots of French red wine.

Grace was stunning to behold and one of those rare individuals whose vitality and dignity add an extra aura of allure to her already incomparable natural beauty. Never has anyone ever been so aptly named: she truly was "grace" personified.

Prince Rainier was a horse of another color. He was charming in his own way, though he kept telling me about the good-looking stewardesses he'd had on a recent flight. When the evening was over and we couldn't drink or eat or talk anymore, we stood up to leave. Prince Rainier leaned forward to say good-bye, so I leaned in assuming, *Hey—we're in Europe. He's friendly. It's going to be kiss-kiss on the cheeks.*

Apparently I'm not as fluent as I thought I was when it comes to regal body language. As I leaned forward to receive what I assumed would be a friendly farewell, Prince Rainier stiff-armed me, pushing me away and reminding me that he was, after all, a prince.

Not so fast, lady, he seemed to be saying, his arm outstretched like a barricade. *I'm saving that for the stewardesses.*

· · ·

IT WAS HARD ON CLAIRE WHEN JONATHAN AND I LEFT FOR Europe. She had been my traveling companion before he came on the scene. Now that Jonathan and I were married, the trip may have seemed like just one example of the way she could expect to get squeezed out of my life. After all, by this time she had been abandoned more than once, by a parent who had moved away and by another who had grown debilitated and died before she was in her teens. Loss had defined her young life.

Then to top it off, she got me as the consolation prize. It must have been scary to have grown up with a high-strung, singer-actress aunt-mom. On film I may have already transitioned to playing mothers, but figuring out how to be a good one in real life was harder. I was sure that I was screwing up the job, trying to use volume and authority to make up for my lack of experience.

I consciously wanted to be different from my dad—a good man who loved us all but also scared us with his quick temper. We never knew when his wrath would show up. I'm afraid that

I had inherited that temper. Like my dad, I could be unpredict-able—joyful one moment, angry the next—and I could tend to assign equal blame to every infraction, no matter how minor. It took me too long to grow up, and Claire was along for the bumpy ride. It's amazing to me how much she overcame, and with so much grace.

I went to my shrink one day, sobbing that I was ruining Claire with my temper.

"Why don't you quit?" he asked. "That's what your sister did."

I knew right then that I never would. But not quitting doesn't make me a hero; it just makes me a human being. I was the only one Claire had.

Soon she had Jonathan, too. Claire moved home for her last year of high school, and soon after we married he adopted her. I had had her all to myself for some time now, and sharing me would be an adjustment. I hoped I could give her more of a nor-mal, stable family life. God knows, I was going to keep trying.

I thought I had to teach her everything so that her life would work out perfectly. But in the end Claire was the one who taught me. She taught me about love.

•   •   •

THERE WAS ONE THING I WAS LEARNING ABOUT MY NEW HUS-band: when Jonathan put his mind to something, there was no stopping him.

"I like your friends better than mine," he used to say. "I'm going to get into show business and get you the jobs you deserve."

"Right," I thought. "I'll be eighty-two by the time you break into show business."

But Jonathan was serious. We knew Blake Edwards from group therapy; he was married to the gorgeous and talented Julie An-drews. Blake was already well established in Hollywood as a writer and director, with a long line of successful film and televi-sion credits, including *Breakfast at Tiffany's*, *The Days of Wine and Roses*, *The Pink Panther*, and *10*, among others. Now he was working on a film called *Victor/Victoria*, in which Julie would star as a woman pretending to be a man pretending to be a woman—and it would turn out to be another huge hit. Blake liked the studio money but not the constraints; temperamentally, he was very independent and headstrong. Knowing this, Jonathan—who at this point had zero experience in show business—formed a plan to help Blake gain more self-determination as an artist.

To pitch the plan, Jonathan decided to fly to London, where Blake was filming. He booked himself on one of those no-frills, brown-paper-bag-it flights. When he left the house, he was a sight to behold. Handsome? Yes, always. But his glasses were taped together on one side and kept creeping down the side of his face. It was my fault: I had accidentally knocked them off and stepped on them, then faked a good cry as I was laughing so he wouldn't be mad. So off he went, glasses taped and cockeyed. But Blake clearly liked what Jonathan had to say: he flew Jonathan home on the Concorde with a deal. Jonathan began executive producing Blake's films. Jonathan was happy, Blake was grateful, and their venture began to take off. But Jonathan, who is always pushing himself, wanted more. He decided to start his own management company.

This time I believed him and began spreading his name around. The minute someone said, "I wish I had a manager . . ." I would immediately put the person in touch with Jonathan.

• • •

MEANWHILE, I WAS WORKING CONSTANTLY, WHICH IS A LOT TO be thankful for. For a while I was mostly doing television movies. I got to sing in *Dempsey*, the story of the prizefighter, with Treat Williams and Sam Waterston. I had met Treat during my run at the Rainbow Grill and loved working with him. While shooting a very emotional scene, I asked the director for a second take.

"We don't have time," he said. Then, from the other side of the set, I heard someone say, "Don't forget! We have to get that promo." They needed me to do a promo for the film's release in

Europe. For the promo they wanted to shoot me in bed with Treat. I got the same old assurance: "We won't see anything but the side of your leg. . . ."

Oh, time for a promo shot, huh? I thought. *Naked leg?*

"Gosh," I said. "If there's time for a promo shot, I guess there's time for a second take?"

We did the take. Then it was on to the naked leg.

Flashes of *Venus* came back to me as the makeup artist began shading my arms, fingers, and rib cage, working her way around my thong and pasties. Meanwhile, the assistant director was yelling, "Come on, we're running out of time." "It's okay," I kept telling the makeup artist. "I don't need any more shading." But she was a professional—bound and determined to give me body makeup circa 1932.

All shaded, I finally got to the set and climbed into bed in my thong. Treat walked toward the bed, and out of the corner of my eye I saw him drop his underwear.

"Okay, let's go," the director, Guss Trikonis, called. At that moment it hit me that, with Treat naked and me in my thong and pasties, we might as well be fucking. Not that that would have been a terrible thing, but I was married now. So I froze. Much as I wanted to be a team player, I couldn't even go through the motions. So after stalling and wasting everybody's time, I said, "I just can't do it."

"Good," Treat said, and he jumped out of bed, put on his pants, and left.

Luckily, my contract had a "body double" clause, which meant that I could have a stand-in for such scenes. Jay Benson, the producer, told me that I could choose my body-double. The "auditions" were held in his office. Jay and I were both a bit shy. As the women came in, we'd ask, "Where were you born? . . . Oh, lovely. How many children do you have? . . . Uh-huh . . . How do you like Los Angeles? What do you like to eat?"

We asked everything we could think of to avoid having to raise the obvious question, "What do you look like naked?"

The first two women got out without shedding their clothes. The third body double came in and asked, "Where would you like me to drop my dress? Right here, or should I take Sally in the other room?"

"No, that won't be necessary," we said.

If I couldn't even ask what they looked like naked, I certainly couldn't stand having to see them naked.

I don't know who finally picked the body double, but it sure wasn't Jay or me.

Other TV films had me working with lovely people like James Brolin in *Hotel* and Geena Davis in *Secret Weapons*. I was awful in that one, stiff as a board. If I had been cast as a wooden Indian outside a cigar shop, I would have been spot on. During the filming of *KGB: The Secret War* I was, after about thirty years in the business, in my very first shootout. My gun stalled, and they told me to keep shooting. So naturally, I started making gun noises with my mouth: *Pew! Pew pew pew!!*

"Cut!!!"

I had now ruled myself out of gunfights and sex scenes.

Moving Violations was a violation, all right. I played a judge but also wore an S&M get-up. My outfit was so tight and revealing that I had to be tied to my trailer during meal breaks to keep from eating anything. I told the director, Neil Israel, whom I adore, that "I can't run down the street in my heels in this awful outfit." Like all great directors, he said, "Yes, you can. You're a comedian—start running." Another role I resisted but was glad in the end that I did it. When you're a painter, you have the luxury of going through your blue period, a mediocre stretch. As actors, we don't get that break. All our work is on display, in living color, good or bad.

Working with Leslie Nielsen on *Murder Among Friends*, a play filmed for TV, taught me a lot about comedy . . . but not necessarily in the scenes themselves. The morning we started shooting, everybody was hanging out in my dressing room. All of a sudden Leslie let loose with a resounding fart. We all laughed, regained our composure, and moved on. Then another big one ripped free. *Okay…* But on set Leslie just kept farting away, as if he couldn't control himself. At first I felt terribly sorry for him, but by the end of the day I was so disgusted that I never wanted to see him again. It wasn't till I was heading home that someone said, "Didn't you know that was a fart machine?"

Remarkable, I thought. Leslie had timed his "farts" so perfectly and, more importantly, didn't give a damn what anyone thought of him. Now *that's* a comedian—I guess.

In my next film—a feature, not a TV movie—I had a chance to work with the king of comedy: Rodney Dangerfield.

Jonathan found me the script for *Back to School*. I told him I was worried.

"I don't even know if I like Rodney," I said. "How will I get this part?"

When I first met with Rodney and a large group of executives, they wanted me to come back to read for the female lead, Dr. Diane Turner. But we couldn't work out the schedule. So they decided just to offer me a more minor part as Vanessa, Thornton's (Rodney Dangerfield's) shrewish wife, and call it a day.

"I can't do that," I told Jonathan. "I've played that role too many times and I just can't do it again."

"Don't do it," Jonathan said.

So I called my agent at CAA, Mike Menchel, to say that I wanted to read for the lead. "I'll make them see you," he assured me. And he did. I remember walking up the stairs to that meeting, trying to figure out what I could say, knowing that they really didn't want to see me. I opened the door and out of my mouth came, "Good. I see you're all as handsome as I remember. But I gotta go."

Rodney laughed and said, "Readings are hard, aren't they? Did you change your hair?"

"No," I answered. "Did you change yours?"

He laughed again, I read a poem, and that was that. I was cast as Dr. Diane Turner. If all my auditions were as simple reading a poem, I'd get a lot more jobs. Rodney and I had some great scenes:

DIANE: Actually, I'd like to join you, but I have class tonight.
THORNTON: Oh. How 'bout tomorrow night?
DIANE: I have class then, too.
THORNTON: I'll tell you what, then. Why don't you call me some time when you have no class?

Ba-DUMP-bump.

. . .

RODNEY WAS MAGIC. THE DIRECTOR, ALAN METTER, WHO had a real eye for comedy—he discovered Sam Kinison, among others—worshipped Rodney's talent, and rightly so. I had the great fortune to see Rodney perform in Las Vegas. Brilliant. He was like a musician, playing the crowd, winding them up and dropping them down. We were all along for a ride with the maestro of respect.

Rodney was a very serious guy on the set. Every night he'd sit in his robe, writing notes on the script. Alan told me that I helped make Rodney human. That was an easy job—all I had to do was love him.

Back to School was a studio film, and they treated us like gold. Still, Rodney would complain as we drove along in his limo. I remember he was being honored one evening and invited me to come along with him and his date. We had a lot of fun, and when we got back in the car, I said, "You know, Rodney, you're going to have to come up to the house for dinner."

The look on his face said it all: "I'd rather get in a helicopter and jump."

I howled. The rejection wasn't personal. Rodney was a night-club guy. He didn't want to have a nice, quiet dinner with Jonathan and me. He wanted to be in Vegas!

And he was a very good kisser.

For only the second time in my life, I was shooting two films simultaneously: *Back to School* and *That's Life*, which starred Jack Lemmon, Julie Andrews, Robert Loggia, and me.

But *That's Life* represented some major firsts: I was working on it with Jonathan as well my friends Blake Edwards and Julie Andrews—and with the participation of Milton, our shrink. Talk about "all in the family."

"You want to be independent of the studios?" Jonathan had said to Blake, knowing his desire to have more autonomy. "You can make a picture for a million dollars."

"All right then," Blake said.

The film was shot at Blake and Julie's house, making it seem like even more of a family venture, like an extension of the Sunday nights when Blake and Julie would host a group of us for dinner and a screening. Milton had helped Blake develop the script, which was about a woman (Julie) waiting for the results of a biopsy on a weekend when her husband (the amazing Jack Lemmon) is dealing very poorly with his sixtieth birthday. I got to play the ditzy neighbor. Milton was on set too, which was an added pleasure. But it was also a reality check.

One day Milton came up behind me and said, "You're such an asshole."

Well, thanks, Milton. So nice of you to say.

"Why do you have to be the whole wheel?" he continued. "Why can't you be a cog in the wheel? Why can't you realize everybody's job is hard?"

That moment changed me. It seemed I never stopped learning from Milton, and the lesson this time was that I was too self-centered, too focused on *my* life and *my* work.

Milton's words reminded me of what Sydney Pollack had said about working with Meryl Streep on *Out of Africa*. I had met Sydney through my good friend Mark Rydell and had even worked with him for about three minutes back in the 1960s on a pilot that never got off the ground. I had also been in group with Claire,

Sydney's wife, for ten years. Sydney was a great director. There was no subject, from comedy to thrillers to tear-jerkers, that he couldn't do. *Tootsie*. *The Way We Were*. *Three Days of the Condor*. *Out of Africa*. I cherish those three minutes I got to work with him. Such directors are very rare.

What Sydney had said about Meryl Streep was that she was on time, every single day, without fail. She was always prepared, and she never, ever, complained about anything. And they were shooting in Africa. Milton's words underscored that that was the way I wanted to behave, the kind of professional I wanted to be.

So thereafter on the set I became a dream. I told my makeup team on *Back to School* that I was going to be like Meryl Streep. Easy, no worries. One day a production assistant came into the makeup trailer, saying, "Sally's gonna kill me! I called her in at five this morning, and looks like she's not going to work until five tonight!"

The makeup girls said, "You mean Meryl Streep? No, Sally's happy. She loves her trailer. It reminds her of a tract house in the Valley."

What a change!

That's Life was a success, but *Back to School* was a blockbuster. It was HUGE, one of the highest grossing films of 1986.

But you know, what they never tell you when you're working so hard in acting class, doing plays, trying to get into television, and doing some movies is that there is no *arriving*. What is truly difficult in Hollywood—and what really matters—is not achieving success but sustaining it. I know that as well as anybody.

There is no "top" you ever reach. Success just means more hard work, so there is no point to joining the ranks of show business unless you *need* to, unless it's a drive that you can't ignore. Being able to work at what you love is a gift. Jonathan would always say, "Passion first, money will follow." I, for one, am grateful that I still have such a passion for entertaining.

Milton had suggested to me to get discipline and that if I did, I would see results. And I did: a huge uptick in work, a marriage to a lovely man, and, now, two critically and financially successful films. I was excited. Claire was off at college, and my husband was becoming a successful manager. I felt reinvigorated about my career and was looking forward to the next challenge, the next adventure.

God laughs while we make plans.

CHAPTER 15

Two, No Three, Little Surprises

I WAS FIFTY-TWO WHEN JONATHAN SAID HE WANTED KIDS.

This, despite the fact that I had warned him on our wedding day that I would kill him if, when I hit fifty, he told me that he wanted kids.

"I was talking to my shrink about things that have meaning in my life, other than work," Jonathan said. "I know you'll think it's bullshit, but we were talking about kids."

Guess how I replied.

"Well," I said, "lately that's all I've been thinking about too."

We both did a double-take, as if we couldn't believe what had just come out of our own mouths. But it was true: every time I saw a baby or a young child, I just ached.

We were both busy. Jonathan was producing more and more, and he now had his own management and production company, MCEG. And I was about to head off to Chile to shoot a film called *Secret of the Ice Cave*. The two of us decided that if we both felt the same way about kids after I returned from Chile, then we were going to adopt a baby.

I had just come off three films: a cute one called *Three for the Road* with a twenty-two-year-old kid named Charlie Sheen, who was a real joy to work with, then *Meatballs III* with another adorable guy, twenty-one-year-old Patrick "Dr. McDreamy" Dempsey. In *Meatballs* I played "Roxy Dujour," a recently deceased porn star who is working to earn her way into heaven by helping Patrick Dempsey's character lose his virginity. One day Patrick and I went to lunch together, and I remember him innocently asking me how he could get a girl to like him.

I have no idea what advice I gave him, but clearly it's working.

After *Meatballs* I worked on an ensemble picture, *Someone to Love*, with my friend Henry Jaglom. There was no script. Henry simply told me, "You're a movie star who just left her husband. Action!" It was also Orson Welles's last film appearance, and Andrea Marcovicci was in the film as well. It was a memorable experience on a lot of levels.

Chile, however . . . well, if I had known in advance what it was going to be, I never would've gone. But oh, am I glad I did. My first impression was a little rough, to say the least. At our first stop I wasn't even sure what town I was in. "Your suite is right this way," I was told upon arriving, and we made our way to my room. The living room consisted of a wooden board with a little thin pad, which I assumed was supposed to be some sort of couch. From there I headed down the hallway and came face to face with an enormous spider hanging by a single thread of web, right at eye level. In the bathroom I soon learned to focus my attention on the flowered shower curtain rather than the floor, where a team of termites were busy making dust. When Jonathan called to see how I was, I told him I was fine as long as I didn't put my bare feet on the floor.

"I'm sending someone right down there to be with you!" he said.

"Don't you dare!" I answered. "I'm twenty-eight and I'm having an adventure!"

It's important to think young.

When I woke up the next morning in my "suite," I heard birds. *Ahh, birds.* I got up to open the balcony doors. There were birds alright—gigantic black ones diving down to dip into the dirty brown water of the swimming pool to my left, then swooping up to circle the oil derricks straight in front of me.

At our next location some of cast members claimed, "Sally got the good room." *The good room?* No water pressure—it took me a half-hour to rinse the shampoo out of my hair—and some mysterious rug sitting on my bed, hiding God knows what. But I had a great afternoon with fellow actor Norbert Weisser, goofing off on horseback in the middle of the desert in the broiling hot sun. I think that by the time we got back we were hallucinating from the heat.

Next stop: a tiny village, where I was thrilled to have a window in my room. Then finally, at our last stop, we stayed in a giant hotel that looked like something out of *The Shining.*

While I was in Chile Jonathan hopped on a plane to come see me, which he normally didn't like to do while he was working. A film he was producing, *Slipping into Darkness,* was shooting at the time. But he came anyway. When he arrived, I could tell by his behavior—and the fact that he came to see me at all—that he was worried I was having an affair.

I wasn't.

We had a lovely visit, snuggling and talking and continuing our thrilling discussion about having a new baby. So when I got back to LA, we moved into adoption mode.

• • •

I WENT TO LUNCH WITH A FRIEND OF MINE, COSTUME DEsigner Marilyn Vance, to share the news.

"We're going to adopt a baby," I said excitedly. Marilyn leaned right across the table, taking my hand in hers.

"Oh," she said. "I wish you could have twins!"

"Yeah, right," I said, laughing. "*You* have twins and call me later!"

After lunch we walked outside to wait for the valet to bring our cars around. Again, Marilyn took my hand and looked straight into my eyes.

"I'm serious about the twins," she said.

"Don't say that!" I told her. "I feel like they're circling overhead and about to land!" And that's exactly how it felt.

After talking to two adoption lawyers and not feeling right about them, I decided to call Burt Reynolds and his wife, Loni Anderson. I'd known Burt since I was a kid but hadn't been in close contact. I did know, however, that he and Loni had adopted successfully. They agreed to make a referral, but days passed before I heard from anyone. In the meantime I decided to share my decision with my sister Diana.

"I wish you could have twins," she said.

"Why is everyone telling me to have twins? I'm the oldest living mother-to-be!"

Then late afternoon on Sunday the phone rang. It was a woman named Mary Hinton, who Burt and Loni had referred to me. She had news: there was a baby available.

"It was supposed to go to another couple," she told me, "but they've gotten pregnant."

But here was the thing: if we wanted the baby, Jonathan and I had to accept right away. Mary gave me some background about the parents and began telling me what we would have to do to make things happen, but I had already said yes. Before getting off the phone, though, Mary said there was just one more thing I should know.

"It might be twins," she said.

"Jonathan!" I shouted at the top of my lungs. "Jonathan! Twins!"

Jonathan, thinking I had said "friends," yelled back, "Great! We could use some."

Not long afterward Jonathan, Claire, and I were in New York when the call came: the mother was indeed going to have twins. In the ultrasound image they had their backs to the camera, so it wasn't clear yet what sex they were. But Jonathan and I were sure that they were two boys. "Jack and Joe," were the names we'd picked out. But then one day I had had lunch at the Ivy and afterward wandered into a small antique store. I was just browsing, thumbing through some cards on a rack, when one particular postcard caught my eye. It was vintage, a brown tintype card with the image of a boy and girl washing a dog on the beach.

I rushed home to Jonathan.

"We need a girl's name," I said. "It's going to be a boy and a girl!"

And indeed, that's precisely what those two little loves turned out to be. We found the girl's name while looking for a baby nurse. I had called Tom Selleck, whom I didn't really know at all, because I had heard that he and his wife, Jillie, had a nurse they loved. While Jillie was on the phone with me, I heard her call out to her daughter.

"Hanna!"

So there it was. About two months after Jonathan and I decided to adopt, I was the mother of twins: a little boy, Jack, and a little girl, Hanna. It felt like a miracle.

My dear Bud Cort later confessed to me that all of our friends thought I was crazy to adopt at my ripe old age of fifty-two. But so far in my life I'd never done what anyone thought was right or proper. Why start now? Thank God I listened to my inner voice. Happiness and joy arrived in the form of those two, eleven-day-old darlings. I don't think I spoke a word to my children for the first three years of their lives—I sang everything to them.

And I wanted those babies all to myself. Jonathan's stepmother, Bubby, came over the very day we brought Jack and Hanna home. I could hear her from clear across the street when she pulled up in her car.

"Where are my grandbabies?! Let me get a look at those babies!"

My first instinct? *Lock the door!*

Then I wised up and realized just how lucky I was. How blessed my children were to be loved by someone like Bubby, someone who could hang out all day in the playhouse, care for them, play with them, and, when they were older, and teach them skills she treasured, like sewing. I was so grateful to have Bubby and my mother—fountains of support and unconditional love—at my disposal.

I was lucky too that Vivianne Carter, who had been my house-keeper since the days when I was married to Rick, was still with us. She was such a wonderful influence on everyone in her life. Vivianne went to church faithfully every Sunday. Each morning when she awoke, the first words out of her mouth were, "Thank you, God!" She cooked up big kettles of food, which she carted to downtown LA to feed the hungry. She was tall, beautiful, and loud—a proud black Texan, through and through—and my dear friend. Years later, when she got sick, she became just about as big as my finger. But she still had that spunk.

She called me from the hospital: "Sally," she said, in her still-booming voice, "get down here right now before I die."

And I did.

When I got to the hospital, she said, "Tell Jonathan to write me a letter!" And Jonathan did, but Vivianne died before she could read it. I was able to share it with her family at her memorial. In my home her picture and spirit still watch over us to this day.

Knowing that I would need help with the kids when I was on the road, I began looking for a backup nanny to help Vivi-anne. Along came Delmi, another tremendous blessing. In the beginning, when Delmi complained about my unpredictable and "snapping" personality, Vivianne would say, "Honey, tell me about it." I had to laugh. Vivianne had been there, done that, and got the T-shirt with my picture on it.

Delmi was an inspiration in the way she raised her three boys without help, all the while working for my family, then eventually started her own cleaning business. She has made a real success of it. And she has been phenomenally generous and giving to our family. I can't believe I got that lucky twice with the women who helped me take care of my home, of my children, of my life.

When the twins arrived, Claire was already twenty-five and living on her own. She absolutely *adored* Jack and Hanna. I'm sure that when the four of us were out and about, passersby thought she was the mother and I was the grandmother. I didn't care. I knew who I was. This time around I was going to be Mother of the Year. Smooth as silk. Happy every moment. Never a cross word. Just sheer bliss.

I joined a "Mommy and Me" group with some neighborhood moms. I was in my fifties, and they were all in their thirties. I can hardly express how much it meant to me to have a group of women to share experiences with, other moms who were witnessing the same miracles that I was seeing. What a joy it was just to hang out in somebody's yard and watch our kids grow up and play together. There was no rushing—just enjoying the children and each other's company.

Jack and Hanna's childhood was like a second one for me. At first I wanted to mother the kids totally on my own. I taught Jack and Hanna to swim. I made a bowling alley out of cardboard boxes. I crawled under the bushes again, just like when I was small, pretending with my children that we were in a jungle. I set up tents and sleeping bags in the backyard and invited all the kids' friends over to play. I still had my good middle-class values—no cliché Hollywood mom here!

By the time the children were six, I had brought in pony rides, disc jockeys, and inflatable bouncy houses—I did everything to entertain them short of hiring Barnum and Bailey.

But like many of the other mothers in the group, I remained a working mom. In between acting gigs I was working on my music and singing a couple nights a week in a local club. My home office had a big bay window, so I could rehearse and watch the kids play in the backyard. The rule was that they could come in to interrupt me any time—and they did. My keyboardist would play "London Bridge," and Jack and Hanna would take turns singing with the mic.

Though I am sure that was fun, I talked with Milton about how guilty I felt for continuing to work.

"Live your life," he told me. "Make your appointments. If you love the kids, they'll know it. The best thing you can do for them is to give them an example of how to live an independent life."

• • •

A FEW YEARS AFTER THE TWINS ARRIVED JONATHAN AND I DID *Boris and Natasha* together, a film based on the *Rocky and Bullwinkle* TV show.

"Sally would be a great Natasha!" our friend, writer Charles Fradin, had said.

Thus began our underfunded saga, fueled by a lot of creative enthusiasm. I loved being around that.

Charlie was a darling guy who worked on the script with Brad Hall. Charles Martin Smith directed. *SCTV* alum Dave Thomas played Boris. Andrea Martin and John Candy—well, what can you say? All Canadian, all funny, all the time.

I actually had the chance to meet with the woman who had voiced Natasha for the original *Rocky and Bullwinkle* show. When I asked her what Natasha was about, she didn't give me a lot to go on. All the woman said to me was "She loved Boris," in that famous deep, guttural voice. It didn't seem like much, but it was actually an important tip. When I saw the final product in the theater, I actually thought we did pretty good.

I then had the opportunity to work with the wonderful German director Percy Adlon on *Younger and Younger*. I'd been a fan of his since his Oscar-nominated film, *Baghdad Cafe*. Donald Sutherland, Lolita Davidovitch, Brendan Fraser, Julie Delpy, and Linda Hunt were all in the film, and Jack and Hanna were a big hit on the set.

The shoot was a dream. I got to dance with Donald Sutherland in our first movie together since *M*A*S*H**. Julie, then about twenty-five years old, was lovely, and I'm so impressed with her career now as she's grown into a director. Linda Hunt remains one of my favorite people. And my little boy, Jack, played my grandson in one scene, in which he comes running toward me yelling, "Grandma! Grandma!" Talk about heaven.

Best of all, on that film I got a demonstration of how, when you're not demanding love and attention, you can get it in spades.

I was still following Milton's advice about being a cog in the wheel, and my new attitude had been working well. While on the set I was relaxed about costumes and makeup and call times. I would even just sit there when I wasn't working, quietly observing. The results were remarkable.

One day Percy approached me.

"Are you all right? Have everything you need?" he asked.

"Yes, of course," I said. "I'm great."

"Do you know how much I love having you in this picture?" he said.

"Well, that's how much I love being in it," I replied.

Love and support were coming to me—without me having to beg—in my work, from my kids, from my mother-in-law, from my friends. . . . Pretty cool, huh?

Then came my third surprise.

• • •

ALTHOUGH I HAD LIVED MY ADOLESCENCE BEFORE I GOT MARried, it turned out that Jonathan was living his afterward: he was having an affair.

When I first got wind of the marital interloper, I practically opened my own detective agency. No pants pocket was left unturned, no ticket stub unexamined. Back when I had had my affair with a married man—I was single, he was married—it never occurred to me what it would be like if the shoe were on the other foot. Now I knew: It was hellish. I was outraged, betrayed, devastated, humiliated. As ye sow, so shall ye reap.

Jonathan and I separated twice as a result. The first time I was busy, which was probably a good thing. I was doing back-to-back plays, one in Boston and one in Edmonton, Canada. I had just finished a couple films and needed a theater fix as well as some distance from my damaged marriage.

First I did *Who's Afraid of Virginia Woolf* at Hasty Pudding Theatricals in Boston. Larry Arrick was directing. At the outset he nearly changed his mind about using me as Martha, the troubled female lead. But I called and said, "I need to do this. I am doing this. I'm coming. Just get ready."

Now, I didn't know this guy from a hole in the wall, but I knew in my core that the play was just what I needed, for distraction and to keep up my chops. So off to Boston I went, with my little darlings in tow. Rejection was not an option.

Soon the twins and I settled in at the Mount Auburn House at Harvard, along with Vivianne and Bubby. I really enjoyed working with Larry: another director, another approach. The first time we sat down for a reading, he said, "This is not the Bible." He was trying to tell us that Albee's text wasn't the most precious thing in the world. He took the idolatry out of that famous work, reminding us that it was "just" a really good play and that we should approach it like a really good play, instead of "My God! *Virginia Woolf!* A classic!"

Still, it was an honor when the playwright Edward Albee came out to see our production.

After that play Larry asked me to come to Edmonton, Alberta, for two months to do a two-character play called *Lay of the Land*, opposite the lovely Michael Hogan. The play was good, but I spent the entire first act talking to a chair. Now I wanted to work, but a chair? I was so desperate that I would have taken a walk-on role in an after-school special to keep from doing the play. But here I was, talking to an empty chair for an entire act.

After opening night Larry flew immediately to New York for another job. We were left with our stage manager, a very proper Englishman who said the same thing every night:

"And that is the close of the show. Matinee tomorrow at two."

That was the extent of his feedback. No more, no less. We

weren't told if we needed to pick up the pace or whether I wasn't concentrating in the first act. Nothing. So every night after the show, Michael and I held a version of this conversation:

SALLY: I didn't feel so good in the second act.
MICHAEL: No? I thought you were good.
SALLY: Really?
MICHAEL: Yeah.
SALLY: Okay, let's go have a drink.

And the next night, in reverse:

MICHAEL: I didn't feel so good in the second act.
SALLY: No? I thought you were good.
MICHAEL: Really?
SALLY: Yeah.
MICHAEL: Okay, let's go have a drink.

We did eight shows a week. Thank God that, at end of those two months, Michael and I really liked each other. Neither of us knew another soul in Edmonton.

While we were in Edmonton I had the kids in preschool, where they studied Halloween in class for two months and played in the snow. When I didn't have a matinee, I'd be home with them. Mondays we were dark, and though I was half-dead on those days off, I dragged along like a zombie behind them as they rode their bikes or whatever.

See? You *can* have it all.

Then Jonathan, the last person I wanted to see, showed up with some crushing news: Richard Martini, Luana's partner, had told Jonathan that she only had a year to live. I refused to believe him. I finished out my run, then hurried home to face whatever awaited me there.

Luana had breast cancer. She had decided to reject traditional medical care in favor of holistic treatments. Both her mother and her aunt had died of breast cancer, and she had seen what they had gone through. I would have loved to have screamed, "Luana, *please* go to a hospital!" But for the first time in my life I just shut up and supported her decision. She was determined to handle things in her own way.

Doctors warned her not to go to Mexico for an alternative treatment, but Luana didn't listen. She came back crippled. It was so clear that no matter what anybody said, this was what she needed to do. If she was going to die, she was going to do it on her own terms, making her own choices.

From my earliest days as an actor, when we shared secrets in the closet of my first apartments, Luana had always been there for me. I'd call her up crying, and she'd say, "Do you need me? I'll be right there." Now I was grateful to have the chance to do something for her.

That Thanksgiving, when I was just sitting down to dinner with my fourteen guests, the phone rang. It was Luana.

"Sally," she said weakly, "I need you to come clean the cat boxes."

"I have a house full of people," I told her.

"I need you to do this," she insisted.

I was glad. It was a gift that Luana was asking me for such a simple thing. I had longed so much to help her, but how you can help someone so ill? You can't ease the pain. You can't dispel the fear. You can't cure the illness. But this I could do.

So I left my guests to eat their turkey and dashed over to Mar del Vista, where Luana lived. When I arrived at her beautiful little Craftsman home, the cat boxes did, indeed, need changing badly, and I took care of it. I loved having that time with her. When she asked me if I could get her some water, I teased her gently.

"Well, okay," I said, "but you know that means I'll have to touch the glass."

For as long as I can remember, Luana never liked anyone to touch food on her plate—it almost brought her to tears. I always assumed it came from her childhood in foster homes.

To the end of her days Luana was so well loved. By Richard Martini, with whom she had had such a wonderful relationship, by Jack Nicholson, by Morgan Ames, by Charles Grodin, by Jonathan and me. When I told Jennifer Jones about Lu, she jumped on board immediately, providing nurses for Luana so she could die at home. We all helped out as best we could.

One night something woke me up. I opened my eyes and saw Luana lying sideways right in front of me, with a beautiful smile on her face. I looked at the clock to make sure I was awake. When I looked back, she was gone.

I went back to sleep, and a few hours later the phone rang. It was Richard. Luana had died. I was so glad that she had come to say good-bye. She looked so peaceful.

. . .

JONATHAN AND I WERE SEPARATED IN EARLY 1994 WHEN I went off to Paris to shoot *Prêt-à-Porter* with Bob Altman, a film about murder, mystery, and backstabbing during Paris fashion week. The usual suspects, Bubby, Vivianne, and the kids, came along with me. None of them had been to Paris, and I was excited to show it to them. We arrived in February, and Jack asked, "How come there are no trees in Pairs?" But soon spring had sprung.

On the first day of production I stopped by the offices, excited to see Bob. But when I caught my first glimpse of him, he had his back to me. *Oh my God*, I thought. He was so thin and frail. He looked like he was dying. He was having some health issues, he said, but he would take care of everything after we finished shooting.

Then, my first day on the set I was so nervous. *I just did Virginia Woolf!* I thought. *Why am I so insecure?* And I was with Bob, my favorite director of all time. But the cast of that film was stellar enough to intimidate anyone: Sophia Loren, Marcello Mastroianni, Julia Roberts, Tim Robbins, Tracy Ullman, Stephen Rea, Kim Basinger, Linda Hunt, Rupert Everett, Richard Grant, Forest

Whitaker, Lili Taylor, Lauren Bacall—what a lineup. No wonder I was shaking in my boots, standing there on set.

Just then, who should arrive but Sophia Loren, flanked by a posse of press. It was Fashion Week in Paris, and we were supposed to be there watching the shows while Bob filmed us for the movie. Sophia walked up and grabbed my hand.

"Sally, you are my daughter," she said. "Come with me."

I didn't know Sophia at all, but I loved her instantly. She walked me through the maze of photographers (who were really there to shoot her more than anyone). She proved to be as warm and generous and playful as she is stunning.

Once I got over my initial attack of nerves, I loved making that picture. The whole experience of being in Paris with my kids and working with all these fabulous talents—not to mention Bob and his darling wife, Kathryn—was invigorating. Bob's pictures never had big budgets to pay actors, but we all wanted to work with him. He was that brilliant.

And what fun we had. Richard Grant babysat Jack and Hanna, building couch-cushion forts and letting them pretend to be dogs, drinking milk out of bowls on the floor. I had a beautiful suite with blue-and-white étoile curtains and a balcony overlooking the Champs-Élysées that was just high enough so I could see everyone without them seeing me. On my days off I'd walk the children in their double stroller across Paris to Miss Lennen's bilingual school.

Kathryn Altman hosted dinners, serving fried chicken, chili, and potpies so we wouldn't feel lonely away from home. On the weekends there might be thirty of us or ten, but those dinners were always interesting. Other nights, after shooting, a lot of us would duck into this quiet little restaurant we had nicknamed "the Val," with red-checked tablecloths, and I'd sit down to a plate of sautéed spinach, *pommes frites,* and a glass of red wine. Perfection.

During the shoot Bob flew Lauren Bacall and me back from

Paris on the Concorde to take part in an event honoring him at New York's Lincoln Center. Lily Tomlin, Robin Williams, Jack Lemmon, Susan Sarandon, Tim Robbins, Keith Carradine, and others all took the stage to talk about working with Bob and to give him a little good-natured ribbing. Keith Carradine opened the festivities and then I was next. I told a story about Bob and me after *M*A*S*H*, when he asked me to test for a film. Then he said he'd rather hang himself than do the film with me. There was a lot of laughter that night, but mostly I just enjoyed talking about Bob. When I went back to my seat, Jack Lemmon grabbed me and said, "No one will top you tonight." I was riding high. Everyone had great stories, and when they showed clips of Bob's films, it was evident why he was so revered, so loved.

That's what I loved about Bob: his films didn't always rock the box office, but he smiled right through it. A picture would come out, be a flop, and the next week he'd be celebrated at Cannes. Another film would come out, get panned by the critics, and the following month he'd be the toast of Lincoln Center.

"Giggle and give in," he'd always say. Those are words to live by.

. . .

IT WAS HARD NOT FEEL LET DOWN WHEN I RETURNED TO LA. I was worried about Bob, who went in for a heart transplant as soon as shooting wrapped. And I was wondering what the hell to do about Jonathan and my marriage.

Jonathan is smart. He knows when to let me be and when to reach out. Faithful or not, he was deeply invested in our relationship. The minute I said that our marriage was over, he wanted to know how soon he could come home. But the first time we separated I wasn't strong enough to make him understand that I would never again tolerate such a betrayal.

During that period, when there were some unexpected extra people in my marriage, I was so lucky to have Milton. If it hadn't been for him, Jonathan and I never would have stayed together.

I didn't have a natural instinct in my body about how to make a marriage last.

"Fill yourself up!" he'd say to me. "Get to know yourself."

He told me that if I wanted my marriage to endure, I had to be loving and kind, even in the face of all I was feeling.

Are you kidding? I thought. I mean, when Jonathan was away on location with the marital intruder, I was in a state of rage.

"Who is in that room with you?!" I wanted to yell over the phone.

But on Milton's advice, I stayed loving and kind when we spoke. When Jonathan came home, I was still as sweet as I could be. Nothing else had worked—not anger, not recrimination. I kept my cool. But that only lasted so long—I hadn't grown that much. One more infraction and suddenly the kind and loving bullshit took a backseat to fury and hurt.

"You sonofabitch!" I railed at him. "I know this, and I know that, and if you're not completely honest with me right now, I'm gone!"

With that, I jumped in the car and tore off, going about one hundred miles per hour. Jonathan called me in the car.

"Come home!" he said. "Please! I'll talk to you!"

When I got there, he told me how floored he was that I had been so loving to him, despite what I knew. My behavior surprised him so much that he was moved to apologize and to regret what he'd done.

Oh my God, I thought. *Milton! It worked!*

But Jonathan still hadn't gotten whatever it was out of his system. The second time he dabbled outside our marriage, it was right in my face. In fact, it was in the newspaper. He was seeing somebody in the business, a name people knew, and it turned out the other woman wanted to get a house with him. I was through.

Of course, I rushed back to Milton.

"Okay, Milton," I demanded. "What? I'm supposed to be sweet now?"

Milton said, "Well, if I were you—and I'm not and I'll back you in whatever decision you make—I would have enough self-esteem to separate."

So Jonathan and I separated again.

It's funny. Whenever an actor's marriage hits a bump in the road, the media blames Hollywood. They mock the fleeting marriages of the Kim Kardashians but never bother to praise the longevity of the Christopher Plummers or the Jeff Bridges or the Martin Sheens. I don't know if it's Hollywood's fault when show business marriages don't work. That seems like an excuse. Maybe people living elsewhere in the world don't have the same distractions and temptations that we do. I don't know whether it's any harder to make a marriage last here than it is in Vermont. But I grew up here, and Hollywood is all I know.

I don't know how easy it is to be married in Seattle.

CHAPTER 16

Lost and Found

OFTEN LOSS CAN REUNITE PEOPLE WHO ARE ESTRANGED. I didn't know if it would happen to me.

I am so grateful that my mother lived until the twins were seven years old. Fifteen years after dad died, she married a lovely man named Howard Benjamin. They were together thirteen years and having a wonderful time until she had a ministroke. (I love the way they try to make those sound less serious than they are.) Nevertheless, Mom rallied from that. I'd bring Jack and Hanna over to visit her at the assisted living center, and they would wander the halls, stopping in everyone's rooms, leaving smiles in their tiny wakes. But then another, slower decline began for Mom, and soon we were having birthdays in her room instead of out at a restaurant. She just kept getting tinier and tinier, and she was only five-foot-two to begin with.

Toward the end she was in wheelchair, someplace I never thought I'd see her. I spent a whole day at Macy's one time, trying to figure out what would be comfortable to wear for a five-foot-two woman in a wheelchair. I was so proud of the way she was handling the confinement, and I found her some pretty things she really liked, doing for her what she had done for me when I was little.

Mom was always in such good spirits. I slept in her room sometimes, and I sang to her, just as I used to in the backseat of the car. On one of the last nights of my mom's life my sister Diana and I went to Marie Callender's and brought back a chocolate meringue pie to share with her while sitting on her bed as we talked about all our happy memories. Mom and chocolate. Some things never change.

Mom listened to my troubles with Jonathan and surprised me by confiding, "If only I'd ever had the courage to walk out on your father just once . . ."

As Mom's days drew to a close, I phoned Jonathan in New York to tell him. He went straight to the airport and flew out to Los Angeles. He was shocked by the agony she was in when he saw her. Mom had a "do not resuscitate" order, but the nurses were leaving her gasping for her last breaths.

"DNR doesn't mean she has to suffer!" Jonathan yelled, and they finally gave Mom the oxygen she needed, allowing her to pass quietly.

Mom had always said that she never wanted to be a burden to her children, and she never was. Instead, she was truly generous, spiritual, full of life, warm, and humorous right up until the very end.

So many of the things she said throughout my life come back to me on a daily basis.

Everything we need is within us . . .
Nothing is too good not to happen . . .
We are surrounded by love. . . .
You are God's perfect child . . .
Ingratitude is the back door through which all our blessings
    escape . . .

She had about a hundred more sayings, and Jonathan has heard them all. One that has come to me over and over while writing this memoir: "Darling," she would say to me whenever I overshared, "do you have to tell everything you know?"

Yes, I do, Mom, at least where you're concerned.

I wish she could hold this book in her hands, to read it and know how much she meant to me in her unassuming delightfully inspirational way. At five-foot-ten, I wish I were half the woman my five-foot-two miracle of a mother was. Maybe someday I will be.

• • •

AFTER MY MOTHER'S DEATH JONATHAN AND I GOT BACK TO-gether. Yes, I endured the humiliation of his extracurricular activities. I know some people thought of me as a woman who should have walked. "One disrespectful incident, and I would be out of there," you hear people say—usually these people have no experience at all with infidelity. I'm certainly not the only person in the world who has stayed in a marriage rocked by an affair. Although in the end Milton thought maybe I should get a medal. In any case, my marriage has survived.

My decision to try again with Jonathan began as an experiment. He always said he loved me and I believed him. And I've always wanted to see what happens if you let love grow. Marriage can be painful, it can be angry, it can be funny, loving, and hot. It can be all those things at once. And in the end the experience of laughing, fighting, making love, talking, arguing, and seeking counseling ultimately deepened our relationship. On the good days—and there are more good than bad—I'm so glad we stuck together.

Jonathan and I are so well suited for each other. He said he likes me a little needy. Well, honey, you're in luck! He believes in my music—always has. He doesn't let me wallow in self-pity. I remember that when I used to ask Rick if I looked good, he'd get frustrated and say, "Stop asking those rhetorical questions!" When I ask the same thing of Jonathan, to this day—even if he isn't looking at me—he says, "Sure honey, you look great . . ." My kind of guy.

Of course, more recently, when I've asked him if I look too thin—which at my age makes you look a lot older—he says, "Darling, I have just spent the last twenty-five years assuring you that you are not too fat. I'm not sure I can spend the next twenty-five years telling you that you are not too thin."

Jonathan has said, "I'm so proud of you having a great life in spite of me." In truth, he's a major part of why I have such a good life. However, we're all responsible for our own happiness. If something isn't working, we'd better start by looking at our part in it.

Younger people sometimes ask me how to stay married thirty years. Well, you're either stupid or you love each other. But one thing is for sure: both people really have to want to make it work. Now, with all those years behind us, Jonathan and I have just about seen it all and, because of that, truly know why we want to be together.

• • •

IN 2000 JONATHAN AND I RENEWED OUR WEDDING VOWS, again at Jennifer Jones's house. We had planned to host the ceremony ourselves, but we were a little disorganized. When it was only a week away, we still hadn't finalized our plans. So we decided instead to have Jennifer join us for a lovely dinner, to commemorate our marriage at her home.

Well, Jennifer wouldn't have it.

"Absolutely not!" she said. "You had a big wedding, and you'll have big renuptials too."

Within a week she had her entire place redone and florists on call. The vows renewal was going to be beautiful.

Jonathan and I quickly got on the horn to invite people. Oddly enough, everyone was free: the Altmans, Milton, Marilyn and Allen Bergmans, the Rydells, my sister Diana and her partner,

Gloria, Claire, Jack and Hanna, Morgan Ames, Bob Esty, Sydney and Claire Pollack, Henry Jaglom, James Coburn and his wife, Beverly, and so many other close friends, many of whom were there the first time around.

On the big day I got dressed with Jennifer. She was sitting at the makeup table with three magnifying mirrors. I said I didn't know how she could stand it, all that reality staring you in the face.

"Honey," she said, "I do the best I can, then I walk away."

Thanks for the tip, Jennifer, because now I'm the one with the three magnifying mirrors.

The vows renewal was one of the happiest, funniest nights of my life. Hanna was rushing around, grabbing hunks of the centerpieces and handing them to my "old" bridesmaids, the ones who were in my first wedding. Bob Altman, Mark Rydell, and Henry Jaglom were there, directing the action. Milton, who saved our marriage, again walked me down the aisle, prompting the joke, "Look! Milton's still trying to give her away."

The ceremony had everyone in stitches. Jennifer had lined up a federal judge, Matt Burn, on short notice. When he forgot the words to the ceremony, Jonathan had to help him out. Hanna and her best friend, Vanessa, Lorna Luft's daughter, began pelting us with roses, and all I could think was, *Oh no, I'm going to have to replace all the carpeting in Jennifer's house.* Well, I didn't have to. At the end of the evening Jonathan and I sailed home on a cloud with the kids asleep in the backseat. What a blast!

· · ·

I AM SO PROUD OF OUR LOVE AND ALSO PROUD OF THE SUCCESS Jonathan made of himself in his second career. "Passion first and the money will follow," he always said. And it had followed for him, that's for sure. After working with Blake Edwards and starting MCEG, he got into distribution. Our friend Marilu Henner introduced him to John Travolta. The two really hit it off, and

Jonathan began managing John's career and producing a string of hit films, like *Look Who's Talking, Face/Off, Phenomenon, The General's Daughter, Michael, Swordfish*, and others.

Jonathan produced *Look Who's Talking* for $7 million, and it made $500 million worldwide. Actually, from the minute Jonathan started working with Blake Edwards, our lifestyle started changing. At first, when the money began rolling in, I actually got depressed. Money—real money—made me uncomfortable.

"I don't want to be an alcoholic!" I wailed at Jonathan one night. I had this image in my head of self-destructive behavior brought on by idleness and wealth. I'd think of Palm Beach and all the huge mansions that line Ocean Boulevard, and I would imagine well-to-do drunks lying in their foyers—all those money-eyed drunken wives I had played in my early days on television.

Needless to say, I got over my distress. We didn't go hog-wild on luxuries but instead started upgrading what we had.

We asked Frank Gehry, whom we knew from ten years of group therapy, to come in and do our home. Years earlier, in group, Frank was always worried about going bankrupt at any minute, always questioning whether he was an architect or an artist. Then Frank went on to become one of the most famous architects in the world.

The first time he came out to our house he did not seem all that impressed. "This is how you live, big movie star?" he said.

That made me laugh. Then I started to tick off the changes I hope to make.

"I'd love a balcony outside our bedroom," I began.

"You can't have that," Frank countered.

"I've always wanted a family room off the kitchen," I went on.

"You can't have that either," he said. "But here's what you can have . . ."

Frank began making drawings and models, showing us all the best possible renovations. He was there for what seemed like forever, but we ended up with a rooftop garden, a screened-in porch off the master bedroom, a master bath with a big window on the curve of the street, measured so precisely that I could take a shower without giving everyone the Hot Lips show.

Ultimately, Frank changed everything in the house. He even took out my one-of-a-kind, custom-made, Harrison Ford book-cases. In the new old house of my dreams, the screened-in porch off the bedroom is my favorite; it's like a tree house. When I can relax for a minute, I sit out there and read and look out on the hills. After working with me for two years, Frank decided he never wanted to do another house again. So, actually, I'm respon-sible for his success. And P.S., we're still friends.

• • •

DESPITE OUR NEW INCOME, I CONTINUED ACTING, OF COURSE. I love working, plain and simple. Doing *Boynton Beach Club* was a wonderful experience with a fabulous female director, Susan Seidelman. It also gave me the chance to work with so many gifted old friends, like Dyan Cannon, Joe Bologna, and Brenda Vaccaro, as well as meet new ones, like Len Cariou.

I also got more serious about my longstanding voice-over career, doing Sears, JC Penney, Volvo, Cadillac, Mercedes, Woolite, and more. Voice-overs are fun when the copy is good—it all starts with the writing. It was fun to work with documen-tarian Ken Burns on *Not for Ourselves Alone: The Story of Eliza-beth Cady Stanton and Susan B. Anthony*. When Bob Altman did his pilot for a television show based on Bill Gates, he featured a talking computer with a screen sporting a pair of big red lips—my lips, my voice.

Funnily, I once got a call from Lena Horne's people, saying they were going to sue me for using her voice. Here I thought I had been using my voice all along, from moaning in ecstasy for Quincy Jones to singing the praises of Hidden Valley Ranch. (I still remember Howard Stern calling me during a radio broadcast, saying, "Sally, come on. Say 'Hidden Valley Ranch' just once.")

Over the past forty years I've had an amazing ride that's still going strong. Not long ago I voiced Principal Stark on the FX animated series, *Unsupervised*. And for the first time, after hawking everything from Woolite to Hidden Valley Ranch, my voice-over work was recommended for an Emmy.

At one point the *Wall Street Journal* called me the industry's most sought-after female voiceover artist. That makes me proud. But the voiceover field is getting crowded today. When my friends' children come up to me to say, "Sally, I'm taking voice-over lessons," I want to tell them, "Beat it, kid."

• • •

THANKS TO JONATHAN'S ADDED INCOME AND THE SUPPORT OF friends, I also had the time, money, and confidence to invest in music, my serious passion. The same year we celebrated our re-nuptials, Bob Altman hosted a show for me at the El Portal Theatre in North Hollywood. Hanna bought me a glass figurine and a pink lipstick she thought would match my suit, and Jack wrote me a little note that makes me weepy to this day.

Dear Mom, You're the best mom because you've reached your goal.

Both kids have been so supportive. One day I told Hanna I might have to be in and out of town quite a bit because of some music commitments.

"I don't care if you're gone for a whole month, Mom," she said, "because I know you love it."

In the 1970s, when I was trying to break into music, actors who sang were not popular. It can still be a struggle for actors to cross over unless they're doing Broadway or singing on prime-time television. But during the slow times my music has kept me from being a victim of "having to be hired." As long as I can pay the piano player and I can sing, I'm okay.

There have been bumps in my music career, for sure, but a lot of excitement too. In 2001 I did a show in Manhattan at Feinstein's at the Regency that got panned by Stephen Holden of the *New York Times*. In essence, he said I couldn't carry a tune, had no musicality, and I was desperate to seem young. When Bob

Altman saw the review, he called me from London, where he was shooting *Gosford Park*. "Even if I didn't know you," he said, "I'd know there isn't one word of truth to it."

My next performance, the night after the *Times* review, I caught sight of Elaine Stritch—not just an actress but also an incredible singer to boot—in the audience. After the show, as I was greeting people at the door to my dressing room, Elaine stuck her head in.

"Kellerman, I saw that review in the *Times*," she said. "I knew that the woman whose body of work I'd known all these years couldn't be the one that the reviewer was talking about. And I was right."

Then she turned around and left. I'd always liked her. Now I loved her.

But a *New York Times* review carries a lot of weight. The club's management now wanted to cut short my run. I was in my hotel room packing to leave when I got another call. It was the critic Rex Reed, asking if I'd seen his review. I hadn't.

"You can't leave!" he said. "My review just ran, and this is the week that everyone will be coming to your show!"

As I was talking to Rex, my assistant at the time, J. J., was literally rolling my luggage out the door, and the concierge was ringing to say that the limo was waiting downstairs. I got off the phone with Rex, but the whole way to the airport I kept telling J. J., "I don't want to go."

I called LA to find out when Michael Feinstein's manager, who supposedly ran the club at the Regency, was flying into town. His office said he was arriving around 5:30, but they wouldn't tell me what airline he was flying. It was 3:30 P.M., and I had a 5:00 P.M. flight to LA. I called Jonathan.

"Jonathan, I don't want to leave."

"Well, then don't," he said.

I told him that my luggage was already heading down the conveyor belt. "Tell J. J. to go get it!" he said. So I sent J. J. running after it. He snagged it just in time, and we went and booked a hotel room at the airport. We got hold of all the LA–NY plane schedules and found the one landing closest to 5:30.

Bingo!

When Feinstein's manager got off the plane, I was waiting.

"Oh hi, Sally," he said. "What are you doing here?"

I laid it all out. Why have the club dark, especially with Rex Reed's great review, and so on. Finally, he told me, "Get in the car."

I got all resettled at the Regency—just hours after checking out—and the phone rang. I was getting only Friday and Saturday night, not my entire contracted run. Well, what the hell—I was going to make those nights count.

I called all my New York friends, like Dan Aykroyd and his wife, Donna Dixon. They all turned out and packed the place. There were standing ovations, crowd whistles, and, more importantly, those shows were *fun*. J. J. and I were very proud of ourselves. I hadn't been desperate; I was determined. It might have taken me a long time to learn the difference, but I knew now.

Closer to home, I played the Roxy for a year, singing standards, thanks to Lou Adler and his son, Nic, who now runs the legendary club on my beloved Sunset Boulevard. Then I did three years at Genghis Cohen, bringing in new material all the time. No scripts, no rules, no way to make a mistake—Bob Altman's influence. We called it the "antishow," and it was a blast. If I dropped a lyric, so what? You can always go see a show where the singer knows all the words.

These shows were all about getting free and finding myself in the music. Industry people—Val Garay, the Grammy-winning producer of Kim Carnes's number-one hit "Bette Davis Eyes," and performers like James Taylor, Linda Ronstadt, and Bonnie Raitt—started coming in to Genghis Cohen when I sang. I was also working with legends Jerry Leiber and Mike Stoller. Mike and Jerry were there for the beginning of rock and roll, the songwriting team behind hits like "Hound Dog," "Stand by Me," "Jailhouse Rock," and "Love Potion Number Nine." Their contributions to music were immortalized in the Broadway play *Smoky Joe's Cafe*. I was a little intimidated, to say the least, but I felt so lucky to be able to work with them.

Over the years I've had the good fortune to work with great talents and legends in the business: Along with Jerry and Mike, there was Mike's wife, the legendary pianist and harpist Corky Hale. They've always been so supportive and special to me. Not to go on endlessly, but music is so important to me that I just have to thank people who helped me get this far: Kenny Vance, still a big hit out on the road singing doo-wop, would take me into a studio in the middle of the night so I could work; and Richard Perry, who had to hear every note of every song I ever sang to give me his critique. So shoot me, but I have to say one more time: I would have never been a singer if it hadn't been for Bob Esty.

Everyone has something to offer if you're willing to listen. Take singing teacher George Griffin, who once told me to take a "surprise breath" while I was singing: "Like you're saying 'hi' to someone," he explained.

I gave it a shot. It worked.

I'm in the mood for—GASP! Oh, hi!—*loooove . . .*

I got an invaluable lesson in performance from Moon Unit Zappa, who is a talented director and also an author. In 2004 I appeared in a short film she directed called *Ugly*. I'd known Moon most of her life. At one point the Zappas lived down the street from us and went to school with Claire.

At one of my shows in Glendale, Moon heard me ad lib something along the lines of "I'd love to pay the band, but in lieu of that, could you just applaud . . ."

Later she told me, "This thing about paying the band . . . Would you rather be thought of as somebody who couldn't pay the band, or would you rather be thought of as the Dalai Lama come to Glendale?"

Out of the mouths of babes.

Hal David, my dear darling friend, was another source of love and constant support in regard to my music. He showed insight (not surprising) when he insisted I work with musician Chris Caswell. Chris wrote many good songs, and along with Bob Esty, helped me put together a selection of songs. Then I had the pleasure of having my CD, *Sally,* produced by the brilliant Val Garay, whom I adore.

After hearing my CD, Barry Manilow sent me the nicest letter, which I cherish to this day. Burt Bacharach called me to say he listened to the CD. I thanked him. And he said, "No, I wanted to listen to it because I know how important music has always been to you."

I still remember when I heard the CD for the first time. Val played it for me.

"Is that who I am?" I asked, hearing myself really *sounding* like myself.

Singing is so much fun, such a rush, once you find your real voice. A little jazz, a little blues, a little rock and roll. Breaking free.

• • •

THINGS WERE GOING SO WELL WHEN THE MONEY I HAD finally gotten used to started to disappear—and not because I was an alcoholic languishing on the floor of a Palm Beach mansion.

I've never known anyone as driven as my husband, Jonathan. He went to St. John's College, reading all the classics in the languages they were originally written. He's a genius, winning scholarships, fellowships, graduating from Yale Law School. Once he turned his hand to show business, he achieved tremendous success as a manager and producer. He had his own company—which went public—and produced over forty feature films. He won a Hollywood Visionary Award and a People's Choice Award, just to name a few of his many achievements.

But after so many years of working nonstop producing and managing—oh, and teaching at UCLA too—he told me that he needed a change.

"I can't do this anymore," he said. "I'm an intellectual. I have to let my mind wander and follow it."

With that, he retreated. He holed up in his home office for almost three years. Not that he wasn't busy. He wrote a textbook about the movie industry, he wrote scripts, and he mapped out his plan for the future. Still an achiever, he kept teaching movie production, and he set up a graduate film school in Florida. As always, he kept setting goals for himself and meeting them.

One day he said, "I have a new financing idea." Then came the first-class trips to Europe, to Germany and Cannes, all in pursuit of financing. We were investing in my music, we were investing in Jonathan's new venture, and the kids were still in school. But it took us a while to grasp that, though we were living the same lifestyle, we weren't earning quite the same as we had in the past. To make matters worse, one day we turned around, and the entire American economy had bottomed out. And so did we.

When the money is gone, and you're down to a song . . .

That's a line from one of my favorite numbers, one that I perform in my show. And that's where we were suddenly: down to a song.

We know we're not victims. The whole world is hurting. What this period of our lives has given me is a compassion for those who have always struggled financially. Though I had been young and broke, I had no idea what being grown up and broke felt like—until now. But not to worry, nothing has ever stopped my husband. We're already back on our feet.

From my friends I've learned about *real* giving, real thoughtfulness. People thinking beyond themselves. It quickly became clear how truly lucky we were when our friends lined up to help us. Our friends Laura and Larry Worchell really did save our lives. At one point we needed help, and when I called Laura to ask about a loan, she reacted as if I was calling to borrow a cup of sugar. Because of her giving spirit, there was no embarrassment, no shame. My friend Esther Rydell—who still gets a call from me every day of the week—I relied on her for so much. How do you cook this? What do I put in that? "I have a brisket for you . . . I always have a twenty here if you need it," she would say to me. So many little, thoughtful, wonderful gestures. We've been blessed with so much generosity. "What do you need? Here take this. Here, let us pick this up for you." The kindness that's been shown to us is beyond words.

We spend more time at home now instead of going out. When it is time to cut loose just a little, we say, "Let's splurge! Let's go to El Pollo Loco!" We have a full meal for $3.99 and feel like we've been to the palace. We are learning all over again how to have cheap fun.

Listen: money doesn't make you happy. But there's no denying it makes things easier. Throughout my life, however, I've learned more from the downs than I have from the ups. I've learned I have friends and even acquaintances willing to go above and be-yond for me. My relationship with Jonathan has deepened. My children have rallied and grown up from this experience. Jack bought his own car, and Hanna's finding her own way. They're both discovering their own talents, facing their own challenges. They are learning, as we have, that you make your own happiness.

So far we've made it through. We have survived. Boy, surviving sure does put a spin on things. *If this experience doesn't get me out of myself and my petty woes*, I think, *I'm doomed*. But all anyone has to do is go out into the world for a second to see that if you have a roof over your head and people who love you, you're doing just fine.

CHAPTER 17

The Next Chapter

HAS HOLLYWOOD CHANGED?

When Jack and Hanna were little, around five or six, they'd ask me, "Mom, what was it like in the olden days?" I said, "I don't know. I wasn't there." But that wasn't quite true. I was there.

I think of the way they lit Greta Garbo, Ingrid Bergman, and Joan Crawford in the films I saw as a little girl. As a kid, I looked up to them in awe. I didn't want to know what Garbo looked like when she was shopping for groceries. I didn't want to see close-ups of any cellulite Crawford might have on the back of her legs. But today that's all the supermarket magazines focus on. Magazines are always trumpeting stories like, "How I got my body back" instead of "How thrilled I am to have my baby."

See what stars look like without their makeup!

Look how hideous they look on the beach!

"Celebrity," whatever that means, has changed. So has society. Sometimes it seems as if audiences don't want celebrities to be larger than life anymore. The paparazzi have created an atmosphere in which everyone is watching and waiting with bated breath for someone to fail. I certainly do feel grateful I grew up in a time before the tabloid madness and the Internet. We had the freedom to live with nobody looking.

I remember rolling down Fairfax Avenue in a shopping cart pushed by Bob Sampson, my friend from Jeff Corey's acting class, both of us with television and film roles under our belts, and there wasn't a camera in sight. You could go to work dressed like a bum and nobody was the wiser. So I was spared the twenty-four-hour entertainment news cycle and paparazzi at every corner, I'm lucky. I have good timing in life. If *M*A*S*H* had come out today, I probably couldn't go to El Pollo Loco without pictures landing on the Internet of me and a burrito.

I honestly don't know how people who work in this town have adjusted to this new level of intrusion—or whether they still manage to have private lives at all. I loved the little picket fence of my Cape Cod house, which was all I needed to keep me and my children safe from the world.

I've always gotten star struck—still do—so I understand the fascination with celebrity. I remember one night when Jonathan, John Travolta, and I were going to a party. John and I were so excited. Why? *There would be a lot of movie stars!* We were thrilled about seeing people we admired on screen. It didn't matter that we were in the same business.

Another night, when I was having dinner with Jonathan and John, a crowd of fans gathered waiting for John to sign autographs. John was gracious and charming, and after signing for a while, he said, "Okay, I've got to go now. Thanks."

Cut to the very next day on Venice Beach. Jonathan and I were walking along when two guys asked for my autograph. "All right," I sighed, and signed half-heartedly. As we walked away, Jonathan turned to me and said, "Right, Sally. Be mean to your fans. You have two."

I've grown up a lot since then, and I love my fans. I adore getting to meet them, signing autographs, and, now, interacting with them on Twitter and Facebook. It's very touching, and it's a responsibility. And without fans, you've got *bupkis*, kid. It's that old giving-back thing that I'm still learning about.

Sometimes, it's not just the bigness of Hollywood—sweeping back lots, soft lenses, and stars up on pedestals—that I miss, but the smallness of Hollywood too. That neighborhood feeling. From the front porch of my Cape Cod house, I'd see Cass Elliot of the Mamas and Papas drive by, slow down in her big Cadillac convertible, top down, to say hi. After she died, Ringo Starr bought her house. Talk about a thrill. I remember watering the plants in the front yard when, lo and behold, Ringo himself pulled up in his convertible. He invited me to stop by sometime. (I never did—I was too chicken.)

That kind of neighborliness doesn't really happen anymore. Now we all have tall, prickly hedges and gates around our properties. But when I open my gate, there's still a neighborly face to be found.

It is still so hard for me to let go of saying, "MGM," no matter how many times I catch myself. I used to love driving onto that lot, feeling welcomed into another world the minute I passed through the gates. There was a little parking area, simple and accessible, before any security, any barriers. Now it's the Sony lot; you park three stories underground, and you'd better have a passport and your running shoes to get where you need to go.

I look back with such fondness at my television years at Universal, wandering past the bungalows, bumping into people I hoped to see. It felt like a real community, dedicated to doing the work we all loved.

Even events like the Cannes Film Festival used to be more intimate. When we went to Cannes for *M*A*S*H*, I wore a Levis skirt with a multicolored rope belt and a red bandanna around my head. When we won the Palme d'Or, I switched to a pretty yellow long-sleeved gown—but I still kept the red bandanna. The lobby of the Hotel Carlton had these big comfy couches. Lunch was mellow at the beach club, the patio serene. It was all warm, wonderful, and French. Now the lobby of the Carlton Hotel is a place of business. No couches—just signs and movie posters.

In those days there was a "petite" Grand Palais with 500 people. Today, the Grand Palais has 150,000 fans lined up for blocks. Cannes used to feel like it was all about the films and the fun; now it's just about your next deal.

. . .

LA. I'VE LIVED HERE ALL MY LIFE. I'VE DONE ALL MY RISK TAK-ing, heart breaking, lovemaking, and mistake making here, right in my own hometown. I still live in the house I've been in for the last forty years, just twenty-five miles from where I was born and raised. Though I've stayed in the same place, I've traveled miles in terms of growth and learning. It seems that's what life is all about.

Someone said that you can do anything you want in life as long as you're willing to take the consequences. Life is definitely more challenging when you're not doing what's expected or what seems like the strategic, smart thing to do. But ultimately, it's your life, so the choice is up to you. So I will go ahead and advo-cate following your passion.

If I hadn't done that and lived my own way, mistakes and all, look at all the experiences I would have missed out on: singing in honor of Mike Stoller and Jerry Leiber, who passed away not long ago, at Carnegie Hall alongside Natalie Cole and Donald Fagen. Performing at the Music Center in LA. Singing at shows with Paul Williams, Ben E. King, James Ingram, and Patti Austin. Not long before she died, Rosemary Clooney came up to me after a show and took the time to tell me that she enjoyed my perfor-mance. I was thrilled to hear that from her, because I'd listened to her all throughout my childhood. Those moments were possible because I followed my passion and somehow didn't worry about the consequences.

. . .

ONE NIGHT IN LA I EVEN GOT TO PERFORM WITH DAVID GATES from the band Bread, my imaginary serial killer–cult neighbors back in the 1970s. Funny how life sometimes comes full circle.

My family—Jonathan, Claire, Jack, and Hanna—inspire me to

keep chasing my passions. Now when I pass a mirror, I think about all my good fortune, all the dreams that have come true for me, and, luckily, all the ones I have left to work on. Like I say to my husband about my music, "Honey! I'm almost there. All I have to do is live."

Because my world hasn't changed much geographically, I am surrounded by reminders of the past, and I love this. There's not a street that I drive down that doesn't hold memories for me. Some of those memories are terribly poignant, because in a short, recent stretch of years I lost Luana Anders, Robert Altman, my mom, Edith Kellerman, Milton Wexler, and my fairy godmother, Jennifer Jones.

I last saw Bob Altman about a month before his death in 2006. We were at Bob and Kathryn's home at the beach, enjoying Kathryn's usual sumptuous spread of macaroni and cheese and sausages—all homemade, all beautifully prepared. Konni Corriere, their daughter, was there, along with their good friend Joan Tewksbury, who had written Bob's movie *Nashville*. Bob and I sat together, smoking grass and laughing at everything. We were like the two bad kids at the dinner table, the only pot smokers. (By the way: two years now, and no grass. It feels good.) I was still as mesmerized by his hands as I was on the first day I met him, by those long Dickensian fingers, like birds flying to the heavens.

I was blessed to spend a lot of time with Jennifer Jones toward the end of her life. She was living at the beach with her son Bobby Walker, his wife, Dawn, and their two darling children. She was happy, relaxed, and without a hairdresser in sight. She had never looked more beautiful.

I'm counting on the fact that they are all looking down at me from heaven because I'm still talking to them. And I feel that they too keep cheering me on. Sometimes I have to remind myself to call a few people who are still alive.

I still have a lot of my friends from the old days too: my partners in crime Bud Cort and Morgan Ames. I see darling Elliot Gould, and whenever we get the chance, we sing Bob Altman's praises. Kathryn Altman, still a very dear friend of mine, comes to my shows, and her amazing daughter Konni has worked with Jonathan and me.

But there's a lot that's new in my small-town world too. Driving down my beloved Sunset Boulevard, I marvel at how it has changed. No more drive-by window shopping—there's too much traffic. No more Chez Paulette. No more neighborhood hangouts where screen legends sit and sip a cappuccino; now they're crowded with tourists. I pass Sweetzer and Doheny and Havenhurst, still picturing Googie's and Schwab's. Thank goodness the Chateau Marmont is still going strong. I'm sure the young actors have their haunts and their own screen legends. They're just not mine. They grew up in this environment and I'm sure they're having as much fun as I did.

In the mornings I take walks in the Hollywood Hills. When it's clear enough, I look out over the valley, where the orange groves that I knew are just a memory.

Singing to myself, as I often do, I sometimes thank George Griffin as I take a surprise breath and, squinting into the sun, think about change.

Won't Hollywood be great once it's finished?

Won't we all?

Acknowledgments

I NEVER THOUGHT I WOULD BE AN AUTHOR OR THAT IT WOULD even be possible to write and publish a book of my own. But here I am—better late than never! However, I didn't do it all by myself, and I am incredibly grateful to everyone who helped me realize this dream; so many wonderful people and happy accidents came together to make this book possible.

I am forever indebted to Yfat Reiss Gendell of Foundry Literary + Media who shepherded this project from start to finish. From our very first conversation, Yfat immediately understood the essence of what I wanted this book to be. Her efforts landed me a stupendous publishing team: Editorial director Amanda Murray and publicity director Georgina Levitt at Weinstein Books have given my book un-wavering attention and support. I am so thankful to them for them taking this on. The Weinstein team harnessed the eagle-eye of editor Elisa Petrini, who whipped this book into shape, and the talents and design flair of production head Christine Marra, who made sure the book you hold in your hands not only got to press on time, but looked fantastic when it came out the other end.

I am lucky to have had my co-writer, Denise Kiernan, working with me throughout this brand new experience. I have never met anyone like her. Denise took the fear out of this unfamiliar process and eased my troubled mind time and again. She brought no ego to our writing together, no matter what I red-lined. She is quite an amazing woman and writer and I thank her for her wisdom and kindness.

I would not have had the pleasure of working with any of these people had it not been for Elliott Gould and Scott Yanover. I have to thank Elliott for introducing me to Scott, who in turn connected me with both Yfat Reiss Gendell and Marty Gepsman, the latter of whom helped make my proposal possible. Scott has become a good friend and I've always loved Elliott.

It is no mystery to anyone who knows me that computers and I aren't the closest of friends. Many people came together to assist me with everything from typing changes to printing drafts and wrangling emails. My dear friend Konni Corriere was there from the beginning of this project, keeping the office running and always offering support and encouragement. Her enthusiasm for this book means the world to me. My manager, Charles Lago, and his partner Christopher Johnson at Polimedia have been unwavering in their support for this project. They are always available, and had kindly "loaned" me members of their office staff when I desperately needed them. I thank Jonathan Aleman and especially Jayel Aheram, who was patient and responsive and helped me meet my tightest deadlines. Ellen Houli-han, a talented young filmmaker, volunteered her time and typing as well. I am indebted to them all, especially Charles who is such a wonderful manager and always in my corner. I adore him.

There are so many individuals in countless areas of my life who just helped keep my world going through all the craziness. Looks may not be everything, but the especially talented photographer Alan Mercer knows how to make the most of mine. I am so fortu-nate to have had Alan's talents at my disposal for many, many years, keeping me looking good. There are doctors and dentists who have been so patient with my sometimes unpredictable life circumstances. Dr. Pitt has taken excellent care of my animals while I work. The lovely, caring Benny Mena, whom I've known since he was just a boy, is so much more than the man who takes care of our pool—he's family. My friend, the amazing Mary Ellen Kay, has cut my hair for years and gives me the confidence to keep going out in public. Patrick Foley, it's taken a village to keep me looking good, and in this case you're the chief; thanks so much for your taste and talent. Dyan Can-non—your warmth, your spirituality, and love—you really walk the walk. And thanks so much for testifying. It is difficult to express the depths of my love and gratitude for the kindness and generosity of my friends Laura and Larry Worchell who, as well as Esther Rydell, have helped keep my life going during tough and uncertain times. I also have to thank Sandra and John Stephenson for their many years of true friendship and spiritual guidance. My darlings Delmi Batres and Vivianne Carter, you both know how I feel about you. All of these people have made life livable, and without their support I know I would not have had the time, space, or sanity to finish this book.

My sister Diane and Gloria, for their emotional support and friendship. Bud Cort for forty years of friendship and all the gifts, the laughs, and the love. Kathryn Altman, what can I say? I just love you to pieces. Aren't you my soul sister? Isn't June 2nd? I think so.

I had often thought about doing something with all my stories, but never knew how to begin. My friend David Rudnick once suggested I just write a letter to somebody I care about. I did, and it helped me get started. For a good 20 years, my dear friend Richard Martini hounded me about writing down my stories, and even volunteered his own time helping me organize my thoughts. He sat me in front of a tape recorder years ago and got me talking. Now he has written a book of his own, *The Flipside: A Tourist's Guide on How to Navigate the Afterlife*. I am so proud of him, and so grateful.

Jonathan. My partner, my love, my darling husband. Jonathan kept pushing me and prodding me to write a book, often threatening to write it for me if I didn't get my act together. He is my hero, my friend and my support system. Our life may not be perfect, but I've never been bored. My family—Jonathan, Claire, Jack, and Hanna—inspires me in ways that I am still discovering. Hanna, my sweet bright loving spirit, I've learned a deeper way of living because of you. I love you so much. My funny Jack, in these challenging times, you've shown your-self to be a man of great caring. We couldn't have made it through without your help. And you are funny, I love you, too. Claire, you've been my spiritual guide, my nutritionist, and I'm proud to have been your mother all these years. You've been an inspiration and what a beautiful voice. I love you. I would not be who I am or have achieved what I have without you.

Well kids, I guess that's it. I've had the most wonderful ride, I feel like the luckiest woman in the world and you all are the reason. With all my love and thanks, Sally.

Index

Academy Awards night/dress (1971), 105–106, 108, 109–113
Actor's Studio, 65–66, 97
Adams, Dawn, 5, 13
Adice, Keith, 195
Adler, Lou, 100–101, 129, 144, 234
Adler, Nic, 234
Adlon, Percy, 215, 216
Adventurers, The (Robbins), 109
After Dark magazine, 161
Airport (film), 103, 112
Albee, Edward, 73, 217
Alda, Alan, 79
Aldridge, Virginia, 33, 36–37, 39, 44
Alfred Hitchcock Hour, The (television), 77
Altman, Kathryn, 112–113, 221, 228–229, 243, 244
Altman, Mike, 90
Altman, Robert
    Brewster McCloud/Kellerman, 98, 99–100, 101, 102
    health problems/death, 220, 222, 243
    Kellerman and, 180, 228–229, 231, 232–233, 234, 244
    Lincoln Center ceremony and, 221–222
    M*A*S*H/Kellerman, 78, 80–81, 82, 84–86, 87, 88, 89–91, 102, 103, 105, 111, 112–113

Nashville/Kellerman, 146–147, 243
    Prêt-à-Porter/Kellerman, 220–221
    Welcome to LA/Kellerman, 168, 169
Altobelli, Rudi, 94, 95, 96, 144, 147, 149, 150
American Graffiti (film), 157
Ames, Morgan
    grandmother's couch, 70, 71
    Kellerman and, 39, 50, 51, 54, 57, 58, 59–60, 108–109, 136, 137, 160, 184, 194, 220, 228–229, 243
And God Created Woman (film), 36
Anders, Luana
    background/description, 10, 39, 66
    illness/death, 218–220, 243
    Kellerman and, 3, 10, 31, 39, 46, 48, 51, 52, 55–56, 58, 76, 94, 165, 184, 194
Anderson, Loni, 211
Andress, Ursula, 137
Andrews, Julie, 199–200, 205
Annie Get Your Gun (film), 22
Anthony, Joe, 73
April Fools, The (film), 79–80, 105
Arkin, Alan, 116, 162–163
Armstrong, Neil, 93
Arrick, Larry, 10, 217
As the World Turns (television), 101
Ashley, Elizabeth, 71
Astaire, Fred, 136

Austin, Patti, 242
Aykroyd, Dan, 234

Bacall, Lauren, 220, 221
Bacharach, Burt, 136, 137, 236
Back to School (film), 203–205, 206
Baghdad Cafe (film), 215
Baio, Scott, 190
Ball, Lucille, 29
Balsam, Martin, 88
Barbarella (film), 36, 68
Bardot, Brigitte, 36
Baretta (television), 11
Barmak, Ira, 184
Barrett, Rona, 139
Barry, Philip, 13
Barrymore, John, Jr., 34
Basinger, Kim, 169, 220
Beatty, Warren, 35, 74, 129, 130, 145, 176
Beautiful People (play), 9
Belson, Jerry/Joanne, 139–140, 151, 159
Benjamin, Howard, 225
Bennett, David, 30, 62–63, 101, 118, 132,
    142, 164, 194, 195
Benny, Jack, 29
Benson, Jay, 201–202
Bergen, Candice, 95
Bergman, Allen, 228–229
Bergman, Ingrid, 1, 69–70, 106, 137, 239
Bergman, Marilyn, 228–229
Bernstein, Carl, 176
Beverly Hills Diet, The (Mazel), 187
Bewitched (television), 56
Bianco, Tony Lo, 175
Bice, Bob, 48, 49, 50, 51
Bick, Jerry, 65
Big Blonde, The (film), 195–196, 197
Big Bus, The (film), 167
Billboard magazine, 144
Bisset, Jacqueline, 130
Bistro, 128
Black, Barbara, 5
Black, Karen, 112
Blake, Robert, 11
Bob & Carol & Ted & Alice (film), 87, 171
Bob Hope Presents the Chrysler Theatre
    (television), 89

Bogarde, Dirk, 67
Bogart, Humphrey, 1
Bologna, Joe, 231
Bonanza (television), 81
Boomy the script supervisor, 79–80
Boris and Natasha (film), 215
Boston Strangler, The (film), 79, 191
Bowen, Roger, 84
Boxing Helena (film), 169
Boyer, Charles, 73, 136
Boynton Beach Club (film), 231
Bradford, Dick, 57–59
Brando, Marlon
    acting/films, 1, 9, 71, 145
    Kellerman and, 2–3, 35–38, 41, 67,
        181
Bread, 121, 242
Breakfast at Tiffany's (musical/film),
    71–72, 73, 199
Brewster McCloud (film), 98, 99–100,
    101, 144
Bridges, Jeff, 224
Brolin, James, 202
Brown Derby restaurant, 88
Brown, Jerry, 132, 138
Brown, Jim, 110
Browning, Kirk, 196
Brute Force (film), 8
Bubby (Jonathan's stepmother),
    212–213, 217, 220
Bud and Travis, 39
Burghoff, Gary, 83, 84
Burn, Matt, 229
Burnett, Carol, 184
Burns, Ken, 231
Burrows, Abe, 73
Butch Cassidy and the Sundance Kid
    (film), 179
Byrnes, Eddie, 7, 8, 31, 55

Caan, James, 124, 125–126, 144
Call Me by My Rightful Name (play),
    63–64
Camino Real (play), 63
Candy, John, 215
Cannes Film Festival, 111, 222, 241–242
Cannon, Dyan, 231

Capitol Records, 30, 33
Capra, Frank, 136
Cariou, Len, 231
Carnes, Kim, 234
Carol Burnett Show (television), 170
Caron, Leslie, 142
Carradine, Keith, 221–222
Carrie (film), 169
Carter, Vivianne, 194, 213, 217, 220
Casino Royale (film), 137
Cassavetes, John, 34
Caswell, Chris, 235–236
Catcher in the Rye, 86
Cavett, Dick, 103
Chamberlain, Richard, 11, 12, 63, 72
Chase, The (film), 71
Chateau Marmont, 7, 59, 244
Chez Paulette, 30–35, 37, 38–39, 41, 50,
    51, 55, 64, 244
Chi, Greta, 54
Chinatown (film), 12
Christian Science, 19–20, 27, 28, 60
Christie, Julie, 130
Claxton, Bill, 49
Clooney, Rosemary, 242
Coal Miner's Daughter (film), 169
Coburn, James, 11, 228–229
Coburn, Beverly, 228–229
Cocker, Joe, 150
Cohen, Herby, 31, 152
Cohen, Stuart
    Altobelli's home/Manson murders
        and, 94–95, 96
    Kellerman and, 66–67, 71, 73, 140,
        141, 142, 144, 147–148, 150–151,
        153, 163–166, 167–170, 183
Cole, Nat King, 5
Cole, Natalie, 242
Coleman, Carol, 184
Combat (film), 64–65
Comer, Anjanette, 68, 184, 194
Company of Angels, 63
Conversation, The (film), 157
Cooke, Sam, 100
Coombs Hardware store, xiii
Coppola, Francis Ford, 11, 157
Cord, Alex, 68

Corey, Jeff
    background, 8
    Kellerman and, 8, 9–10, 15
    Professional Actors Workshop/
        students, 8, 10, 11–12, 13–14, 62,
        111, 178, 240
Corman, Roger, 11, 53, 66
Corriere, Konni, 243, 244
Cort, Bud, 86–87, 98–100, 159–160,
    167–168, 194, 212, 243
Cosby, Bing, 1
Cosmo Alley, 1–2, 36, 37
Cosmopolitan magazine, 161
Cotten, Joseph, 88, 127
Crawford, Joan, 239
Crenna, Richard, 69
Currie, Cherie, 190
Curtis, Tony, 79, 190, 191–192

Daisy (dance place), 66
Dangerfield, Rodney, 203–205
Dark Side of the Moon (television), 53
Dashiell, Bud, 39
David, Hal, 136, 137, 139, 235–236
Davidovitch, Lolita, 215
Davis, Bette, 106
Davis, Clifton, 134
Davis, Geena, 202
Davis, Jerry, 56–57
Day, Doris, 1, 24
Days of Wine and Roses (film), 106, 199
Dean, James, 8–9, 45
Delmi, 213
Delpy, Julie, 215
Dementia 13 (film), 66
Dempsey (film), 200–202
Dempsey, Patrick, 209
Deneuve, Catherine, 79
Devil and Daniel Webster, The (film), 8
Diamond, Neil, 143, 153
Dick Van Dyke (television), 139
Dietrich, Marlene, 7
Dino's restaurant, 31
Dirty Dozen (film), 87
Dixon, Donna, 234
Donahue, Troy, 56
Duchin, Peter, 176

Duel in the Sun (film), 185
Duffy, Bill, 57–59, 62
Dukes, David, 180
Dunaway, Faye, 145, 171
Dunbar, Hooper C., III, 6
Duvall, Robert, 86, 126
Duvall, Shelley, 100
Dylan, Bob, 32

Eastman, Carole, 10, 12, 39, 111
Eastwood, Clint, 162
Edelstein, Rick, 101–104, 106–108, 109,
    110, 112–113, 115, 116, 118–119,
    121–122
Edwards, Blake, 184, 199–200, 205, 229,
    230
Egyptian Theatre, 62
Eisenstaedt, Alfred, 102, 144
Eklund, Britt, 130
Elizabeth, II, Queen, 142–143
Elliot, Cass, 241
Ellsberg, Daniel, 131
Empire Strikes Back, The (film), 11
Enemy of the People (play), 55, 56, 64
Erickson, Leon, 86
Esty, Bob, 147, 149, 164, 228–229, 235,
    236
Everett, Rupert, 220
Eyes of Laura Mars, The (film), 11

Face/Off (film), 229–230
Fagen, Donald, 242
Fall of the House of Usher (film), 11
Feinstein, Barry, 31–32, 40
Feinstein's at the Regency, Manhattan,
    232–234
Feld, Donald Lee, 105, 106, 108, 109,
    114, 147
Finch, Peter, 142, 143
Finwall, Mary, 5
Fisk, Jack, 169
Five Easy Pieces (film), 10, 111
Fleming, Erin, 160
Flying Nun (television), 68
Folger, Abigail, 94
Fonda, Henry/Shirlee, 70–71, 95, 131
Fonda, Jane, 36, 68, 71, 128, 131

Fonda, Peter, 69
Ford, Harrison, 156–158, 231
Forrest, Dickie, 19
Forster, Robert, 79
Foster, Jodie, 190, 192
Four Freshmen, 5
Fox, James, 67
Foxes (film), 190
Fraker, William, 64, 124
Frankenheimer, John, 127, 194
Franklin, Aretha, 152
Frank's, 2
Fraser, Brendan, 215
Fred MacMurray Show, The (television),
    64
Frost, David, 103
Frykowski, Wojciech, 94
Fuller, Samuel, 47, 50
Funny Girl! (musical), 72, 102

Gallery Bar, 12
Garay, Val, 234, 236
Garbo, Greta, 1, 7, 239
Garden of Allah Hotel, 7
Gates, Bill, 231
Gates, David, 242
Gehry, Frank, 127, 184, 186, 194, 230–231
General's Daughter, The (film), 229–230
Genghis Cohen, 234
Georgy Girl (film), 68
Getz, Stan, 2, 47
Gielgud, Sir John, 136, 137, 142, 143
Gilardi, Jack, 163, 168
Gleason, Jackie, 29
Godfather, The (film), 2, 124
Golden Globes, 111
Gomer Pyle (television), 139
Gone with the Wind (film), 69
Googie's Coffeehouse, 40, 48, 49, 244
Gordon, Ruth, 167–168
Gosford Park (film), 232–233
Gossett, Louis, 190
Gould, Elliott, 87–88, 90, 111, 130,
    243–244
Graham, Ian, 54, 58, 60, 70, 76–77, 119,
    121, 154–155, 156, 158–159
Grant, Cary, 1, 13, 128

Grant, Lee, 112
Grant, Richard, 220, 221
Granz, Norman, 5
Great Escape, The (film), 11
Great Performances series, PBS, 173, 195
Green family (Lori Ann/Jean), 26–27
Griffin, George, 235, 244
Griffin, Merv, 111
Grodin, Charles, 220
Guardino, Harry, 35
Guinness, Alec, 157, 158
Guttman, Dick, 172
Guys and Dolls (film), 1, 38

Haas, Millidge Marie, 19
Hackman, Gene, 130, 145, 146
Hale, Corky, 235
Hall, Brad, 215
Hall, Conrad, 64
Harold and Maude (film), 86, 167–168
Harper's Bazaar, 103
Harris, Richard, 114
Harrison, George, 32
Harry O. (television), 192
Hart, Bobby, 100
Hash tea, 191
Hauben, Larry, 97–98, 113–114
Hawaii Five-O (television), 73
Hawn, Goldie, 130
Hayes, Helen, 112
Hayward, Brooke, 176
Hayworth, Rita, 127
Head, Edith, 106
Heckman, Don, xii
Hello Dolly! (musical), 72
Help, The (film), 169
Hemingway, Ernest, 7
Henner, Marilu, 229
Hepburn, Katharine, 13, 71
Hereditary Disease Foundation, 185
Heston, Charlton, 132
Higher and Higher (television pilot), 78–79
Hill, George Roy, 179, 180, 181
Hiller, Arthur, 172
Hilton, James, 136
Hinton, Mary, 211

Hippies arriving in West Hollywood, 92–93
Hoffman, Dustin, 79
Hogan, Michael, 217, 218
Hoge, Warren, 176–177
Holden, Stephen, 232–233
Holliday, Billie, 174
Holly Harp's, 114–115, 151, 193
Home of the Brave (film), 8
Homosexuality and 1950s, 54–55
Hopper, Dennis and family, 69
Horne, Lena, 231
Horrocks (Wilcox-Smith), Tamara, 83–84
Hotel (film), 202
House Committee on Un-American Activities, 8
Howard, Ron, 11
Hubbard, Liz, 101
Humphrey, Hubert, 129
Hunt, Linda, 216, 220
Hunt, Marsha, 62
Hunter, Ross, 138–139, 140–141, 184
Huntington's chorea, 185
Hurry Sundown (film), 171
Hurt, William, 173
Hush, Elizabeth, 65–66, 137, 139, 194
Hussey, Olivia, 136, 137
Hutton, Betty, 22

I'm Dickens, He's Fenster (television), 172
Ingram, James, 242
International Review of Music, xii
Invaders, The (television), 11
Israel, Neil, 202
It Rained All Night the Day I Left (film), 190–192
Ivar Theater, 2
Ivy, Clayton, 152–153

Jaglom, Henry, 209, 228–229
Jan and Dean, 100
Janssen, David, 192
J.J., 233, 234
Joan of Arc (film auditions), 6, 9
Johnson, Ben, 114
Jones, Chris, 95

Jones, James Earl, 130
Jones, Quincy, 5, 108–109, 129, 130, 138,
    231
Jones (Simon), Jennifer, 1, 69–70, 123,
    126, 127, 176, 183–184, 193, 194,
    220, 228, 229, 243
    daughter (Mary Jennifer), 193
Joplin, Janis, 32
Jourdan, Louis, 69

Kardashian, Kim, 224
Kashfi, Anna, 41
Kaye, Danny, 1
Kazan, Elia, 9, 35
Kellerman, Diana
    background/description, 17, 18, 21,
        33, 131
    daughter Claire and, 70, 76–77, 158,
        172–173
    Gloria and, 76, 116, 119, 158, 170,
        228–229
    marriage to Ian Graham, 54, 58, 60, 70
    Sally and, 7, 17–18, 23, 54, 55, 58, 60,
        104, 170, 172–173, 211, 228–229
Kellerman, Edith
    background/description, 15–16, 115,
        117, 135, 175
    as Christian Scientist, 19–20
    grandchildren and, 213, 225
    health problems/death, 225–227, 243
    marriage, 16–17, 115, 116, 117, 189, 226
    remarriage, 225
    Sally/Diana and, 8, 15–16, 19–20, 24,
        30, 33, 60, 61, 76, 102–103, 114, 193,
        194, 225–227
Kellerman, Jack
    background/description, 16, 45–46,
        60, 115–116, 198–199
    illness/death, 115, 116
    letters to Sally, 61, 115, 116
    Sally/Diana and, 8, 21, 22, 24, 33, 46,
        52, 60–62, 114, 115–116
Kellerman, Sally
    Claire (daughter) and, 158–161, 165,
        167, 173, 175, 180, 181, 183, 186–187,
        198–199, 211, 213–214, 228–229,
        235, 243

Claire (niece) and, 119–121, 123, 134,
    138, 154–156, 158
early jobs, 30–35, 37, 38–39, 41
first audition, 6
Jack and Hanna (children), 210–215,
    216, 217, 218, 220, 221, 228–229,
    232, 238, 239, 243
J.R. and Holly, 72, 133
losing "snowflake," 57
losing weight, 66
pregnancy/abortion, 58–61
swimming, 19, 21, 33, 174, 181–182
*See also specific films; specific plays;
    specific television shows*
Kellerman, Sally/childhood
    description, 17–19, 29
    Granada Hills, 3, 17–18
    high school, 3–6
    ice cream incident, 18
    Jennifer/Jennifer's father, 22–23, 24–25
    mirror pep talks, 4
    move to Los Angeles, 28–29
    move to San Fernando, 20–21
    school clubs, 4–5, 22–23
    school studies, 5, 22
    Shadow (dog), 17, 18, 20–21, 22, 28
    singing/performing, 5, 16, 22, 23
    size, 3, 5, 21, 23–24
Kellerman, Sally/singing
    Academy Awards, 108, 110
    career (2000s), xi–xii, 232–236,
        242–243
    childhood, 5, 16, 22, 23
    films, 99–100, 136, 137, 173, 200
    first album, 118, 144
    Quincy Jones and, 108–109
    tour, 143–145, 147–153
    Verve Records, 5, 12–13, 14
    Vitello's on Halloween, xi–xii
Kellerman, Sally/therapy
    Corey suggesting, 15, 28, 178
    sessions/advice, 28–29, 35, 58, 59,
        83, 178
    Wexler/group therapy and, 176,
        177–179, 182–186, 187–188, 189,
        199, 205, 206, 214–215, 216,
        222–223, 227

Kellerman, Vicky, 25–26, 27–28
Kelly, Princess Grace, 106, 197–198
Kennedy, Bobby, 93
Kennedy, John F., 93
Kerr, Deborah, 69
Kershner, Irwin, 11
Kert, Larry, 67–68, 72
Kessel, Barney, 14
KGB: The Secret War (film), 202
Kidd, Michael, 72
Killers, The (film), 8
King, Ben E., 242
King, Carole, 100, 129, 144
King, Martin Luther, Jr., 93
Kinison, Sam, 204
Kissinger, Henry, 123, 126–129, 131–134
Knife and Fork, 40
Knight, Sandra, 39, 66, 76
Knight, Shirley, 10–11
Krane, Jonathan/Kellerman
    affairs/separations, 216, 222–224
    careers, 193, 199, 200, 205, 206, 207,
        208, 210, 215, 229–230, 236–237
    financial difficulties, 237–238
    marriage, 195, 196, 197, 198, 199,
        206, 208, 209, 210, 211–212, 213,
        215, 218, 220, 226, 227–228, 233,
        237–238, 240, 243, 244
    marriage proposal/wedding, 192–195
    meeting/early relationship, 186–189,
        192
    renewing wedding vows, 228–229
Kroll, Jack, 169
Kupcinet, Irv, 192, 193

LA City College, 8
LaBianca murders, 96
Ladd, Cheryl, 197–198
Lancaster, Burt, 130
Landau, Martin, 65, 66
Lane, Diane, 179–180, 190
Lardner, Ring, Jr., 89, 90–91, 112
Lasser, Louise, 144
Last of the Red Hot Lovers (film), 116–117,
        146, 162
Last Picture Show, The (film), 115
Laurel Canyon General Store, 46

Lautner, John, 40
Lay of the Land (play), 217–218
Lazar, Swifty, 113
Leary, Timothy, 98
Legend of Billy Jean, The (film), 57
Legend of Jesse James, The (television), 95
Leiber, Jerry, 234–235, 242
Leigh, Vivian, 1
Lemmon, Jack, 79, 205, 221–222
Lettieri, Al, 2
Lewin, Max, 31, 32, 34, 35, 37, 41
Lindstrom, Pia, 69–70
Linville, Joanne, 93, 184, 194
Lipton, Peggy, 100, 130, 138
Lithgow, John, 196
Little Romance, A (film), 179–181
Little Shop of Horrors (film), 11
Loggia, Robert, 184, 205
Long Goodbye, The (film), 90
Look Who's Talking (film), 229–230
Loren, Sophia, 220, 221
Los Angeles Times, 114, 185
Lost Horizon (film/tour), 124, 135,
        136–143, 184
Love Story (film), 103
Lucy Show, The (television), 139
Luft, Lorna/Vanessa, 229

M*A*S*H (film), 81–91, 97, 98, 99, 103,
        105, 111, 112, 126, 127, 146
    See also Oscar night/dress (1971)
Machine Gun Kelly (film), 53
MacLaine, Shirley, 130
Magee and the Lady (film), 175
Magnificent Seven, The (film), 11
Majorga, Lincoln, 5, 13
Malibu, 69
Malick, Terry, 69
Mamas and Papas, 100, 115, 241
Mandel, Johnny, xi
Mandelker, Phil, 157
Manilow, Barry, 236
Manson, Charles/murders, 93–96
Marcovicci, Andrea, 209
Marley, John, 55
Marquand, Christian, 36–37
Marriage-Go-Round (play), 62–63

Marshall, Garry, 139, 151
Martel, Ed, xi
Martin, Andrea, 215
Martin, Dean, 31
Martini, Richard, 218, 219–220
Marvin, Lee, 168
Marx, Groucho, 29, 159–160
Mastroianni, Marcello, 220
Matthau, Walter, 75
Maxwell, Ron, 174
Maynor, Asa, 8
Mazel, Judy, 187
Mazursky, Paul, 170–171, 175
McDowell, Roddy, 78
McGovern, George, 128, 129–131, 133
McGuire, Dorothy, 127
McQueen, Steve/Neile, 34–35
Meatballs III (film), 208–209
Medeiros, Lyman, xi
Meet Me in St. Louis (Hollywood High
    production), 5–6, 9
Melcher, Terry, 95
Melnick, Dan, 69
Men, The (film), 1, 38
Mengers, Sue, 118, 145, 147, 161
Merrick, David, 71–73
Merrill, Bob, 72
Metter, Alan, 204
Mexican trip/peyote, 105, 106–108
Michael (film), 229–230
Miller, Harvey, 151
Milwaukee Journal, 50
Mirabella, Grace, 117–118
Mitchell, Joni, 130
Moffitt, Peggy, 49
Montand, Yves, 69
Moore, Dudley, 184
Moore, Mary Tyler, 72, 73
More American Graffiti (film), 57
Morrissey, Wendy Stark, 132
Morrow, Vic, 63, 64–65
Motion Picture Association of America's
    rating system, 82
Moving Violations (film), 202
Mull, Martin, 196
Murder Among Friends (film), 202–203
Murphy, Michael, 100

Murrow, Edward R., 29
*Music of Antonio Carlos Jobim, The:
    Music from the Adventurers*,
    108–109
Musso, 2
My Friend Flicka (film), 8

Nashville (film), 146–147, 243
Nelson, Ozzie and Harriet, 63
Network (film), 142
New York Times, 171, 176, 232–233
Newsweek, 169
Nichols, Mike, 130
Nicholson, Jack
    girlfriend Georgiana, 12–13
    Kellerman and, 12–13, 39, 51, 57,
        58–60, 66, 68, 94, 111, 115, 130
    Luana and, 220
    Sandra Knight and, 66, 68, 76
    See also specific films
Nielsen, Leslie, 202–203
Nielsen, Norma Jean, 5, 8
Nilsson, Harry, 143
Nimoy, Leonard, 63, 73
1950s repression, 7–8, 9, 54–55, 60
Niven, David, 73
Nixon, Richard, 126–127, 128, 129, 134
Norm's, 58
North, Sheree, 47
*Not for Ourselves Alone: The Story of
    Elizabeth Cady Stanton and Susan B.
    Anthony* (documentary), 231
Nudity in films, 82

Odd Couple, The (television), 56
Oliver! (musical), 72
Olivier, Sir Laurence, 180–181
On Golden Pond (film), 71
On the Waterfront (film), 1
One Flew Over the Cuckoo's Nest (film),
    97
O'Neill, Donna, 184
Oriental Theatre, 67
Orr, Bill, 56–57
Oscar night/dress (1971), 105–106, 108,
    109–113
Our Gang (television), 11

Out of Africa (film), 205, 206
Outer Limits (television), 64, 65, 66, 67, 84, 89, 124

Page, Gene/Billy, 144
Page, Joy, 56
Pan, Hermes, 136–137
Pantages, 2
Parent, Steve, 94
Parker, Dorothy, 7, 195
Patton (film), 88
Patty's, 100
Paul Kohner Agency, 56
Peck, Gregory, 1, 130
Penn, Arthur, 71
Peppard, George, 59, 71, 78
Perry, Richard, 144, 235
Persky, Bill, 196, 197
Peters, Jean, 1
Peyote/Mexican trip, 105, 106–108
Pflug, Jo Ann, 82
Phenomenon (film), 229–230
Philadelphia Story, The (play/film), 13
Phillips, Mackenzie, 163
Phillips, Michelle, 115, 130
Pico Playhouse, 7
Pink Panther, The (film), 199
Pittman, Tom
  death/father's lawsuit against police department, 47–52
  Kellerman and, 45–52
Playboy, 99
Playhouse 90 (television), 45
Pleshette, Suzanne, 59, 70
Plummer, Christopher, 224
Polanski, Roman, 95
Polka Parade (television), 33
Pollack, Sydney/Claire, 205–206, 228–229
Porter, Don, 62
Poseidon Adventure, The (film), 146, 153, 167
Preminger, Ingo, 89
Preminger, Otto, 6, 171, 172
Prêt-à-Porter (film), 220–221
Professional Actors Workshop/students, 8, 10, 11–12, 13–14, 62, 111, 178, 240
Prymus, Kenny, 84

Psycho (film), 64
Pupitch, George, 21

Quaid, Randy, 190

Rafferty and the Gold Dust Twins (film), 162
Rainbow Room/Grill, Rockefeller Center, 140, 151, 200
Rainier, Prince, 197, 198
Raitt, Bonnie, 234
Rayfiel, David, 73, 74–76, 97, 101, 102, 140
Rea, Stephen, 220
Redgrave, Lynn, 68
Reds (film), 74
Reed, Rex, 233, 234
Reflection of Fear (film), 124
Reform School Girl (film), 55, 135
Renaissance, 47
Rey, Alejandro, 68
Reynolds, Burt, 211
Richards, Dick, 162–163
Righter, Carroll, 34
Rivera, Chita, 65
Robbins, Harold, 109
Robbins, Tim, 220, 221–222
Roberts, Julia, 220
Rocky and Bullwinkle (television), 215
Rocky Horror Picture Show, The (film), 100
Rogues, The (television), 73, 111
Roll with the Feelin' (album), 144
Ronstadt, Linda, 234
Rosemary's Baby (film), 167
Roxy, 234
Rudolph, Alan, 168, 169
Russell, Brian, 197
Rydell, Esther, 237
Rydell, Mark/Joanne and children, 69, 71, 93, 194, 205, 228–229

Sage, Will, 34
Saint Joan (play), 6
Saks, Gene, 116
Sampson, Bob, 53, 57, 58, 59, 62, 63–64, 67, 240
Sanford and Son (television), 101–102

Sarandon, Susan, 221–222

Saroyan, William, 9

Sarrazin, Michael, 130

Sayonara (film), 1

Schwab's, xiii, 39–40, 244

Scorsese, Martin, 11

Scott, George C., 88

Sea Witch, 40

Seberg, Jean, 6

Sebring, Jay, 93–94

Secret of the Ice Cave (film), 208, 209–210

Secret Weapons (film), 202

Selden, Tom, 63–64

Selleck, Tom/Jillie, 212

Selznick, David O., 69, 126

Serial (film), 196–197

Servant, The (film), 67

77 Sunset Strip (television), 7, 31

Shadow, The (radio), 19–20

Shatner, Bill, 73

Shaw, George Bernard, 6

Shaw, Robert, 124

Sheen, Charlie, 208

Sheen, Martin, 224

Shirlee, stewardess, 70–71

Shonberg, Burt, 40, 50, 51

Shurtleff, Michael, 63

Shyer, Chuck, 149–150, 151, 155, 156, 158, 167

Signoret, Simone, 69

Simon, Jennifer Jones. *See* Jones (Simon), Jennifer

Simon, John, 171–172

Simon, Neil, 116

Simon, Norton, 126, 127, 194

Sinatra, Frank, 129

Sinclair, Dick, 33

Skerritt, Tom, 85, 86

Slattery's People (television), 69, 70, 71, 93

Slipping into Darkness (film), 210

Slither (film), 124–125, 144

Smith, Charles Martin, 215

Smith, Donald, 174

Smith, Liz, 176

Smoky Joe's Cafe (play), 234–235

Smothers Brothers, 170

Smothers, Tommy, 196, 197

Solms, Kenny, 170, 171

Someone to Love (film), 209

Song of Bernadette, The (film), 69

Southern, Terry, 69

Spacek, Sissy, 169, 173–175

Spencer, Diana, 54

Spivak, Susan, 186

Splendor in the Grass (film), 35

Springfield, Dusty, 137

Stanton, Harry Dean, 124

Stapleton, Maureen, 73, 112

Star Trek (television), 73

Star Wars (film), 158

Stark, Ray, 132

Stark, Wendy, 132

Starr, Ringo, 40, 241

Starsky and Hutch (television), 101–102

Stefano, Joe, 64, 65, 84

Steiger, Rod, 68, 89

Stern, Howard, 231

Stewart, Jimmy, 13

Stewart, Rod, 143

Sting, The (film), 179

Stoller, Mike, 234–235, 242

Streep, Meryl, 205, 206

Streetcar Named Desire (film), 38

Streisand, Barbra, 102, 129, 130, 131, 132, 145, 147

Stritch, Elaine, 233

"Suicide Is Painless," 90

Surfside 6 (television), 56, 58

Sutherland, Don, 85, 87–88, 90, 111, 131, 215

Swordfish (film), 229–230

Tate, Sharon, 93–94, 95, 96

Taylor, James, 129, 234

Taylor, Lili, 220

Tehran Film Festival/trip, 170–172

10 (film), 184, 199

Tewksbury, Joan, 243

That Girl (television), 72

That's Life (film), 205, 206

They Shoot Horses, Don't They? (film), 106

Thinnes, Roy, 11, 62–63, 66

Third Day, The (film), 71, 78, 79
Thomas, Danny, 132
Thomas, Marlo, 72, 130
Thornbirds, The (television), 11
Three Days of the Condor (film), 206
Three for the Road (film), 208
Tomlin, Lily, 221–222
Tootsie (film), 206
Tora Tora Tora (film), 88
Towel Head, 40–44, 46
Towne, Bob (Robert), 12
Travolta, John, 215, 229–230, 240
Trikonis, Guss, 201
Twilight Zone (television), 53

Ugly (film), 235
Ullman, Tracy, 220
Ullmann, Liv, 136, 137–138, 139, 140
Unmarried Woman, An (film), 171
Unsupervised (television), 231–232
Ustinov, Peter/Helene, 181

Vaccaro, Brenda, 170, 171, 231
Vadim, Roger, 36–37, 68
Vance, Kenny, 235
Vance, Marilyn, 210–211
Vanity Fair, 132
Variety, 65, 111
Venus (film), 98, 113–114, 201
Venza, Jack, 195–196
Verboten (film), 47, 50
Verna: USO Girl (film), 173–175
Verve Records, 5, 12–13, 14
Victor/Victoria (film), 199–200
Vitello's, xi–xii
Viva Zapata! (film), 1, 38
Vogue, 117–118
Voice-overs, 79, 189, 231–232
Voight, Jon, 130, 131
Vreeland, Diana, 118

Walker, Bobby/Dawn, 194, 243
Walker, Robert/Ellie, 68

Wall Street Journal, 232
Walters, Norby, 113
Warner Brothers, 56–57
Waterston, Sam, 200
Way We Were, The (film), 132, 206
Wayne, John, 128
Weinstein, Harvey, 139
Weisser, Norbert, 210
Welch, Raquel, 130
Welcome to LA (film), 168, 169
Weld, Tuesday, 196
Weller, Dick, xi
Welles, Orson, 7, 209
West Side Story (play), 67
Wexler, Milton
    death, 243
    Kellerman's wedding/vow renewals,
        195, 228, 229
    That's Life, 205
    therapy work, 176, 177–179, 182–186,
        187–188, 189, 199, 205, 206,
        214–215, 216, 222–223, 227
Whitaker, Forest, 220
Who's Afraid of Virginia Woolf (play), 217
Wilcox-Smith (Horrocks), Tamara,
        83–84
Wild One, The (film), 1, 38
William Morris, 65, 71, 171
Williams, Paul, 242
Williams, Robin, 221–222
Williams, Treat, 200, 201
Winters, Shelley, 146
Wintour, Anna, 118
Woodford, Terry, 152–153
Worchell, Laura/Larry, 237

York, Michael, 136, 137
Young, Gig, 73, 84, 111–112
Younger and Younger (film), 215

Zappas/Moon Unit Zappa, 235
Zieff, Howard, 124–125
Ziffren, Paul/Mickey, 127, 132, 133, 162